BRAINWASHED

BRAINWASHED
Challenging the Myth of Black Inferiority

Tom Burrell

SMILEYBOOKS

Distributed by Hay House, Inc.

Carlsbad, California • New York City
Sydney • London • Johannesburg
Vancouver • New Delhi

Grateful acknowledgement is made to Diane Allford-Trotman for the art and photo research for the Brainwashed Timeline.

Art and Photo Credits:
Branding Slaves, Declaration of Independence, Wedgwood Slave Cameo, and Thomas Jefferson: Courtesy of The Granger Collection, New York; Negro Slave Ad: Courtesy of The New York Public Library

Coon, Coon, Coon sheet music, Cream of Wheat, Black, White, political cartoon: Courtesy of The New York Public Library; Gorton's Minstrels: Library of Congress Prints and Photographs Division

Civil War recruitment: Courtesy of The Granger Collection, NY; Fredrick Douglas: Courtesy of The New York Public Library

KKK: Library of Congress Prints and Photographs Division; Hanging: The Granger Collection, NY; Ida B. Wells: Courtesy of The New York Public Library

Whites Only sign: Courtesy of Dolph Briscoe Center for American History, The University of Texas at Austin; MLK, Credit: The Granger Collection, NY
Right On fist, Hulton Archives/Getty images; Olympic runners and Malcolm X: The Granger Collection

"JJ" Jimmy Walker, Good Times: CBS/Photofest; King Kong: Courtesy Everett Collection; Flavor Flav: Flavor Flav-Arnold Turner/Getty Images

ISBN: 978-1-4019-2592-5
Digital ISBN: 978-1-4019-2669-4

28 27 26 25 24 23 22
1st edition, February 2010

Printed in the United States of America

To my wife,
Madeleine,
gentle force

Baby daddy, negro, bred to be led, white superiority, high yella, smother love, chew-i-cide, buy now pay later, black ball, sluts, good hair, helpless, uncle toms, D's will do, homey-cide, studs, darkie, uppity, buy now pay later, disunity, dis-eased, diss-unity, uglified, mammy, shiftless, lazy, crabs in a basket, negro, heavenly fodder, lazy, studs, Neo-coons, baby daddy, negro, uppity, bred to be led, white superiority, high yella, smother love, chew-i-cide, buy now pay later, black ball, sluts, good hair, helpless, uncle toms, D's will do, homey-cide, studs, un-think, darkie, uppity, buy now pay later, disunity, dis-ease, diss-unity, uglified, mammy, shiftless, lazy, crabs in a basket, heavenly fodder, lazy, studs, Neo-coons, baby daddy, negro, uppity, bred to be led, white superiority, high yella, smother love,

Contents

Introduction

...You've been misled
You been had.
You been took.

— MALCOLM X

We are strong. Survivors of the Middle Passage, the whip, and the chains. We have survived centuries of terror, humiliation, vilification, and deprivation.

We are smart. Even when our literacy was illegal, we learned quickly, invented, discovered, built, taught, and excelled against all odds.

We are creative. Making a way out of "No way!" and constantly birthing and rebirthing American art and culture.

So then why, after all this time, when calculating the achievement of the "American Dream," are we still ranked at the bottom of almost every "good" list, and at the top of the "bad" lists? Why, despite our apparent strength, intelligence, and resourcefulness, do we continue to lag behind and languish in so many aspects of American life?

The answer is intricately linked to the hundreds of years blacks have lived with white guilt and black shame. It lurks just beneath the surface of the American consciousness, like a cancer that can't be healed because it can't be discussed honestly and openly.

Forty-five years in the advertising industry have given me personal and professional insight into the power of propaganda—positive and negative—and the use of words and images to influence, change, and even transform people's lives. The knowledge and insights I've gained have inspired me to provoke an honest discussion in the hope that the healing process can finally begin.

:::

I was born and raised on the South Side of Chicago. It was at the beginning of the New Deal, the "second coming" of black dependency. Throughout my community, we Negroes were indoctrinated with the idea that we were unable to take care of ourselves, and that we needed help and handouts from Mr. Charlie in the form of government programs, including public assistance, food stamps, and any other "gifts" the government bestowed. This unquestioned dependency—what psychologists call "learned helplessness"—was, I believe, one of the many reinforcements of a deep-seated, race-based inferiority.

The message was clear, consistent, ubiquitous, and loud. It was subtly broadcast by the white mass media, and bluntly and repeatedly echoed by its black recipients: "A nigger ain't shit!" It was, for the most part, an advertising pitch not much different from the ones used to sell beer, laundry detergent, or life insurance. The two main ingredients of this campaign created a toxic blend of white superiority and black inferiority. Sold!

In 1971, I and my partner, Emmett McBain, launched what would become Burrell Advertising, a full-service advertising agency specializing in promoting products and services to the then largely ignored African American consumer. Burrell Advertising became an industry leader because of its positive, realistic, and compelling depictions of black life and culture, particularly in the medium of television. We were keenly aware of the power of culturally relevant language and images to influence perceptions and attitudes toward my clients' products and services.

In other words, we created and disseminated "positive" propaganda.

Many years later, while minding my own business—literally—as chairman and chief executive officer of Burrell Communications, I coined the phrase, "Black people are not dark-skinned white people." It was a concise summation of the basis of my business: that black Americans, because of our heritage and history, have a unique culture that could best be reached through strategies, words, and images subtly or overtly related to those historical and cultural factors.

All ad agencies employ creativity—writing, art, photography, and music—to capture the public's much-divided attention. However, the most important part of what we do is study people: why they do what they do and why they buy what they buy.

Understanding what motivates people is a crucial part of my profession. But, being a black man, I was compelled to understand the way blacks are viewed in this country and the way many of us unconsciously view ourselves. Connecting the black dots on a larger level early on—from slavery and Jim Crow segregation to commercial and social propaganda—became my passion.

Burrell Communications' research of the '70s and '80s showed that African Americans have distinct psychosocial needs, desires, fears, hopes, and aspirations, all born of the circumstances arising from our experience as chattel slaves in America. We discovered, for example, that:

- Black preference for high-end status brands was driven by the need to compensate for feelings of low self-esteem.

- Our penchant for a lopsided spending/savings ratio grew out of our need for immediate gratification, based on a chilling pessimism about an uncertain future.

- We "over-indexed," spending disproportionate amounts in every product category related to cleanliness (from feminine douches and scented laundry detergent to car deodorizers and household disinfectants), primarily to compensate for being historically stereotyped as dirty.

The genesis of all these attitudes can be traced to American slavery. It was in America, in the "Land of the Free" that Africans were chained and branded, both physically and psychologically, as subhuman beasts of burden. It was here that we were first indoctrinated with the idea that we were, in fact, not humans at all, but property.

I determined to gain a clearer picture of the various ways that our painful history in America manifests itself in present-day attitudes and behaviors. Yes, there were intergenerational and historic factors determining African American purchasing patterns. But might there be similar factors influencing our daily lives, our relationships, our institutions?

In 2004, I sold the company and left the advertising business... but not completely. I found myself consumed by what I had learned and applied from my years of real-life African American cultural anthropology. How could I utilize what we knew—that we'd been branded physically and mentally from the beginning—to enable further exploration? How had that branding been perpetuated even after our physical chains were broken with the end of legal slavery? How were our intensely torturous enslavement and indoctrination transformed into the powerful, pernicious, all-pervasive, mass-media-driven brainwashing that still goes on today?

As a marketing professional who respects and admires brilliantly conceived and deftly executed propaganda, I eventually recognized that one of the greatest propaganda campaigns of all time was the masterful marketing of the myth of black inferiority to justify slavery within a democracy.

Ingenious.

I also became fascinated by the timeline of this perverse but brilliant campaign. The brainiac of his day, Thomas Jefferson—propagandist extraordinaire, chief strategist, and creative director, along with other powdered-wig power brokers—sold the idea of white supremacy to the masses—all the masses. They conspired to make this out-and-out barbarity America's first big brand. The early American ruling class used every available tool—religion, law, politics, art, literature, even the nascent field of science—as tools of their sales promotion and PR strategy.

The goal was to rationalize and reconcile the development of a single society with two outrageously contradictory parts: one built on the concept of human freedom, the other built on a vicious, governmentally sanctioned destruction of human freedom—all with the same history-making quill pen.

Think about it: America had grappled with the moral dilemma of slavery ever since the first Africans landed in Jamestown in 1619. The Founding Fathers found themselves at a serious moral crossroads. They desperately needed a way to justify the gaping divide between their God-fearing, freedom-loving rhetoric and the nation's increasing addiction to cheap slave labor.

The solution: an effective marketing campaign created to not only force the institution of slavery to fit within the budding democracy, but one aimed at convincing both master and slave that blacks had always been and would forever be mentally, physically, spiritually, and culturally inferior.

On a personal level, I'm revolted. Yet, as a marketing man, I find it to be an audacious and ingenious strategy. It's as though the original colonial elites hired a PR agency to sell the concept that Africans were innately inferior and it was indeed completely justifiable to treat them as subhuman beasts. The last several centuries still haunt us, and hinder our advancement and achievement. It has separated successful blacks from "disposable" blacks, those who simply refuse to "act right" and prosper.

In our effort to prove our equality, we unconsciously chased the master's dream, adopted his values, moved into his neighborhoods, went to his schools, and danced to his tune. While in assimilation and survival mode, we had no time to consider the price we'd pay for leaving our communities and leaving behind so many who look like us.

In the '60s and early '70s, we paid lip service to being black and proud, but the sudden conversion was not supported by the necessary psychological machinery to make the change permanent. Even today, we have woefully inadequate countermeasures, no permanent cultural mechanisms to undo what a 400-year marketing campaign has achieved.

Our insistence that we have broken free from the negative propaganda is wishful thinking. It takes much more than big afros, clenched fists, and danceable slogans to fight the centuries of unremitting exposure to twisted images and dehumanizing messages.

While I was writing this book, something happened that few of us in our wildest dreams ever imagined. A black man became president of the United States of America. Some may look at that and say, "See. Black Americans have overcome! As Dr. King predicted, we 'as a people' have gotten to the Promised Land."

In this day and age, imagery is power. Never before has the country had the image of a black man occupying the highest office in the land, delivering the State of the Union address, drafting and promoting national policy, or disembarking from Air Force One with his black wife and daughters. From a marketing perspective, this is powerful, life-altering stuff.

Yet anyone who looks beyond the glow of the moment will understand that neither we, nor our situation, will change overnight. A few of us have always succeeded, somehow, in spite of the failure of our American Dream. Barack Obama, through intelligence, will, self-determination, and yes, not a small confluence of favorable circumstances, may have reached his Promised Land, but most black Americans are still wandering in the wilderness.

The black inferiority/white superiority campaign has morphed exponentially in the New Media age—a vastly different, highly technological phase of instantly communicating messages and images has changed the landscape forever. Now a click of a mouse, a push of a button, or a finger slide across the screen of a portable media device defines what's an opportunity and what's a lost cause, what's stagnant and what's progress, what's valuable and what's worthless.

In the so-called "post-racial era," internalized black inferiority combined with this new media reality means the rules of engagement have changed dramatically. America's racial fatigue, coupled with the election of the nation's first African American president and the illusion of the acceptable exceptions, present new challenges for the best of us and, most importantly, for the rest of us.

The illusion of racial progress paves the way for a nationwide survival-of-the-fittest mentality. It will be okay to uproot urbanites so suburbanites can reclaim valuable metropolitan areas—gentrification is still unrelenting. Efforts to diversify the workplace and neighborhoods will become needless distractions. Affirmative action or any other race- or class-based efforts will become moot issues, of no value. After all, racism and prejudice died with the 2008 election. In a "post-racial" society, with New Media as its weapon, the brainwashing campaign now enters a phase that threatens to totally destroy our way of being.

At a time when the global economy is a touch screen away, when a fractured, dispirited nation is forced to once again dig deep and tap into its innovative roots to save itself, creative, time-tested black people can ill afford to sit on the sidelines besieged by a dormant, invisible virus. Now, more than ever, we have to come to terms with this devastating campaign. We've been programmed to deal with serious issues at a topical, epidermal level instead of going into deep tissue, to the root cause.

President Obama, utilizing a savvy New Media campaign to change hearts and win minds (and votes), has opened the door for a counter-propaganda campaign—one that benefits not just black people but whites as well. Now we are at a point in history when the opportunity for moving ahead has never been greater. We can seize this moment if only we take charge of our own destiny, our own reprogramming. If we pool our resources, we have the critical mass—the numbers, the voting power, and the persuasive skills—to enable us to combat the ills that derive from lingering racism. The same skills that have allowed us to survive, if used less passively and more pro-actively, can enable us to thrive.

I've experienced race-based lack of self-esteem first-hand. I know that it was not based solely on low income or poor education. As upwardly mobile as I was, that sense of lack was right there, climbing every rung of the ladder of success right beside me. Over time, I've learned that the root of the problem wasn't what was being done to me—it was what I'd been brainwashed to feel about myself.

We cannot cure the symptoms without acknowledging the disease. These pages examine the roots of why, more than 140 years after the Emancipation Proclamation, so many of us still think like slaves. I interviewed and incorporated the thoughts and experiences of many people throughout this book. Although I've changed names and ages of some of these interviewees to protect their identities, their honest input was invaluable in illustrating the modern-day impact of black inferiority conditioning. In Brainwashed, we will question why we still think so little of ourselves, why our grandmothers still put their savings in a special offering plate to help pay for the pastor's new luxury automobile, why our children answer when called "ho" and "nigga," why our one-time civil rights, business, and political heroes succumb to "crabbin' and backstabbin'," and why we, all too often, avoid critical thinking about any of this. This book examines our subconscious perpetuation of the myth of black inferiority by asking these fundamental questions:

- Why can't we build strong families?
- Why do we perpetuate black sexual stereotypes?
- Why are "black" and "beauty" still contradictions?
- Why do we keep killing each other?
- Why are we killing ourselves?
- Why can't we stop shopping?
- Why do we expect so little of each other—and ourselves?
- Why do we give up our power so willingly?
- Why can't we stick and stay together?
- Why is the joke always on us?

Even at this unprecedented and powerful point in American history, friends, colleagues, and well-wishers still express their frustration with black America's ever-worsening dependency on handouts, corporate sponsorships, and our kids' lack of respect for anything and anyone, especially themselves. They finally convinced me that my advertising-based discoveries about the brainwashing of my people, and my ideas about how to finally reverse its effects, could fill a book.

Well, here it is.

Chapter 1

The Scorch at the Bottom of the Melting Pot

*But in the propaganda against
the Negro since emancipation in this land,
we face one of the most stupendous efforts
the world ever saw to discredit human beings,
an effort involving universities, history, science,
social life and religion.*

— W. E. B. DU BOIS

The marketing of black inferiority and white superiority as building blocks for the founding of America is a chicken that has finally come home to roost. Now we must ask ourselves: Did the world's greatest brainwashing campaign work?

Fast-forward 233 years. "Yes, it worked brilliantly."

That response, however, is incomplete. To discover the real answer, we must strip away multiple layers of complex conditioning. Part of the black inferiority marketing campaign is to convince us that we can't handle the truth… that we're better off not knowing. It's an extremely patronizing message. We are capable enough and strong enough to handle the truth. More importantly, if we are to reverse the mindless perpetuation of the "black inferiority" or BI campaign we must go to that painful place so that we may claim our peace.

Let's examine the effects of the brainwashing campaign from a visual perspective. Imagine a video collage of contemporary black

1

images, delivered in a flashing, rapid, 60-second sequence. Try not to think in terms of good and bad or right and wrong but rather how familiar these scenes are.

- A syncopated, heart-thumping hip-hop beat pulsates while music video-style images explode on the screen with increasing tempo.

- A ghetto corner cordoned off with yellow police tape.

- On the six o'clock news, a mother wails over the body of a black boy felled by another black boy with a gun.

- Ivy League African Americans from Princeton, Harvard, and Yale running Fortune 500 companies.

- Prisons engorged with mostly dark-skinned inmates under twenty.

- Forlorn teenage girls with swollen, pregnant bellies and scowling, pubescent boys sporting saggin' pants zooming in and out of the picture.

- The 21st-century American Dream in black: Oprah Winfrey, Maya Angelou, Will Smith, Whoopi Goldberg, Condoleezza Rice, Colin Powell, and other role models.

- Tattooed rappers, half-naked, booty-shaking women; and hilariously funny but race-debasing comedians.

- Halle Berry seducing.

- Tiger Woods swinging.

- Michael Jordan flying.

- Beyoncé singing.

- Flava Flav bling blinging.

- Stressed-out, hard-working, underpaid workers walking through an economically depressed neighborhood.

- Empty faces of neglected and abandoned elders, emaciated adults, and obese children, malnourished in the land of plenty—all disproportionately suffering from junk food diets, diabetes, heart disease, HIV/AIDS, and other long-ignored, untreated yet preventable diseases.

- An urban school resembling an outdated factory with armed guards.

- A teacher/warden in an overcrowded classroom attempts to instruct children, who run the gamut from hyperactive to comatose.

- Photo gallery: Thurgood Marshall, Martin Luther King, Jr., and other Black History Month politicians and dignitaries.

- The montage slows to its finale with "Hail to the Chief" soaring in the background. Dominating the screen is a glorious photo of Barack Obama with First Lady Michelle by his side. Images fade to black with the voice of the nation's 44th president repeating the now familiar phrase: "It's our time."

:::

Exceptional Exceptions

Of all the faces in my video collage, which ones were most likely influenced by the inferior black/superior white brainwashing campaign?

All of them.

I can just hear the critics: "Whoa, whoa! Hold up, Burrell. Sure, there's black negativity on a grand scale, but how can you say *all* blacks are brainwashed to feel inferior when you just noted inspiring examples of prideful, positive, and progressive African Americans excelling and accomplishing historic feats?"

As an African American who has made his living understanding and utilizing the power of propaganda, I have unapologetically used the principles of psychology and emotional persuasion to promote products and agendas. I recognize marketing brilliance and am cognizant of the country's addiction to feeding its illusion of being a free and equal society, where anyone and everyone can succeed despite cultural and economic obstacles. Training the spotlight on well-deserving African American achievers clouds the realities that they grapple with daily.

The illusion that anyone can succeed—what I call the "paradox of progress"—solidifies the myth of a "post-racial society." It weakens the impulse to understand or help those still scorched at the bottom of America's melting pot. It fuels the perception that all is well and "racism is dead," and suggests that those still wallowing in poverty made conscious choices to live in that stratum. If not, many reason, they'd simply follow Halle, Tiger, Oprah, or even Tom Burrell's lead. They'd quit bellyaching, grab those bootstraps, and go to work!

Hold on. It's even more convoluted. Blacks, who've been conditioned to expect less from people who look like themselves, automatically insert these high-profile black achievers into the "exceptional exceptions" file. Many are positioned on pedestals, with no demands of accountability toward those they left behind.

After all, these people have achieved so much. They're different! They're exceptional! Some prominent black achievers have actually opened their own Kool-Aid stands. They, too, consider themselves the "exception" and, in many instances—consciously or unconsciously—have begun to regard blacks of lesser social status or achievement as inferior. Ironically, in many ways, the progress paradox is an impediment to substantive collective progress.

Consider recent FBI crime statistics, census figures associated with poverty, or the conclusions found in the book put out annually by the National Urban League, *The State of Black America*. They reveal the same ongoing, depressing themes: social chaos, irresponsible spending, economic stagnation, and disproportionate death and incarceration rates. No matter what the category, blacks statistically trail behind whites and other ethnicities, and in some areas, such as educational achievement and overall life expectancy, our numbers are actually getting worse.

Regardless of our individual social, economic, or media success, it has not affected the black bottom line. Therefore, though black progress is more visible today than ever before, I maintain that the unwritten, audacious promotion of white superiority and black inferiority was (and still is) the most effective and successful marketing/propaganda campaign in the history of the world. African Americans, no matter how savvy, educated, or financially privileged, could not completely avoid the conditioning that resulted from increasingly sophisticated bombardment of subtle and not-so-subtle messages created to reinforce how different and inherently inferior blacks are when compared to whites.

In this perpetual state of "otherness" there's no disputing our unequal status. Like Coca-Cola, the black inferiority product has been modernized and updated with time. But don't be mistaken, the intent is to keep the original message firmly embedded in our psyches: white superiority was, is, and (unless we block the negativity) will always be "The Real Thing."

Early indoctrination into my own inferiority fueled a determination to succeed. I remember coming to a conscious decision when I reached adulthood that, rather than continue internalizing the hurt and humiliation, "I'd just show them."

I tried to deal with it in a variety of ways, starting with the idea of fooling "the man," making all believe that I was something other than what "they" said. Some days I tried my best. Other days, I'd just want to give in, accept the lesser status and engage in cynical behavior. Ultimately, I chose the "fake it till you make it" approach, spoofing the public until I was financially secure enough to retire into a category of my own design. This line of thinking continued until I was more than 40 years old, well after I'd established my marketing firm.

Burrell Communications was touted for mastering the skills of positive commercial propaganda. Perhaps it was because of our commitment to understanding, mastering, and utilizing savvy techniques required to sell products and influence behavior that certain realities finally clarified and eventually inspired this journey. All I know for sure is, at some point it dawned on me that I was not faking. I was, indeed, just as smart, just as brave, just as disciplined, and just as beautiful as what I thought I was pretending to be. The more I learned about the origin of my own issues, which had been festering from the legacy of chattel slavery, the more I was able to see the same wounds in others.

It was then I realized that I, like most Americans, had been brainwashed.

Propaganda Campaigns

Maybe I'm expressing a sense of atonement or maybe it's just that I don't want to leave this planet without putting my life's skills to the ultimate test. I've decided to adopt a strategy similar to that of Edward Bernays, the nephew of the famous psychiatrist Sigmund Freud.

Bernays was considered by many experts to be the first public-relations professional. In fact, he takes credit for inventing the term. Bernays adapted some of Uncle Sigmund's revolutionary psychological studies to aid the government's World War II media offensive and helped manipulate the American masses for fun and profit.

Bernays didn't call himself a propagandist. Back then the Germans had already given the word the negative taint it still carries today.

Instead, Bernays called himself a public-relations expert. In a very real way, his first propaganda triumph was to change the image of propaganda itself. In a way, this book follows Bernays's lead. The intent is to thoroughly dissect this white superiority/black inferiority phenomenon, demonstrate how it still retards our social, personal, and economic advancement, and then help Americans flip the script—to neutralize the techniques.

Unlike Bernays, I have no intention of shying away from the term *propaganda*. I say we use it—take what was thrown at us, shuck it off, and replace it with "positive" propaganda. Propaganda is the outer layer of this brainwashing onion. After all, in the marketing world, propaganda is the first tool utilized to achieve a desired outcome. Brainwashing is the outcome, but propaganda got us here, and its continued use keeps the inferior/superior mind game in play. Instead of using torture and other coercive techniques, the stealthy, media-savvy propagandist uses mass media and other forms of communication to change minds and mold ways of thinking.

In the United States, the first society in theory governed by popular opinion, propaganda became a critical tool of the wealthy, governing elite. For instance, the powerful words *freedom and justice for all* overshadowed the reality that both were denied to black slaves. Yet those words, as propaganda tools, helped solidify the image of a burgeoning nation.

There are many propaganda principles. But here are a few that I believe were of prime importance in the 18th-century black inferiority marketing strategy. These principles were employed throughout the colonial period of the late 1700s, Reconstruction in the late 1800s, the 20th-century civil rights movement, and still survive in modern times.

The Big Lie—the repeated and consistent articulation of a partial, distorted, or manufactured "truth."

- **Colonial era:** Black slaves are subhuman beasts.

- **Reconstruction era:** Emancipated blacks are still inferior to whites.

- **Civil Rights era:** Blacks are angry, dangerous, unemployable, and addicted to welfare.

- **Modern era:** Low-income blacks are innate failures, responsible for their own moral and economic decline.

Appeal to Fear—the purposeful effort to instill apprehension and panic.

- **Colonial era:** Changing the status of black slaves will threaten our livelihood and destroy our way of life.

- **Reconstruction era:** Emancipated blacks will seek revenge and rape white women.

- **Civil Rights era:** Blacks are revolutionary communists. They're moving too fast and want too much at once. "Black power" really means "race war."

- **Modern era:** Low-income blacks are violent and prone to crime. They threaten property values and must be contained or incarcerated.

Appeal to Prejudice—attaching a value or moral label to flawed but well-established perceptions.

- **Colonial era:** Whites are physically, mentally, and morally superior to blacks.

- **Reconstruction era:** Blacks want and need to be subjugated. They cannot function in free society.

- **Civil Rights era:** Whites have earned economic and social privilege through hard work, discipline, high morals, and family values.

- **Modern era:** Social and economic woes are attributed solely to irresponsible black parenting, crime-coddling communities, and a sense of perceived "victimization."

Stereotyping—exaggerating established perceptions of physical or cultural traits, attaching negative attributes to an entire group.

- **Colonial era:** Black slaves are uncivilized, childlike, and content with bondage.

- **Reconstruction era:** Emancipated blacks are buffoons, lazy, illiterate, and rapists.

- **Civil Rights era:** Blacks are angry, impatient, and murderers.

- **Modern era:** Low-income blacks are drug-addicted, criminal, oversexed, dependent on government assistance, and irresponsible.

Anti-Jewish Propaganda

Perhaps the only other group subjected to such an extensive, calculated, and government-funded propaganda campaign were the Jews under the reign of Germany's leader, Adolf Hitler, in the '30s and '40s. The Führer found propaganda a handy tool in spreading the dogma of Aryan superiority, achieving his military goals, and justifying the mass eradication of Jews. The "Ministry of Public Enlightenment and Propaganda," headed by Hitler's propagandist, Joseph Goebbels, churned out posters, films, and books that spread Hitler's bile.

Although Jews, like blacks, suffered under a deadly campaign of propaganda and brainwashing, the effort doesn't seem to have hampered their long-term cultural evolution or caused stifling psychological impairment. Jews don't rank with blacks in social and economic dysfunction.

It's not that Jewish people are better or stronger than black people. The Holocaust under Hitler—as deadly and horrific as it was—lasted about 12 years. Even by conservative standards, the black holocaust had a solid 250-year run.

When examining Jewish culture, we understand that their physical and mental survival was attributed to their foundations in culture, family, and rituals. Among Jews in Egypt, Persia, Germany, America, and elsewhere, there is common ritual, common belief, common values, and a common religious thread.

As later chapters will illustrate, such cultural riches were stolen from blacks. Slaves and their descendents had no assumed permanent structures to maintain their cultural roots. They continuously cobbled together culture based on white dictates. Slavery, Jim Crow, and segregated society were not solid foundations. Blacks were programmatically stripped of their cultural identity and brainwashed into a mindset of black inferiority—a double whammy that's tough to overcome.

Propaganda in the Modern Era: Branding and Marketing

The principles of propaganda withstood the test of time. But propaganda by itself is just angry, vile, vicious sentiment. Just as a car's engine works best with additional, intricate parts, propaganda, coupled with other promotional tools, such as marketing and branding, made the black inferiority crusade a long-lasting success.

Take *marketing*, for example. Think of it as the commercial, for-profit, businessend of brainwashing and propaganda. It's what all major companies use to sell products and services. Although marketing encompasses many endeavors, advertising is its most familiar form.

Branding is another word with diverse meanings and nuances. Several of these apply to this book's premise, including branding a product with a trademark or branding of skin as an identifying mark. Branding also helps the consumer associate products with a widely accepted name, distinguishing it from similar products.

In today's world, companies spend hundreds of millions, if not billions, to establish, promote, and protect their brands—Nike shoes, McDonald's hamburgers, Apple computers, Starbucks coffee, United Airlines, Ivory soap. However, one of the first high-value brands in America was not an inanimate product. It was humans. African Americans were turned into *animate* products: slaves. And the brand that the early ruling class literally and figuratively burned onto black Americans, as they did with livestock, was the permanent identifier of "subhuman inferiority."

While some might argue that racist media practices died with the Jim Crow era, a few thousand folks stranded for days on sweltering rooftops or in neck-deep, toxic floodwater in the aftermath of Hurricane Katrina in 2005 might disagree. We now know that many of the 24/7 news accounts of black-on-black sniper attacks, mass murders, and the rape of women and babies were largely unfounded.

What influenced seasoned journalists, policemen, and emergency workers to initially sidestep humanity and propagate exaggerated accounts of black crime?

Again, media propaganda.

Norman Coombs, author of *The Black Experience in America: The Immigrant Heritage of America*, wrote about the genesis and ultimate result of this grand scheme:

> Not only did white America become convinced of white superiority and black inferiority, but it strove to impose these racial beliefs on the Africans themselves. Slavemasters gave a great deal of attention to the education and training of the ideal slave...At every point this education was built on the belief in white superiority and black inferiority. Besides teaching the slave to despise his own history and culture, the master strove to inculcate his own value system into the African's outlook. The white man's belief in the African's inferiority paralleled African self-hate.

In short, we were brainwashed.

Chapter 2

Relationship Wrecks

Why Can't We Form Strong Families?

*The shattering blows on the Negro family
have made it fragile, deprived, and often psychopathic.*

— DR. MARTIN LUTHER KING, JR.

On Father's Day, June 15, 2008, Barack Obama, then only a candidate for the U.S. presidential nomination, stood before a black congregation at a Chicago South Side church and delivered an important message to the black community:

> Of all the rocks upon which we build our lives, we are reminded today that family is the most important...But if we are honest with ourselves we'll also admit that too many fathers are missing from too many lives and too many homes. They have abandoned their responsibilities, acting like boys instead of men. And the foundations of our families are weaker because of it.

While Obama was congratulated for boldly taking absentee black fathers to task and condemned for taking an opportunistic shot at black men for political gain, all sides missed the most important points. Black men are not just absent from their children's lives; too many black men and women are absent from each other's lives.

13

In other words, it's not just a fathering problem; it's a "family-ing" problem, another casualty of our addiction to the black Inferiority brand. The major challenge, therefore, is to discuss and seriously dissect the black family-ing problem.

Songs to the Beat (down) of Black Life

Hit the road, Jack. The kid is not my son, who's making love to your old lady? Papa was a rollin' stone. We sing, dance, and make love to catchy beats that endorse, reinforce, and promulgate our most self-destructive habits.

The messages are not only telegraphed through our music. The muddy milieu of black relationships seemingly splash across the front pages of tabloids, on Internet pages, on the nightly news and TV dramas, and in everyday advertising. The media gleefully amplified the exploits of a wildly successful R&B singer beaten bloody by her equally popular boyfriend. Of course, the juicy story of the black televangelist strangled and stomped by her preacher husband on a hotel parking lot also received plenty of media play.

Flip the channel or turn the page and there are the "baby mamas" and "baby daddies" so ubiquitous in common American culture that they become plot points or titles for mainstream comedies and movies.

And there, on the news, backed by respected research, are the products of all this ingrained promiscuity and violence—young children seemingly running amok in urban cities that breed violence, some left to raise their own siblings in the absence of negligent or missing parents.

The syndicated television program *Maury*, hosted by Maury Povich, is known for its "Who's Your Daddy?" segments. Much of the content is based on issuing paternity tests to teens and young adults in hopes of determining fatherhood. In just one week during the summer of 2009, I watched these scenarios:

Three young African American women—girls really—accused a young man of fathering their three children—all born within a month of one another. The young man had another 7-month-old child with his current girlfriend. In another segment, a young girl slept with two men at the same time, and was unsure who fathered her child. Then, there was the story about a mother who paid her daughter's boyfriend for sex.

Many of *Maury*'s guests are black, and the sheer number of these cases is damning. Shows like these, along with court television shows that promote the same dysfunction, are very popular. I couldn't help but imagine the vast numbers of people indoctrinated by these images of black family chaos. And it's not like we can put 100 percent of the blame for this public buffoonery on the producers of these shows. These situations aren't fabricated; they're just carefully picked realities of black life. Sadly, it's art (and I use the word loosely) that imitates life. We watch these programs like a gory train wreck because they involve so many people who look like us.

Blacks not only dance to the beat of family destruction, we patronize films by black producers and directors that bombard our brains and reinforce all the bad we've been fed about ourselves—first by the white ruling class, and now abetted by our brainwashed brethren. Whether it's sagas like Rihanna and Chris Brown, or negative, self-demeaning movies, or characters like those depicted in HBO's gritty urban drama *The Wire*—black relationships and families are seen as hopelessly at odds, dysfunctional, violent, and unsubstantial.

Yet we accept and share these perceptions without question or qualm. Passionate conversations about "no good black men" among groups of black women are not irregularities. What *is* a rare occurrence, however, is our willingness to go to the historic root of negative black male behavior or discuss how fatherless homes help shape the sentiments shared by so many black women.

Likewise, black men are not aware of the unconscious motivators that cause them to demean black women. Nary is an objection raised when gaggles of these men depict evil, mean-spirited, materialistic, or impatient black women, and then expound on why they're better off with white women. Little attention is paid to the daughters

these men bring into the world. Not only are they conditioned to live the stereotype of their mothers, many do so in homes with absentee fathers.

It's assumed that black women are supposed to have a slew of children with multiple men who will eventually abandon them. These women are quickly relegated to "supermom" status, expected to serve as both the foundation and as the black family's doormat. This, too, is a topic that receives little discussion, as is the mystery of how and why black women become enablers, molding black boys who will someday emulate the actions of their wayward fathers.

At a very young age, black men and women are inundated with messages that they cannot trust or depend upon one other. Children hear comments and jokes about lazy, greedy, irresponsible, or otherwise flawed black adults. They are warned to be tough, trust no one, and always, always be prepared for the doomed relationship. Is it really a revelation that incompatibility, lack of love, and oftentimes violence become the inevitable conclusions of these tainted individuals' relationships?

Black Family Dysfunction

We hear them. We see them. We feel them and, ultimately, we tune them out.

Distrust and contempt; physical, verbal, and psychological abuse; infidelity; emotional distance; and mutually disabling partnerships—these are the five most destructive dynamics that lead to fractured black relationships and broken families. To tackle our Black Inferiority Complex as a purposefully embedded condition, it's important that we approach the subject in the manner in which I've taken on projects as a marketing and advertising executive for 45 years.

In a sense, BI Complex is the competitor's product. My goal is to break its dominance in the black mindset and introduce a better, uplifting brand. This means that we first have to dissect the brand's staying power and understand how it continues to wreak havoc on black families and relationships. So let's start peeling the onion. First, let's define the five dynamics that hamper the development of strong, healthy black families.

Relationship Wrecks—Dynamics

1. **Diss-respect**
   Words of mutual contempt, ridicule; wide mistrust of mates, mothers, and fathers.
   We hear this in everyday conversations among black men and women, parents and grandparents, at parties, and in the privacy of our homes. Words of mutual contempt, the casual dissing of one another that seed the notion that black men and women are to be ridiculed, put down, and widely mistrusted as mates and as parents. The effect of self-inflicted disrespect is indicative in the 43.3 percent of black men and 41.9 percent of black women in America who have never been married (according to 2001 Census Bureau statistics), compared to 27.4 percent of white men and 20.7 percent of white women who have never married. The overall U.S. marriage rate, from 1970 to 2001, declined by 17 percent, but the rate among blacks fell by a whopping 34 percent.

2. **The Beat-Down**
   Disproportionate rates of physical, verbal, spiritual, and psychological abuse in black relationships.
   Physical, verbal, spiritual, and psychological abuses are disproportionate factors in black relationships. Today, reported incidents of family violence are highest in African American households, according to data from the American Bar Association's Commission on Domestic Violence. The number one killer of African American women aged 15 to 34 is not cancer, not car wrecks, but dying at the hands of "loved ones." Overall, from 1993 to 1998, black females experienced intimate partner violence at a rate 35 percent higher than that of white females, and *about 22 times the rate of women of other races.*

On the other side of this spectrum we find that black males experienced intimate partner violence at a rate of about 62 percent higher than that of white males and *about 22 times the rate of men of other races*. Of course, verbal, psychological, and spiritual abuse has not been documented, but coupled with physical violence, we glimpse the full-body assault far too many black women, men, and children must endure. Recognizing the beat-down is one thing—understanding its destructive opposition to forming and maintaining healthy family relationships is the real task at hand.

3. **"Can't Be True to My Boo"**
   The acceptance and expectation of infidelity.
   Infidelity is another popular subject in relationship conversations. Additionally, in song and through mass media messaging, we advertise our inability to remain true to one another. And, like self-fulfilling prophecies, these repeated messages are like bricks paving the walkway to wrecked relationships.

4. **Icing**
   Emotional shutdown and distance that fosters unhealthy relationships. Icing results in embracing anti-intimate behavior, even in intimate relationships.
   We are a tough, strong, resilient race. Our elders remind us that "life ain't no crystal stair." We're expected to "suck it up" and deal with the cards we're dealt in life. The "icing" process is encoded in our DNA. Therefore, we embrace anti-intimate behavior even as we seek intimate relationships. We shut down and keep emotional distance, hoping to avoid hurt at all costs. In reality, we only avoid true romanticism, opting instead to survive relationships instead of enjoying healthy ones.

5. **Mutual Dis-enabling**
   Irresponsible black men and overprotective black women perpetrate negative emotional trends with sons and daughters. Children continue the cycle of unhealthy relationships.

Irresponsible and absent black fathers who won't (or can't) protect or provide for their families mate with the black superwomen—over-responsible, addicted to no-account black men, and woefully empty partnerships, they assume roles of "Mama," "Daddy," and "family provider." Their fragile children will someday procreate and continue the cycle of unhealthy relationships. The results were evident in the 2005 National Center for Health Statistics data showing that nearly 70 percent of black children in the United States were born to single mothers, compared to 25.3 percent to non-Hispanic white women, and 48 percent to Hispanic women.

We acknowledge these and other negative statistics, but what has not been thoroughly explored is *how* we collectively came to behave in destructive ways and *why* the cycle continues unabated.

Question, Analyze, Unplug, Reprogram

Are these statistics indicative of our natural state of affairs, or do they reflect a self-fulfilling prophesy? Are we stuck on a path of low expectations that legitimizes the disintegration of black families? Are we so "iced" and emotionally toughened that we expect abusive, violent relationships, high percentages of unmarried couples, and out-of-wedlock children born to parents with no commitment to one another or their children's well-being? Failing to explore the genesis and ongoing ramifications of these issues is like a doctor treating acute pneumonia with a cough suppressant.

The baby mamma/baby daddy drama is laughable, even to a generation of blacks who expect a single mother to raise kids who must fend for themselves and have no extended family members to nurture, care for, or protect them. What kind of indictment is it of black men and women that, based on the number of their sexual relationships, they *don't* know who has fathered or mothered their

children? It's disheartening to watch young black men on shows like *Maury* celebrate when they learn: "You are *not* the father!" Reaction to such life-altering news may be understandable but, for most of the American viewing audience, these young men are celebrating their escape from responsibility. Fatherhood is one of the greatest privileges in any society. Yet, this very serious issue is trivialized through spectacles like *Maury* and other popular TV shows. Trivializing black life has become all too common a sport.

Why are stable, normal black families considered the exception, not the rule? Perhaps it's because constantly marketed, predetermined negative expectations prepare black men and women to expect the worst from one another. Perhaps it's because history takes us directly to a place that inspires white guilt and black gloom, a place many want to ignore and few want to recognize as the source of much of today's black angst. It's time to look past the depressing headlines and gloomy statistics, and begin dealing with the acute factors that cripple black families and relationships. First, however, we must honestly look into what contributed to this state of affairs.

Where the Beat-Down Began

To be blunt: disproportionate black family dysfunction is directly linked to American chattel slavery, the Founding Fathers, and the barbaric entrepreneurship of a nation.

As black abolitionist David Walker argued in his 1829 pamphlet, *Appeal to the Coloured Citizens of the World,* American slaveowners, unlike their counterparts in some other slave-based economies, had no regard for familial attachments. In fact, they made a conscious, willful decision to control slaves' minds through decimating the black family. Deconstructing the very concept of "black family" was central to the massive enterprise to build a new economy, and to lay the cornerstones of personal fortunes.

Assessing this from a marketing perspective, to achieve their strategy, enslavers could not leave Africans with any vestige of the "family" brand. In laymen's terms, the black family had to be destroyed and the first order of business was to annihilate the black family's designated protector—the black man.

My granny taught me a lot about black men. That they are good for nothing...they don't want to work, they want to sit up and take all your money. And they are ignorant. She told me if I was smart I should be good and go to school and find myself a rich white man.
— Lela

Dehumanizing the Family

By the mid-1600s, with the passage of the first Slave Codes, slavemasters began legalizing the dehumanization of African slaves. Because men in African cultures were an integral part of both the immediate and extended family, branding and breaking any remnant of a rebel spirit in black men became a critical step. If black men were not sufficiently animalized, dehumanized, and broken, they could potentially cause great damage to the lucrative slave-marketing system—as slave revolts in America and Haiti proved.

Slaves had no legal safeguards. Black men were powerless to protect their loved ones from harassment, sexual exploitation, or rape from masters and overseers.

Black women were forced by circumstance to stifle their matriarchal impulses, and to abide and navigate a system that left their husbands and children exposed to unimaginable cruelty. Toni Morrison's book *Beloved* provides but a glimpse into the insane world where a beaten and brutalized runaway slave mother kills her baby girl rather than have the child reared as a slave.

Fear was a constant among slave families. In addition to various other indignities and humiliations, slave families were forced to watch wives, husbands, sons, and daughters harassed, violated, or mutilated. Those who tried to protect their loved ones found themselves abused or murdered.

To my knowledge, the long-term trauma and mental damage to the black family forced to tolerate repeated family abuse under

slavery has never been fully studied or documented. One thing is clear, however: Stripping black men and women of their natural roles as parents and protectors, and conditioning them to accept physical and psychological abuse were initial steps in the brainwashing campaign.

If early American institutions of commerce, architecture, and religion morphed into modern times, is it any surprise that the system that devastated the slave family also snaked its way, in some form, into the 21st century? We have iced over centuries of inherited trauma. Instead, most of us choose the easy route of emotional detachment, refusing to acknowledge a damaging condition we don't understand and cannot control.

The damage still seeps out. It's notable in the abandonment, debasement, and violence we inflict upon ourselves, our spouses, our lovers, and our children.

> *Marcus came from a working class black family—one generation away from the projects. We didn't so much as fall in love, we fell in need. (His) parents fought and were abusive, so we were really doomed from the start. He was used to seeing abuse, and therefore he thought that was what a man was supposed to do. I was used to taking abuse, so I thought that was what I was supposed to do. We were a perfect complement for each other...for disaster.*
> — Tanya, age 52

Family by Another Name

For the slaveowner, keeping black families united garnered less of their attention than breeding and selling livestock. A key component to establishing the "beast" brand was treating and breeding black men and women like farm animals.

The domestic sale and breeding of African Americans for slave markets remained legal until early 1808. However, after the importation of slaves was no longer sanctioned by the government, slaveowners in tobacco-growing states like North Carolina, Maryland, and Virginia earned big profits by breeding and selling excess slaves to farmers "down the river" in the Deep South. The large plantation owners there needed massive numbers of slaves to pick the South's next big thing—cotton—a commodity more and more in demand in England.

Black families existed in a perpetual state of instability. Any number of circumstances easily separated them for a lifetime. Many slaves wound up on the auction block due to their owner's misfortune or death. Slaves labeled "unruly" were often sold as punishment for their behavior. Even if immediate families managed to stay together, there was no guarantee that a niece or grandson would remain on the same plantation as an aunt or grandfather. The system retarded and fractured the basic sense of safety inherent within the family. Slaves found themselves dependent upon the benevolence of their oppressor, the slavemaster, for any semblance of safety.

From Boys to Men

Slavery and its aftermath constituted an unrelenting assault on black male identity. The trauma was a serious blow to the sense of manhood prevalent in male-dominated societies, and which many black men still wrestle with today. It is impossible to understand our current family crisis without examining the historical ways in which black fathers, mates, brothers, and sons were emasculated.

Slavery disturbed the minds of black men who watched their women carry out traditional male duties of West African societies. Black male slaves could not take on any of the roles monopolized by white men, who set guidelines in the home for training and raising children, especially their sons, into adulthood.

Renowned anthropologist Margaret Mead, as noted in the 1965 U.S. Department of Labor report "The Negro Family," explained the consequences of manipulating the family hierarchy:

> With the family, each new generation of young males learns the appropriate nurturing behavior and superimposes upon their biologically given maleness, this learned parental role. When the family breaks down—as it does under slavery...these deliberate lines of transmission are broken.

Who's the Man?

As empathetic as female slaves were to the plight of their husbands, who were deprived of the roles of protector and leader, the fact remained that the slavemaster was, by design, the real provider of safety and security.

Oftentimes she demeaned herself. She grinned, shuffled, and hustled to protect her family. And the power dynamic didn't change after Emancipation. Jim Crow segregation and institutionalized racism cemented the rule of law in white male hands. For centuries, black women understood that the natural order of male/female relationships didn't apply. No matter how much she understood *why* her man couldn't protect her, the unnatural code of survival seeded subliminal contempt: *You didn't protect me. You can't protect me. I have to protect myself!*

Black Woman/White World

The Founding Fathers maintained dominance by waging a mental war to convince themselves and their slaves that blacks were childlike, inferior, and better off under *their* care, discipline, and direction. In a twisted form of mental manipulation and male dominance, white men worked to persuade black women that black men were unreliable, docile, and unsuited for leadership roles. Propaganda reinforced the notion that black women and their children were safer in a white-controlled environment.

Black women—deemed less threatening—were more often assigned roles as house servants. They were allowed indoors to suckle white babies and tend to the white family's every need. This role was seen as a step up from grueling field work. Into the late 20th century, even during the harshest economic times, maid service and house cleaning in white, well-to-do households were always options available for black women.

In caricature, even after slavery ended, black men were depicted as vile, buffoonish loafers who thrived in neighborhoods filled with corruption and vice. Juxtaposed against this were images of black women happily separated from these men, enjoying safety and privilege in the sanctity of calm, well-ordered, clean, and wholesome white environments.

In early American literature and numerous films, black women were portrayed as part of the white family—à la Aunt Jemima—wholly dependent on the benevolence of white men and blissfully serving the family. *The Beulah Show,* America's first television sitcom starring an African American woman (1950–1953), featured black actresses, first Ethel Waters and later Hattie McDaniel. Advertising for the show hyped Beulah as the beloved servant who served as the "queen of the kitchen" and managed the household.

The modern rendition of the black-woman-thriving-in-the-white-world theme is evidenced in the Nickelodeon sitcom *True Jackson, VP.* In this bubblegum series, a black teenage girl (Keke Palmer) wins a prize job at a successful, white-owned high-fashion company. In the first season of the show there was no hint of True's family life or her black parents. Her best friends are not black and she falls for the white nephew of the company's eccentric white male boss.

And who could forget Omarosa Manigault-Stallworth, the hard-edged, independent, and famously stubborn contestant on the TV show *The Apprentice.* Even though it's promoted as a reality show, writers still script the roles for best effect. Omarosa fit the popular stereotypical role of the "corporate black bitch" who would backstab, brown-nose, mooch, and do whatever necessary to win the favor of the white mega-boss, Donald Trump.

The overabundance of these on-screen heroines subtly reinforces the early American mantra that black women are suited to white surroundings. If black men are depicted at all, they are often flawed, powerless, and secondary characters.

Most often, however, black men are invisible, as in the 2008 comedy film *Role Models.* In the film, a black mother (Nicole Randall Johnson) depends on a white, hard-drinking, dope-smoking, womanizer (Sean William Scott) to reform her troubled, foul-mouthed, ill-tempered

"Booby Watcher" 10-year-old son (Bobb'e J. Thompson), who was abandoned (without explanation) by his black father. *Role Models* is but a modern-day echo of a slave-era theme. Of course, a black woman would turn to a boozing, irresponsible white man to save her son. After all, she knows she can't depend on a black man to protect her or raise his own children.

The seeds of mutual disrespect are rooted deep in the foundation of "blackness." Media messages, on a subconscious level, remind blacks of their inferior status and their roles, designated during slavery, of irresponsible, childlike wards of an almighty, all-powerful, superior white society.

> *(Mother) married a Caucasian man, because in her mind, that was going the complete opposite direction...he would be all the things that Daddy wasn't: stable, have a good job, wouldn't cheat on her, etc...She wanted that white picket fence, that stability, and he (Daddy) couldn't do that. She loved him. She loved him so much, but it was not enough.*
> — Tanya

Why We Can't All "Just Get Along?"

Isn't it fairly predictable that men and women who've been bred, branded, and programmed for hundreds of years to avoid traditional roles of commitment, parenthood, and marriage would have a difficult time sustaining these roles today?

It is encouraging that, given this history, so many black men and women have remained "whole and functioning" men, women, and parents. Yet, the current state of relations among African American couples indicates that our gender wars are more intense than in other racial groups, our expectation gaps far wider, and the routes we travel in search of conjugal bliss are planted with more landmines.

Authors Brenda Lane Richardson and Dr. Brenda Wade get to the genesis of this pathology in the book *What Mama Couldn't Tell Us About Love:*

> In the meantime, both your son and daughter have grown into adulthood on other plantations, believing they can't count on anyone for closeness and warmth, that love is temporary. After all, they lost the first love of their lives, and heaped on this are the everyday cruelties and humiliations of being a slave. Under these conditions, they can't love themselves, and so it is impossible for them to teach their children how to love themselves.

Instead of teaching love, most black men and women regurgitate negatives. In barbershops across the nation, where black men can be black men, a common topic centers on the crazy, violent, untrustworthy, overpowering black woman.

Once we look at the traumatic hand black women have been dealt and still shuffle, we can move beyond the stereotypical "angry black woman" and address the issue from the foundations of her frustration. If we dissect the brainwashing campaign, black men may recognize that, inherent in our negative descriptors of black women, we are still grappling with an age-old fear that we are "less than," and cannot meet societal expectations. It's simply easier to write black women off as crazy than confront the white man's "truths."

> *The things men would say about black women: "Black women don't let you get away with anything. They'd always be all up in your shit, attitudinal, all in your face." The stereotypical black experience was a hard-ass life. Black men wanted to escape from that, and unfortunately black women represented that. You can't leave this box you've been painted into unless you leave her behind.*
> — James, 32

"When women get together and talk about men, the news is almost always bad news," writes bell hooks, the feminist social critic, in *We Real Cool: Black Men and Masculinity.* "If the topic gets specific and

the focus is on black men, the news is even worse." Is it any wonder that the pain resulting from fractured relationships infuses art, literature, and song? The black woman, who subconsciously considers herself unworthy, has steeled herself to expect less love, less understanding, less compassion. Bruised and broken, she is fully prepared not to invest too much in the inferior black man. Filled with inexpressible disappointment and disillusionment, she buries her feelings and will even tolerate contempt and abuse.

The black woman's recurring theme is "love and trouble," as expressed by the legendary Billie Holiday in "My Man":

> He isn't true
> He beats me, too

Accepting the lowest common denominator of ourselves, rejecting or not having any reasonable expectation of a loving relationship, or choosing to go it alone because black men and women are portrayed as spoiled goods, all perpetuate the "big lie" expertly drafted to emphasize the inferiority of the black race.

Mama's Baby,
Daddy's Maybe?

Nearly three-quarters of a century ago, sociologist E. Franklin Frazier, in his seminal study *The Negro Family in America* (first published in 1939), described common family patterns in the Cotton Belt that resulted in high rates of out-of-wedlock births, which were tolerated without "stigma in the community."

We are but a few generations removed from this part of our past. A famous Mississippi Delta blues legend was reported to have had 15 children by 15 different women. This is something that cannot be explained solely by the enormous amount of time spent on the road. It is instead an integral part of our cultural heritage.

Although the palimony suit brought against Atlanta-based rapper TI (Clifford Joseph Harris) dominated the media gossip circuit in 2008, few fans questioned why the relationship ended between the 27-year-old artist and the 29-year-old mother who had known each other since their teen years. Few bothered to ponder the fate of the couple's two children left in the wake of the legal dust-up.

Famous absentee black fathers sometimes boast of their "studliness." In the eyes of many of their adoring, unquestioning fans, such recklessness actually brightens, rather than dims, their star appeal. Romanticizing and emulating irresponsible celebrity behavior is just another indicator of a race suffering from an acute addiction to the BI Complex.

Do You Really Want to Hurt Me?

Having lost any normal claim to masculinity and any right to act out the role of man and father, many black men attempt to compensate for their powerlessness by exercising dominance over the only people they can—their women and children, and when possible, other black men. Slavery's abolition translated into freedom to claim the manhood they had long been denied. Many black men seized this new opportunity with a vengeance, using as their model the manliest man they knew: the brutal white, Southern patriarch, supreme master over his wife, his home, and all his property—including his slaves. It was in a slave-dominated society that black men learned it was acceptable to use violence to establish patriarchal power over black women, writes bell hooks in *We Real Cool: Black Men and Masculinity:*

> The gender politics of slavery and white-supremacist domination of free black men was the school where black men from different African tribes, with different languages and value systems learned in the new world, patriarchal masculinity.

Women, who had been raised to be strong, tough, and creative survivalists, were suddenly excluded by black men from public life and leadership roles in church and civic organizations. Newly emancipated

black male leadership instructed these women to let black men finally be men and defer to them on all matters.

In contemporary times, the BI brand convinces black men that this dominant, macho posturing is still essential to their male identity. In reality, it serves as just another relationship killer, contributing to our present-day crisis.

Secondly, this attitude is an assault on the spirit of strong, black women who expect and deserve full parity. It is this culture of male dominance that leads many men to accuse black women of being "ball busters" if they refuse to be subservient.

The image that black women are shackled with feels like a ball and chain. She's a reminder of how the world sees you, and what you can and cannot change. It's scary, and it's a disservice to strong black women, but it's part of what scares men away.
— James

In Search of Manhood

To be black in America is to be tense, anxious, and often fearful if not outright angry. Intimate relationships often become the central arena where black men today can vent racial frustrations. While he struggles to grasp "manhood" in a society that holds it from him at arm's length, the befuddled black man lashes out violently at the woman he feels is undermining his fragile authority. This pattern often intensifies when a black middle-class or professional woman is on the fast track in the white corporate world while the man still struggles merely to gain access.

The black-male-dominance ideology that fuels marital tension and leads to physical or emotional abuse is no new phenomenon. In *Trouble in Mind*, Leon Litwack's history of blacks in the Jim Crow South, the author describes widespread incidents of men lashing out at women "for no other reason than to exercise a male prerogative and to subdue independent spirits."

In his essay "Open Letter to an American Woman," Kevin Powell, a New York writer, offers a contemporary explanation of his attitude toward women:

> And just like most males in America, I too was taught, in school, at home, on the streets and playgrounds, at the churches I attended as a youth, and via popular culture, that to be a man is to forever be in a position of power and advantage over women and girls. That flawed concept of maleness meant not only dominating women or girls, but having little to no regard for their health and wellness, for their safety, for their bodies...

No Men Allowed— for the Family's Welfare

Blacks in modern-day urban areas have seen a world of changes that were not necessarily of their making. As industrial jobs began disappearing from cities, many black men found themselves back in positions of economic helplessness, without the kinds of jobs that allowed a man to support a family.

To survive, many families turned to the government's welfare system for sustenance. In her commentary, "Black Females Raising Black Males," Dr. Arlett Malvo described the ramifications of the welfare state on black families:

> Now during welfare days, early sixties, when black families were able to get welfare, black females with dependent children were allotted welfare, but there were stipulations—no men could be in the house. The welfare agency monitors this situation and agencies randomly search the female's home, at any time of day or night. Many black men left their homes so their families could survive. Many were put out of the home and these families broke up because of money. This was the first destruction of the black family since slavery.

Other external forces contributed to the dissolution of black families during the dawn of the welfare era. A few years later black men began disappearing from their homes and communities in disproportionate numbers, drafted to fight the Vietnam War, and returning home broken men. This was followed by a devastating crack epidemic, with lopsided, discriminatory sentencing for minor crimes that led to further destruction and abandonment of black lives, families, and communities.

Creating the Bad-Ass Boy and the Love-Starved Girl

Our family crisis is inseparable from our black male and female identity crisis, and brainwashing has left a great many of us fearful, confused about our identities, and hopelessly caught in a cycle of relationship underachievement.

Too many black men are still stuck in roles ultimately dictated by slavery. Some, living up to the expectation that they are irresponsible, take pride in making babies knowing they can leave without stressing about the outcome of their actions.

Black boys are not the only recipients of the psychological and physical trauma inflicted on their emasculated fathers. Vulnerable black daughters seeking love and validation from the first man in their lives are often left to fend for themselves, relying on their mothers or society to define black manhood for them. Like their mothers, the girls are saddled with feelings of disillusionment and disappointment in black men that often becomes a permanent fixture of their psyches. On the other end of the parental spectrum, many black women have been brainwashed to be active enablers of irresponsible men, supporting the unhealthy behavior of their mates, leading to future relations fraught with unnecessary drama.

As the old saying goes, black men have been brought up by mothers conditioned to "raise their daughters and spoil their sons." For many black mothers without committed male partners, the son becomes the "little man" whom the mother overindulges and neglects until he gets to an age where she can no longer handle him. Rationalizing that he is indeed a "man," she submissively allows the boy to come and go as he pleases.

Poor young black women with little education pay the greatest toll. Many are tragically retro, stuck in a past where women had little control over their sexuality. Following in the footsteps of their female ancestors, they are brainwashed into believing that motherhood is the means by which they can validate themselves; having babies with no resources is seen as a way out.

These distressing patterns must be acknowledged and addressed if we ever want an inkling of a chance to foster strong black families.

When I was 12, I decided my goal in life was to get pregnant and move to the projects. I thought a baby would be someone that I could care for, someone who would love me, and would never leave me.
— Lela

The Sixth Dynamic of Black Family Destruction

Poverty remains one of the most treacherous barriers to the development of strong black families. It could easily qualify as the sixth dynamic of black family dysfunction. Critics will counter that other ethnic groups were subjected to forms of slavery and tyranny, and yet still managed to excel socially and maintain solid familial structures. But as Harvard University professor Orlando Patterson noted in *Rituals of Blood: The Consequences of Slavery in Two American Centuries*, the "ghetto-ization" and poverty of Irish-American immigrants of the past century, Jews in European ghettos, Chinese refugees throughout Southeast Asia, and Latinos in the U.S. today had "*not* resulted in men's massive abandonment of their wives and children." Travel to poor countries that did not witness America's slavery holocaust and, yes, you will find people living in the kind of squalor that no longer exists

in this nation. However, you are also likely to find family units that are more intact than those families that descended from the slave era.

Without weighing African American generational poverty within the context of a society based on generational wealth and privilege, the observations of other non-white family structures could, in fact, serve as proof that blacks are uniquely flawed. It's important to keep in mind, however, that Jews, Irish, Chinese, and Latinos who immigrated to this country came with their cultural and familial norms intact and were not included in the devious 17th-century plan to embed inferiority into an entire people's psyche.

Secondly, we must take into account the generational black poverty rate. It swelled after Emancipation and, to this day, hasn't significantly changed since the year Dr. Martin Luther King, Jr. was assassinated. It's extremely difficult *not* having money in a society dictated by materialism. According to the University of Minnesota's Institute on Domestic Violence in the African American Community, intimate partner violence occurs more frequently among black couples with low incomes, those in which the male is underemployed or unemployed (especially if he's not seeking work), and among couples residing in very poor neighborhoods.

When considering that blacks are subtly and not so subtly reminded of their inferior status, and lacking the resources to mount an effective counter-offensive, it's a sheer miracle that more of us haven't been driven clinically insane.

A Plan of Action

Far too many of us—deeply confused about what it takes to be whole men and women—remain trapped in behavior that's detrimental to our personal relationships, our children, and society. The five dynamics fueling fractured black personal and family relationships have roots deeply embedded in slavery's soil.

Relationship Wrecks: Connecting the Dots

Contemporary Manifestations	Historical Roots
Diss-respect: Words of mutual contempt, ridicule; wide mistrust of mates, husbands, mothers, and fathers.	Black family life, not conducive to a slave-based economy, was disrupted, disrespected, and destroyed. Black men and women were stripped of roles as parents and protectors. Society, through the welfare system, dismissed black fathers.
The beat-down: Disproportionate rates of physical, verbal, spiritual, and psychological abuse in black relationships.	Slaves and descendents were conditioned to accept physical and psychological abuse. Emulation of slave-era dominant male norms continues today with a misplaced sense of "manhood" and reaction to powerlessness.
"Can't be true to My Boo": The acceptance and expectation of infidelity.	Result of male slaves' emasculation and bearing witness to misogynistic, humiliating sexual crimes against black women. Black men portrayed as unreliable and unable to protect. Black women portrayed as property of white males. Unquestioned belief in black male and female unworthiness.
Icing: Emotional shutdown and distance that fosters unhealthy relationships. Icing results in embracing anti-intimate behavior, even in intimate relationships.	Slaves learned to endure conditions outside their control. Protective mechanism to provide family safety fractured during slavery. Generational acceptance of trauma and instability of black life.

Mutual dis-enabling: Irresponsible black men and overprotective black women perpetrate negative emotional trends with sons and daughters. Children continue cycle of unhealthy relationships.	Parental norms broken during and after slavery. Undiagnosed and untreated feelings of inferiority and anger recycled. Generational feelings of betrayal, disappointment.

The mental shift needed to sever the historical roots that feed our self-destructive contemporary mindsets and behaviors won't be easy. We are a race that has been conditioned to ice over its emotions, to dance, sing, and laugh our way past the blues. However, the first step in getting to that holistic, healthier place mandates that we start scrutinizing all the influences. Consider the following comedy routines addressing personal and family relationships offered by the popular comedians Malik S. and Steve Harvey:

I hate my baby mama. I wanna choke her and slap the shit out of her ass, but I can't afford no domestic violence case right now, you know? But I told her, "When I save $2,500, I'm slapping the shit out of yo' ass, bitch!" Like most of you women don't know, you $200 from getting yo' ass choked right now.
— Malik S., *Def Comedy Jam*/February 24, 2008

I'm not condoning domestic violence in any way. I'm not sho' 'cause I'm not a lawyer...I think when they turn 18 you can put yo' hands on 'em a little harder than when they was a minor. I think if they 18, [it] can just turn into full-blown ass-whoopin's... Check your local law...Find out what you can do. Can you choke her? Can you shake her? Find out how by law what it is you can do...how far can you put your foot up her behind before it becomes a felony?
— Steve Harvey, *The Steve Harvey Radio Show*/February 23, 2009

Funny stuff, right? Well before you laugh, let's weigh the short-term benefits, long-term costs, and ultimate impact on the black psyche.

Short-term Benefits

1. **Free speech/expression:** It's fun to be risky and edgy with material that makes somebody laugh.

2. **Emotional commiseration:** The material elicits a "Yeah, I understand, I have a baby mama or a bad-ass daughter at home, too", response.

3. **Short-term relief:** Helps us vent pent-up anger and/or other feelings.

4. **Commerce:** The comedian makes money. May elicit a "Yeah, it might be harmful, but it's providing a job" response.

Long-term Costs

1. **Endorses violence:** The material condones/legitimizes domestic violence and child or spousal abuse.

2. **Trivializes black life:** Material makes light of life-threatening problems and gives a tacit green light to abuse.

3. **Prolongs the cycle of violence:** Sends message that violence is the way to make someone learn or behave.

4. **Perpetuates stereotypes:** Validates the myth of blacks as lawless and willing to skirt or break the law. Perpetuates the myth of the violent male, the myth of male dominance, and the myth of female inferiority—we do the "white man's dirt," we do the oppressor's job.

The Antidote

We have analyzed the data, questioned and deconstructed the five relationship wreck dynamics, and noted the clear line connecting slavery's indoctrination with today's behavioral patterns. Now that we've separated fact from myth, it's possible for critical self-analysis to lead us to action.

Remember, friends don't let friends stay brainwashed. Seek tactful ways to call out your friends and loved ones if they seem to be poisoning the environment for healthy relationships. Vow to end the legitimization of physical or verbal abuse in the black family. Let everyone—be they family members or comedians—know (verbally or with your wallet) that you no longer tolerate any form of abuse.

Relationship Wrecks— Positive Propaganda Cues

Here's a of list positive propaganda tools designed to help us find antidotes to the BI campaign's poisonous effects on our relationships:

Do your "home" work
Invest quality time and attention to your relationships at home. Home is your base of strength and personal growth, and the springboard for the rest of your successes in life.

Best way to "do it" is to duet
Most people's lives are enhanced and enriched by a healthy partnership. Having a loving relationship leads to a happier, healthier, more productive life.

Staying power
Anybody can get up and leave at the slightest sign of problems within a relationship. The person that has the maturity to stick

around and work it out winds up in a better place than the person who quits.

Flip the Script

With the proper perspective and commitment we can flip the script and utilize the positives that have helped us survive the black inferiority trek. From *Roots* to *Sounder,* from Julia to Roc, and from the Huxtables to the Obamas—images of strong, loving black families are not just in Hollywood. They are evident in the families that gave us Wynton and Branford Marsalis, Serena and Venus Williams, Craig and Michelle Robinson (now Mrs. Obama). If we can see black greatness in the White House, why can't we manage to see it in our own houses? How can we redefine our house without perpetuating the demeaning, outlandish, and negative perceptions attached to the black family? Once we really accept that we are not the way we've been projected for more than 400 years, everything changes, sensitivity rises, and clarity ensues. The possibility of implementing a new campaign becomes doable, at an accelerated rate, with positive propaganda techniques that undo the mass media's damage.

It might seem quaint, but the power of one voice can grow into a movement. The fact that we are in the New Media generation increases the possibility of victory. With mass media power just a computer click away, the black church, civil rights and community organizations, and empowered blacks have the ability to produce and support messages and images that adhere to a new, uplifting standard.

Lamar and Ronnie Tyler didn't wait for another *Cosby Show* to mount a multi-media offensive against negative media portrayals of black families. In 2007, the couple, who live in Washington, DC with their four kids, launched Black And Married With Kids.com. The site offers positive, professional, and informative articles, videos, stories, and links, all designed to strengthen black families and add balance to negative imagery.

Since negative propaganda got us to this point, I maintain that positive propaganda will be the key to our resolution. Fortunately for us, there are many positives examples in the past and present that we can resurrect, emulate and, if necessary, expand.

The reclamation call has already been repeatedly sounded. In 2008, hip-hop artist Talib Kweli, professors William Jelani Cobb and James Peterson, filmmakers Aaron Lloyd and Byron Hunt, playwright Shaun Neblett, and other notable black men contributed poetry, prose, and pictures to the book *Be a Father to Your Child: Real Talk from Black Men on Family, Love and Fatherhood*. In this effort, black men attempt to break from a past of patriarchal masculinity to help future generations of black men be the dads they can be.

Aishah Shahidah Simmons, producer, writer, and director of *NO! The Rape Documentary*, boldly confronts the scourge of racial, gender, and sexual oppression, and its violent manifestations. Simmons, who understands the power of mass media, almost single-handedly put together a film that utilizes individual testimonials, scholarship, spirituality, activism, and culture to bring the reality of rape and other forms of sexual and physical abuse to the forefront of public conversation.

Ultimately, the change needed to halt the self-destructive behavior that results from our victimization must come from within. We cannot undo the past. What we can and must do is move forward with the realization that it is up to us to break the negative cycles.

Chapter 3

Studs and Sluts

Why Do We Conform to Black Sexual Stereotypes?

. . . love seems with them to be more an eager desire,
than a tender delicate mixture of sentiment and sensation
— THOMAS JEFFERSON

By plan or by circumstance, the April 2008 edition of *Vogue* magazine garnered worldwide attention. It wasn't because it featured the first black man ever on its cover. No, the controversy was linked to *Vogue*'s decision to personify a classic American stereotype.

With his towering 6-foot-8 frame, anchored by size 16 shoes, NBA star LeBron James, nicknamed "King James," struck a familiar pose on the magazine's cover—gorilla-like, baring his teeth, flexing his muscles, with one hand dribbling a ball, the other clutching the tiny, slinky waist of white, blonde supermodel Gisele Bündchen.

Kong on the Court

The criticism was swift and furious. Sport columnists and cultural commentators accused editors of the influential fashion magazine

of monkeying around with James's image, evoking the centuries-old stereotype of "the black savage in search of the prized white woman" to give their annual issue devoted to size and shape a little extra thrill.

Others noted that the image by famed photographer Annie Leibovitz was eerily similar to a 1933 *King Kong* movie poster in which the giant, raging, dark ape carries off a fair-skinned damsel in distress.

"I was just having fun with it," LeBron told reporters, dismissing the controversy. "We had a few looks and that was the best one we had. Everything my name is on is going to be criticized, in a good way or a bad way. Who cares, honestly, at the end of the day?"

Who cares? We all should. Here's why: In framing King James as King Kong, *Vogue*, which reaches 1.2 million readers a month, perpetuated one of the most enduring stereotypes of black sexuality—the Brute. He is the oversexed, menacing black man, inherently violent, destructive, and shady. He appears on MTV as the gun-wielding, muscle-bound rapper 50 Cent, in the film *New Jack City* as a vicious crime lord played by Wesley Snipes, and throughout pornography as the well-endowed Mandingo stud ravaging the purity of white women.

LeBron may have been "having fun," but little did he know he was playing with an ugly, debilitating stereotype that dates back several centuries.

Super-Sexed

Two powerful slave-era images are still active, still distorted, still damaging and—thanks to our Black Inferiority Complex—still perpetrated by our own people:

BRUTE (broot): noun: a nonhuman creature; beastial/animal qualities, desires, etc.; adj: animal; not human/not characterized by intelligence or reason; irrational/savage; cruel (source: Dictionary.com)

JEZEBEL (jez-*uh-buhl*): noun: a woman who is regarded as evil and scheming; a wicked, shameless woman (source: Dictionary.com)

Surely, we all know someone who fits the mold of the black brute or the gold-digging black Jezebel. If not personally, we've seen their amplified personas via televised media and marketing images, pop literature, or on saucy music videos. As with black family dysfunction, we are familiar with the contemporary manifestations of the Studs and Sluts phenomenon.

Studs and Sluts Dynamics

1. **Studs on the hunt: Men who define themselves by their sexuality and sexual exploits.**
   They are constantly on the sexual hunt with self-worth directly tied to their conquests and sexual performance. Sex is a higher priority than job advancement, fatherhood, or real relationships. They will risk all in the pursuit of the quarry. They cannot (and will not) get too involved with their conquests. They have an internalized brutish nature: "I'm doing this *to* you, not *with* you" is their mantra. They animalize, dehumanize, and objectify women to reinforce the idea that they are unworthy of emotional commitment and long-term involvement.

2. **Gold-digging slut: Jezebel-like sex objects believe that, to get anywhere in life, they have to be really good at *it*. Sex is their ticket, their money-maker.**
   Gold-diggers allow themselves to be conquests in return for material gain (dinners, jewelry, rent, or a starring role in a video). They are conditioned to devalue sex. Their innate emotions and need for tenderness, compassion, and love are constantly repressed. They believe they are unworthy of love and respect, and avoid disappointment at all cost.

3. **Gotta do whatcha gotta do: Sex as a means of sustenance and immediate gratification. Sex without
   emotion.**
   Defensive self-devaluation justifies their sensation-driven
   life. Propaganda validates their actions. Sexual behavior is
   legitimate and necessary to "make it." They disassociate
   themselves from their bodies and the possibility of a
   legitimate means to holistic, authentic love.

Yes, we know studs and sluts exist. But here, we attempt to
understand why and examine the impact these stereotypes have on a
race still in need of therapy. Let's decode the enduring legacy of the
Brute and the Jezebel.

Ape by Association

*We believe that even among people who aren't particularly
prejudiced, the association between blacks and apes is still strong,
held in place through "implicit knowledge," the result of a lifetime
of conditioning, rooted in historical representations of blacks as less
than human...It was a kind of racial programming, a legacy even
something as progressive as Obama's election cannot obliterate.*
— Phillip Atiba Goff and Jennifer L. Eberhardt, social psychologists

The belief that blacks are sexual savages descended from fiction
rooted in the first impressions of Africans. Englishmen were introduced
to the chimpanzee and black Africans in western Africa at the same
time and place. The startlingly human appearance and movements of
the chimpanzee aroused their imagination.

According to A. Elaine Brown Crawford, as early as the mid-1500s,
English explorers and traders who traveled to Africa "mistook the semi-
nudity of Africans as lewdness. They also misappropriated the cultural
tradition of polygamy as uncontrollable lust."

In European eyes, the warfare, diet, and other aspects of African
life they encountered placed Africans among the beasts. Africa, seen

as the dark continent, possessed a natural landscape upon which lions, zebras, and other exotic wildlife flourished. Therefore, the people in this strange geography surely merited comparison with the beasts with which they co-existed.

The grand pooh-bah of the Founding Fathers, Thomas Jefferson, helped legitimize the belief that blacks are akin to apes. In his *Notes on the State of Virginia*—the most widely read book of the period—Jefferson argued that blacks prefer the "superior beauty" of whites "as uniformly as is the preference of the Oran-ootan for the black woman over those of his own species."

Size Matters

On the South Side, all the white men and white women would come to the clubs to try to get black women and black men. It was a mixer. In those days, the penis thing was so damned powerful that white women were not frightened. They'd come and drive to your neighborhood, coming to look for it. They'd ask you, "Do you have a big one?"
— Ron

Ron, a 74-year-old artist, and I were born in the same era—about 73 years after black slaves were emancipated. It was a time when we still navigated in the dark eddies of harsh racial undercurrents. Loving, interracial relationships were still deadly taboo, especially between black males and white females. White men, however, could use black women for sexual gratification without social condemnation.

These men inherited a system designed to keep them advantaged and empowered. Those cunning 17th-century colonial leaders managed to establish a code of behavior that gave white men the best of both worlds—unfettered access to black women, while barricading black men from white women.

The colonial fathers understood that slaveowners were, first and foremost, men. Rape, at its core, is a power trip, a means to exert control. The institution of slavery provided ample opportunity for

white slaveholders to unleash their puritanically repressed sexual urges on female slaves who were powerless to reject their advances.

Thomas Jefferson provided a moral escape clause that allowed lascivious "Christian" slavers to sexually subjugate black women. Jefferson helped extinguish religious guilt by animalizing slaves, defining them as unfeeling, unemotional beasts:

> They are more ardent after their female; but love seems with them to be more an eager desire, than a tender delicate mixture of sentiment and sensation...their existence appears to participate more of sensation than reflection...an animal whose body is at rest, and who does not reflect...

The slaveholder's carnal, beastly behavior was also legitimized with propaganda so effective that blacks (slave and free) absorbed its messages and, throughout the centuries, acted out the propagandized stereotypes.

Jefferson's obsession with black sexuality overlapped with white scientists' fixation with African penises, specimens of which were collected and studied. In *The N Word: Who Can Say It, Who Shouldn't, and Why*, author Jabari Asim quotes British "niggerologist" Charles White who, in his 1799 anatomy studies, gushed: "That the PENIS of an African is larger than that of a European has...been shewn in every anatomical school in London. Preparations of them are preserved in most anatomical museums; and I have one in mine."

LeBron as the modern-day rendition of the brutish, ape-like menace preying on a fair-skinned maiden does indeed matter, especially in a society still fixated on warped racial images. However, the Brute is but one half of a destructive, diabolical duo. His counterpart in the marketing of black inferiority is the Jezebel.

Skank by Any Other Name

I ain't neber had to pay a fare to ride a steamboat needer. I was a good-lookin' yaller gal in dem days and rid free wherever I wanted to go.
— "Aunt" Charity Anderson, former slave

Singers Justin Timberlake and Ciara are talented young artists. Like LeBron, the entertainers would probably consider their music video "Love Sex Magic" just a bit of youthful, erotic fun…no big deal, right? Wrong again. In the video, Ciara plays a sexual tease—gyrating, crawling on all fours, pole dancing, rubbing her body against the white singer and licking his face, while he sits on a chair in a king-like position. In the opening sequence, Timberlake actually pulls a dog chain attached to Ciara's neck. Throughout the video, he repeatedly slaps the seductress's butt, while she works her sex and magic.

Timberlake seems to be the prototypical Neo-Massa. While performing a musical number during Super Bowl XXXVIII's halftime show in 2004, the singer ripped off a part of Janet Jackson's wardrobe, exposing her bare breast to millions around the globe. The controversial stunt was timed to coincide with the last line of Timberlake's song "Rock Your Body": "I'm gonna have you naked by the end of this song."

The 21st-century Jezebel, as a butt-jiggling, thong-tossing, pole-sliding gold-digger, is nearly as ubiquitous as the "UL" symbol on all things electric. She's the lustful black woman with an insatiable sexual appetite who uses her body for money, vengeance, or power. She was Lisa Raye, the college-student-turned-stripper "Diamond" in *Player's Club*, the gyrating rear in almost all hip-hop videos, and the booty call centerfolds tucked within the pages of *King* and other magazines targeting black readers.

Indeed, no music video seems complete without a Jezebel. She is the flesh-and-blood accessory akin to the flashy cars and iced-out jewelry worn by the rappers for whom she bumps and grinds.

As Deborah Gray White comments in *Ar'n't I a Woman: Female Slaves in the Plantation South:*

> One of the most prevalent images of black women in antebellum America was of a person governed almost entirely by her libido, a Jezebel character. In every way Jezebel was the counter-image of the mid-nineteenth-century ideal of the Victorian lady. She did not lead men and children to God; piety was foreign to her. She saw no advantage in prudery, indeed domesticity paled in importance before matters of the flesh.

Perpetuating the "Ho" Persona

I know this to be true: if you can do certain sexual things better than another person, you tend to get treated better. You get more out of that person: Money, their time, their attention. I learned how, through practice, and by watching a whole lot of movies.
— Lela

The Jezebel stereotype was used to excuse rape and justify the slaveowner's carnal desires. After all, how could it be rape, if the victim is property designed for seedy sexual indulgence? During the first half of the 20th century, the myth manifested itself in the form of everyday objects—from postcards to novelty items. Today, the depiction of black women as Jezebel-like whores continues, thanks in large part to best-selling, black female rappers who probably have no clue that they're playing myth-personified roles.

That particular idea isn't mine. It was written by author Lori A. Tribbett-Williams in her book *Talking Loud, Saying Nothing: Lil' Kim and Foxy Brown, Caricatures of African-American Womanhood.* Trina, Lil' Kim, and Foxy Brown are just a few of the black female rappers who have ridden to the top of the charts by flaunting their sexuality under the guise of women's empowerment.

Much of their music did nothing more than perpetuate the Jezebel mythology and reinforce the idea that black women are hypersexual, one-dimensional playthings for a whole new generation.

WikiMusicGuide.com describes Trina in admirable, defiant tones: She "turned the tables on a male dominated genre...with hit singles 'No Panties' and '69 Ways'...Trina showed her real sexy and naughty personality," the Web site boasts.

Allow me to decipher this colorful marketing lingo: Trina is just another rapping version of Jezebel. In case there's any doubt, here's a sample from "69 Ways":

> Open up my legs, put your head in between 'em
> Till I bust like lead from a heater

In a society that already considers black women as "bitches and hos," such validation should be considered treasonous.

Together, the Jezebel and Brute stereotypes reinforce the ageless idea that blacks are morally loose, culturally retarded, and sexually perverse. This is why we should not only care, but should care enough to change.

The Rap on Rap

I liked being looked at like a sexual object, I had no problem with it. To me, that meant they were looking at me as someone who could satisfy, who could deliver sexually. Sometimes that was all they wanted from me, and I was cool with that.
— James, 33

Vogue was turned into a whipping post, and rightly so, for its racially charged imagery, but the prime culprits for perpetuating these hypersexual images are heavily rotated music videos on networks like MTV and BET.

The "harmless fun" crowd will also dismiss any damage caused by images of oversexed black video vixens by pointing to the sexually explicit acts of white female artists like Britney Spears or Lady Gaga. What they fail to note is that these singers are not linked to a past of sexual servitude. For every Lady Gaga there are dozens of white

female artists like Colby Caillat and Sheryl Crow who add balance that's missing from the acts of black female artists who conform to the "sex sells" maxim. Also, even if rappers use the cop-out, "Well, whites do it, too," there are no corollary, hard-core, Trina-type examples on the white roster. Regrettably, it's a genre black female rappers control.

Most importantly, lewd white images do not add to the mental brainwashing inflicted on young African Americans.

Consider the data released in "The Rap on Rap" report issued in April 2008, the same month as the King Kong *Vogue* cover. The Parents Television Council, in partnership with the Enough is Enough Campaign, analyzed a total of three weeks of content found on BET's "Rap City" and "106 & Park," and MTV's "Sucker Free." When it came to sex, the report released shocking findings, including:

- 746 sexually explicit scenes or lyrical references for an average of 27 instances per hour

- 45 percent of the adult content in the music videos was of a sexual nature, followed by explicit language (29 percent), violence (13 percent), drug use/sales (9 percent), and other illegal activity (3 percent)

- 103 vulgar, slang references to sexual anatomy (e.g., the term "gushy" used to refer to a woman's lubricated vagina) in a one-week period in March 2008

What the report didn't quantify was the vast majority of images accompanying the music of young, blinged-out Brutes and jiggling Jezebels. Among the most-played videos, for example, was the Trap Starz Clik's "Get It Big," from their debut album *Hood Depot*. Surrounded by midriff-baring seductresses, the flesh-obsessed rap trio commands:

Vibrate your body…Make a playa wanna cut [slang for "have sex"].

"Get it Big," however, pales in comparison to the borderline pornographic music videos, including "Pussy Poppin'" by Ludacris, "Wobble Wobble" by the 504 Boyz, or the infamous "Tip Drill" video by Nelly, in which the St. Louis rapper swipes a credit card through the ample butt cheeks of bikini-clad "video vixen" Whyte Chocolate.

As for the butt-swiping incident, Nelly, like LeBron, sidestepped the seriousness of his actions. In an interview with *FHM* magazine, the rapper defended his brute-like behavior by equating it to a Hollywood, Jezebel-esque performance:

"Halle Berry can go on film and get the dog shit freaked out of her, and she wins an Oscar," Nelly said, referring to Berry's role in Monster's Ball. "I swipe a credit card down the crack of a girl's butt, and I'm demoralizing women?"

Nelly, who has a teenage daughter, doesn't seem to recognize his duplicitous role as a demoralizer of black women for the next generation. Consider the entrepreneur's clothing line "Apple Bottom," which, we all know, is a euphemism for a woman's "perfect, round ass." Nelly has found success marketing his jeans and other products to black consumers. Fair enough—I'm assuming they are old enough to make their own clothing decisions. But for what reason does Nelly market twill "bubble shorts" for toddlers, this too with the Apple Bottom logo emblazoned across the butt?

The straight answer? Brainwashing.

Perhaps we can take some comfort in the results from the Black Youth Project at the University of Chicago. In that study, 72 percent of black youth, ages 15 to 25, agreed with the statement: "Rap music videos contain too many references to sex." When broken down by groups, 66 percent of the young black women and 57 percent of young black men surveyed also agreed with the following statement: "Rap music videos portray black women in bad and offensive ways."

However, the effects of brainwashing were evident in the 44 percent of young black men surveyed who disagreed with the statement: "Rap music videos portray black men in bad and offensive ways." One interviewee answered the question this way: "When you're

framed as being 'cool' for being a 'playa,' steady getting money, sex, and power, what's there to disagree with?"

As evidenced in the responses of this young man and Nelly, it's obvious that the mental conditioning of so many of our unfortunate brethren does indeed run deep.

> *When I was coming up, the media messaging told me that black men were overly sexual. I was glad that I had sexual prowess and that I could please women, because otherwise I would have felt like I didn't live up to what I was supposed to be.*
> — James

Bamboozled by Our Own

Though the hypersexual images of black men and women were created centuries ago, studies have shown that, once images are established, they change very slowly if at all. They become part of our collective culture, the DNA of newer, even viler images. "These stereotypes are internalized in society, and therefore become ideals for certain groups. Thus, even media designed specifically by blacks contain images that maintain some of the characteristics of these stereotypes," notes scholar Christina N. Baker in her writings about the portrayal of sexuality in advertisements. In our state of mental confusion, we tolerate and laugh as some black artists paint whole generations of black women with broad Jezebel-lian strokes.

Take for example, this banter from the 2008 Tyler Perry movie *Meet the Browns* (now a TBS sitcom). In the following scene, a family finds out that their late father, Pop Brown, a respected deacon, actually lived an earlier life as a pimp. This news, which surfaced due to Pop's estranged adult daughter, raises questions about his female friends from the family's childhood. Only LB Brown, an older son, can answer these questions:

Family member: . . . remember sweet Sadie?
LB: She was one of his ho's.

Family member: What about Agnes, with the freckles?

LB: Freckle-faced ho.

Family member: What about Shirley, the one who used to make cupcakes…

LB: City ho.

Family member: What about our Mother?

LB: Nasty ho.

Yes, we black people pull the trigger for our own image assassination—from movies and music videos created by black entertainers, producers, and directors to "street lit" by black authors that over-emphasize erotic and violent street life. The latter, interestingly enough, is a $300-million-a-year business built on titles like *Nasty Girls* by Erick S. Gray, *Bitch* by Deja King, and *Thug-a-licious* by Noire. They "are literally flying off the shelves and into the hands of African American women and men ranging in age from 15 to 90," according to *Black Issues Book Review*.

Sadly, too many of us have become the new perpetrators of the brainwash myth.

Of Brutes and Brutality

After Emancipation, proslavery advocates argued that slavery was still needed to control black creatures, otherwise they would revert to their savage, brutish state. This belief was central to the ideology of racism that flooded the South after 1890. Historian George M. Fredrickson wrote in *The Black Image in the White Mind*: "[Whites]… had to contend that many Negroes were literally wild beasts, with uncontrollable sexual passions and criminal natures stamped by heredity." At the beginning of the 20th century, anti-black imagery in "scientific" journals, newspapers, and best-selling novels heavily promoted the "black rapist" thesis. Frederickson also wrote about Dr. William Lee Howard's 1903 medical journal piece in which the scholar explained that the increase in sexual crimes by blacks had a physiological basis—the "large size of the negro's penis [which lacked]"

the sensitiveness of the terminal fibers which exist in the Caucasian." For this, Howard reasoned, black men were prone to habitual fits of "sexual madness and excess."

Film historian Donald Bogle confirms that brute imagery persisted in pop culture most vividly in the late 1960s and '70s with the rise of blaxploitation films—"movies that played on the needs of black audiences for heroic figures." The era gave us movies like *Shaft, SuperFly, Hammer,* and *Trouble Man*—all with black studly heroes who triumphed with blazing guns and/or raging penises. The trend continues today with disproportionate media images of wild, undisciplined, irresponsible, and over-sexed black thugs, pimps, seductresses, playas, and playettes.

Like prized pit bulls on the plantation, young, virile male slaves were trained to stud. While often forbidden to have normal relationships with the woman or child, the slavemaster rewarded the valuable buck for making babies—inhuman property that could be worked or sold for more profit.

Fast forward four centuries and we see the effect of this phenomenon in the disproportionate media images of wild, undisciplined, irresponsible, and over-sexed black thugs, pimps, seductresses, playas, and playettes. Through Hollywood movies and rap videos, we see black men with no meaningful relationships, who still place unnatural value on their sex organs and their ability to stud the black Jezebel.

Stay on the Scene, Like a Sex Machine

During slavery, black men were encouraged to see themselves as licentious heathens, subhuman, simian sex machines, and natural-born breeders with no emotional attachments. Today, our dilemma is an existential crisis that collectively we've been unable to resolve: How can a black male be a *man* in America? If we reflect honestly, we'll concede that our perpetual quest for the next conquest, the need for instant sexual gratification stems from a deeper personal crisis, the compulsive need to scratch an itch that will not go away.

> *When you are in a room with white men who think they are better than you, assume they have more money than you, certainly have more advantages than you, a black man can look at him and know: "Yeah, all that might be true, but I could fuck your woman, and I could take her from you." It is a weapon in male racial warfare. Our sexuality trumps yours.*
> — James

Even today, the media manipulators (black and white) keep us fully duped, focusing on the head between our legs and discouraging us from using our thinking head.

Shake Your Money Maker

Serious self-analysis is not a male-only exercise. Black women must also expose the demons that allow them to tolerate and reinforce the Jezebel image. Perhaps the Jezebel persona would be rejected quicker if more women scrutinized that destructive and demeaning role and incarnations from a historical perspective. She was the "Negress" that German botanist and physician Johann David Schoepf described during his travels to the colonies in the early 1780s, who was honored "to bring a mulatto into the world." The black woman in 1915 was Lydia Brown, the promiscuous mulatto mistress in the racist film *The Birth of a Nation,* who used her feminine wiles to seduce powerful, well-meaning white men.

Later, during the blaxploitation period, Jezebel was reincarnated as the militant, more independent but still "foxy" and hypersexualized woman who bared her butt and breasts while solving mysteries and fighting for justice.

On television sitcoms like *Friends,* where black men were rarities, both Joey (Matt LeBlanc) and Ross (David Schwimmer) woo and win the affection of Charlie (Aisha Tyler), a black paleontologist. Ironically, in one episode of *Friends*, Phoebe Buffay (Lisa Kudrow) confesses a sexual attraction to a black man. In fact, when her pal Rachel Green (Jennifer Aniston) is in search of an unattached sexual encounter,

Phoebe arrives at her apartment offering to share her lover. The fact that the "lover" was really just a man-sized, cardboard cut-out was funny. The character, however, was revealing: The life-size cutout was boxer Evander Holyfield—a Brute.

Bloodsucking Sluts & Studs

The Sluts and Studs theme was written into the plot of *True Blood*, the hit HBO series about vampires and humans co-existing in a small Louisiana town. Pretty and witty Tara Thornton (Rutina Wesley) has trouble keeping a steady job. Stereotypically angry, sassy, and confrontational, she is known for her sharp tongue. She has an unrequited crush on Jason Stackhouse (Ryan Kwanten), the sculpted, white, not-too-bright town gigolo. After fast-talking her way into a bartending job at the bar Merlotte's, Tara propositions the white boss, Sam Merlotte. What starts out as a night of no-strings-attached, legs-up-in-the-air hot sex turns into an in-the-back-office-and-wherever-else series of graphic, "just-because" encounters.

Of course, in a town where vampires and humans mingle, one would expect some pathological behavior. But Tara (who's ironically named after the slave plantation in Margaret Mitchell's 1936 novel *Gone with the Wind*) and the other major black characters in *True Blood* are largely early-American black stereotypes. For example, actor Nelsan Ellis plays Tara's cousin, LaFayette Reynolds. He is not only Merlotte's short-order cook but also the town's resident drug dealer, violent prostitute, and "3-snaps," oh-so-gay, white-man-chasing host of his own homosexual pay-per-view Web site. Then there's Tara's mother, Lettie Mae Thornton (Adina Porter), former child abuser, habitual mean drunk, and Jesus freak convinced she's possessed by a demon. In one episode, while attempting to arrange a bank loan, Lettie Mae sits on the lap of a white loan officer to demonstrate why her landlord doesn't mind when she falls a little behind on her rent.

In a world of equals, there's nothing sinister about interracial relationships. However, in a society where black women have been branded as devoid of healthy black relationships; as lewd, manipulating vixens; and as the white man's sexual conquest—these repeated messages and images slip into the seedy category of subtle propaganda.

> *Sex? I started very early. I know most that I was looking for the love I did not receive from my father. The guys I chose...I thought they were good-hearted people, but you couldn't trust them. They were like my father: male chauvinist, bad boys. They didn't stay around, either. They would get what they wanted and then disappear until they wanted it again. Yeah, I became a booty call.*
> — Lela

Sick and Tired of Being Sick and Tired

I'd wager that some producers of this material actually believe it doesn't matter. Remember, complicit with the BI campaign is a dual component that reinforces white superiority. Without effort, many whites subconsciously perpetuate roles assigned to blacks in Colonial times.

It's part of the human DNA to push the limits. Today's advertising industry says, "If you don't stop us, we'll place erectile dysfunction and male enhancement ads on TV during family hour." The pharmaceutical industry will put products on the market that will kill people ("in case of death, consult your doctor") if regulatory agencies don't say "Stop!"

If entertainers, especially those escaping poverty, get an opportunity to make it in an industry that promotes destruction, they will exploit the rules of the game. For all we know, Trina might be a virgin. But she's going to sell the hell out of the slutty golden showers, "shit in yo' face" schtick until enough of us say "Stop!"

At one point during the 2009 BET Awards show in Los Angeles, someone, anyone should have stood up and shouted, "Hold up. These are our little girls!" During the show, rap artists Lil' Wayne and Drake

took the stage to sing the sanitized version of Wayne's song, "Every Girl," a little ditty in which Wayne (in his words) wishes to "fuck every girl in the world." Accompanying the rappers on stage were young girls who appeared to be 15 years old or under. Social entrepreneur, writer, and editor April R. Silver blogged about her reaction to the routine at clutchmagonline.com:

> I was hoping that a hunched-over stage manager would bust through from back stage to scoop up the children, rescuing them from harm's way…from being associated with this song. But instead, what those girls witnessed from the stage was hundreds and hundreds of adults (mostly black people) staring back at them, co-signing the performance.

Even if Lil' Wayne presented the clean edit of his song, and even if, reportedly, one of the preteen girls on the stage was Wayne's own daughter, the rapper and BET "set the stage for child pornography," as Silver argued in her essay:

> Last night we were reminded that there are few safe spaces for our little girls to be children; that some of us are willing to trade their innocence for a good head nod.

I support the proactive approach Silver described, which includes boycotts, national letter-writing campaigns, and other "activities designed to shame and/or pressure." Silver wrote to persuade BET to improve its programming. Citing Proverbs, Silver concedes that there will always be "fools amongst us." However, she adds, there are also "wise ones…a small group of people concerned about the long-term health and well-being of the community."

Ultimately, a successful anti–BI Complex strategy will serve those affected by both black inferiority and white superiority. However, we must create enough wise ones armed to say, "We've had enough with the Studs and Sluts imagery."

Tracking the Shame

Unlike other ethnicities, blacks are told to get over the past. The shame attached to our journey helps many of us attempt to comply with this directive. To succeed we must arm ourselves by understanding ourselves and the poisonous roots of the Studs and Sluts predicament.

Studs and Sluts: Connecting the Dots

Contemporary Manifestations	Historical Roots
Studs on the hunt: Black men as sexual exploiters, conditioned studs with an internalized brutish nature. Animalizes, dehumanizes, objectifies, and views women as objects unworthy of long-term commitment.	Black male slaves were brain-washed to see themselves as studs. They were rarely allowed to form relationships they could control. This created an ambivalent love/hate relationship between black men and women.
Gold-digging slut: Jezebel-like sexual object, allows herself to be the conquest in return for material goods. Devalues the importance of sex and suppresses her need for tenderness and compassion. She is unworthy of love and avoids disappointment.	The black female slave was always treated as a sexual object. Told that all she had to offer was her body, she had no control over who raped or exploited her. She couldn't afford to connect her sexuality with her emotions.
Super-sized studs & sluts: Super-sexual objects. Every other human quality stripped away. Super-sized studs and sluts identify with and promote familiar sexual stereotypes.	Slaves learned that sex was an effective bartering tool. A good breeder earned the master's praise. A black woman and her family were rewarded if she satisfied the master's carnal urges. Stripped of all self-esteem, slaves clung to the one possession that always mystified, tantalized, and angered whites—their sexuality.

Gotta do whatcha gotta do: Black men and women justify the unjustifiable. They employ defensive devaluation to justify sensation-driven dehumanized lives as sexual objects. Selling sex and hyper-sexualized behavior is legitimate and necessary to "make it."	Sexual subjugation forced black men and women to use the power of their sexuality. Many regarded it as a survival skill. Over time, psychological defenses were erected to block the depression and despair that often accompanied such actions.

The Cost of Our Benefits

How can we honestly face our own mental distortions? A cost-benefit exercise is a good start. For example, let's look at the misogynistic lyrics and music videos put out by hip-hop artists Trina and Killer Mike from their song "Look Back at Me":

I'ma make it rain for you, here's a golden shower
Come a little closer, I wanna fuck your nose

Short-term Benefits

1. **Get paid! On board the hip-hop prosperity train:** The Brute and Jezebel images, lyrics, and product lines generate lots of money! Media producers, directors, actors, rappers, writers, dancers, and others get paid handsomely.

2. **Instant gratification:** Living the life of the Brute or Jezebel provides a basic sense of short-term pleasure and temporary relief, be it sexual or financial.

Long-term Costs

1. Fuels a legacy of sexual brainwashing today and tomorrow.

2. Keeps blacks in a hedonistic mode, reinforces inferior status.

3. Distracts us from other areas of personal, social, and economic development.

4. Reinforces the brainwash like nothing else.

Armed & Ready!

African Americans have been conditioned to see themselves as powerless. Yet, if only a fraction of the 39 million of us in the United States decide we want to *stop* media portrayals of Studs and Sluts, believe me, this part of the BI campaign would end—quickly.

It's a tall order, I know, but we can get there, especially with the proper tools.

Studs & Sluts Positive Propaganda Cues

I am more than my sex
We need to understand that there is more to who we are than our sexuality. We have minds, we have spirit, and we have a need to be holistic human beings.

Lust is not the whole you
My actions will be governed by what's behind my eyes, not what's between my thighs.

From ho to w(ho)le!
Women have infinitely more to offer than just their bodies—more to offer to men, and more to offer the world.

From 'man'-ho to manhood!
Men need to understand that manhood is not gained by sex alone.

Waking Up

Real benefits can be realized when we unplug from conditioned thinking and confront the burden of being defined solely by our sexuality.

Although far too many of us have accepted the role of mythmaker, luckily there are also those who are determined to reverse this form of brainwashing. Some artists, media outlets, and community groups have started efforts to provoke widespread change by asserting healthy images of black sexuality or by simply demanding that programming executives do a better job of presenting well-rounded black images.

A movement known as black erotica argues that it is time for self-defining expression, one that portrays black sexuality as more beautiful than beastly—from *Brown Sugar*, the tastefully written stories collected by Carol Taylor, to the groundbreaking anthology *Erotique Noir/Black Erotica* edited by Miriam Decosta-Willis, Reginald Martin, and Roseann P. Bell to the intimate color nudes of women by renowned photographer Marc Baptiste.

"Black culture is realizing, perhaps hundreds of years or so too late, that we are human first, that we have impulses and feelings and desires to examine and admire and touch and photograph and paint and write about the human body and human sexuality," author Jill Nelson told the *New York Times*. "We are finally dealing ourselves into that kind of dialogue."

In a 2001 interview with ABC News for his film about boxer Muhammad Ali, former rapper-turned-superstar Will Smith talked honestly about the black male image:

> *Tons of women would love to have sex with me. I hate the image of black men as promiscuous and unable to control themselves sexually. I don't like that image.*

The most consistent retort from television and media producers when responding to charges that there are few television programs or mainstream movies that portray blacks as well-rounded couples or in loving relationships is, "Well, there's no support."

It's time for reprogrammed thinkers to deflate this argument. We must compel ourselves to support alternative, more holistic black images in Hollywood, in rap videos, and in consumer marketing messages.

The brainwashing collaborators who serve as the new mythmakers are among us. What's needed are more myth-breakers. To enact real change, the modern-day engineers of the BI campaign, no matter what their color, must understand that myth-breakers are on duty and that we are waking up, we are watching, and we will take action.

Chapter 4

Uglified

Why Are Black and Beautiful Still Contradictions?

It is no secret to many of [us] that we have internalized racist/ sexist notions of beauty that lead many of us to think that we're ugly. And the media have bombarded us with stories... that white children are cleaner and nicer. The white-dominated media presents this knowledge to us as if it's some defect of black life that creates such aberrant and self-negating behavior, not white supremacy.

— bell hooks, *SISTERS OF THE YAM*

In 2006, many of us watched HBO, mouths agape in pained astonishment, as 17-year-old film student Kiri Davis presented her documentary *Girls Like Me*, a re-creation of the famous experiment by Drs. Kenneth and Mamie Clark that was instrumental in the historic 1954 *Brown v. Board of Education* victory. Fifteen of the twenty-one children Davis filmed at the Harlem Day Care Center preferred white dolls over black dolls. Davis's 2005 results were shockingly similar to those of the Clarks, who, during the 1940s, used black and white dolls to study and demonstrate children's internalization of racism. The following description of one of the exercises in the 2005 study was described by the NNPA News Service and published in *The Final Call* newspaper:

> The reassuring female voice asks the child a question:
> "Can you show me the doll that looks bad?"
> The child, a preschool-aged black girl, quickly picks up and shows

65

the black doll over a white one that is identical in every respect except complexion.

"And why does that look bad?"

"Because she's black," the little girl answers emphatically.

"And why is this the nice doll?" the voice continues.

"Because she's white."

"And can you give me the doll that looks like you?"

The little girl hesitates for a split second before handing over the black doll that she has just designated as the uglier one.

The dolls in both Clark's and Davis's studies were identical in every way, except for color. I can't help but wonder if all the kids would have chosen white dolls if they were more African-looking—wide noses, broad lips, and with "natural" hair styles?

More than 60 years after the Clark study, 40 years after "Black Is Beautiful" rang out across the nation, and more than 40 years after Naomi Sims, the first African American supermodel to grace the covers of *Ladies Home Journal* (1968) and *Life* magazine (1969), black girls still prefer white dolls and reject black ones. The one time we see a black doll chosen in the 2005 documentary (and chosen with painful hesitation) is *not* when a young black girl is asked, "Which doll is smarter? Which doll is prettier?" No, it's when she's asked, "Which doll looks like you?"

Slowly, with embarrassment (or maybe it was hurt that twisted her expression), the child selects the black doll.

How is this possible? How could our children still be editing "black" out as it relates to beauty and brilliance? Why do black adults, far too often, do likewise?

Uglified Dynamics

Many of us have been conditioned to believe that whites are the pretty people, that their traits and physical attributes are more suitable than our own ugly features. The modern-day dynamics of this negative propaganda are manifested in these ways:

1. **White is right**
   Black beauty as the antithesis of white norms. The further we are from the European standard, the lower we find ourselves on the beauty scale. We judge beauty by our most significant features—our noses and lips. If a nose is too wide or too flat, it's the direct opposite of the white standard—narrow and prominently bridged. The bigger the lips, the more our appearance becomes the antithesis of the accepted thinner European mouth.

2. **Get back black**
   We are better if we are lighter. We want our children to be pretty because we know beauty will grant them an easier life in a color-coded society. Most of us don't want to be reminded of our past, our ancestors, and where we come from. Many of us boast of having a little Indian, Irish, Italian—any additional blood in our lineage boosts our value. We find ourselves using a sliding racial scale, somewhere between black and white, with lighter or whiter always, always defined as better.

3. **Nappy? Not happy!**
   There is no aspect of black physical appearance that has more psychodynamic value than our hair. Black hair carries extraordinary advertising weight and is among the leading topics used for editorial content for black news articles, books, and magazines. The amount of time and money spent in beauty salons speaks to our obsession with black physicality and beauty standards. Hair repair is the easiest of the inferiority dynamics to transform (a box of relaxer costs under 15 dollars, whereas plastic surgery can be prohibitively expensive). "Fixing that nappy hair" is to cover up, or "cure," the scourge of blackness.

Our impossible obsession to meet white beauty standards is seeded in our trek from servitude to freedom. Emancipation unlocked

physical shackles but the mental bondage forged through centuries of indoctrination keeps blacks strapped to the notion that our looks are somehow connected to the inhumane treatment we endured.

> *I grew up thinking I was ugly, and my mother reinforced that. She'd say things like, "Stop poking out those lips, they are already too big, they look like two sausages." My mother never told me I was a beautiful woman.*
> — Tanya, 52

So What Do You Expect?

Told of Kiri Davis's findings, Julia Hare, a San Francisco psychologist said:

> Our children are bombarded with images every day that they see on television screens and on coffee tables—either the light-skinned female that everybody is pushing or they give preference to the closest-to-white images.

Given the centuries of brainwashing that equated black with *ugly, inferior,* and *undesirable,* it really isn't surprising that many black children—like their parents and generations of blacks before them— reject their own image.

Our analysis should start with these questions:

How do we see ourselves? Why do we see ourselves as physically inferior?

When the colonies became America, the primary campaign to "uglify" African slaves became more intense, pervasive, and codified. The message was reinforced in a myriad of ways, including Thomas Jefferson's *Notes on the State of Virginia*, where he demeaned blacks while defining the standard of superior (white) beauty:

The first difference which strikes us is that of colour...Is it not the foundation of a greater or less share of beauty in the two races? Are not the fine mixtures of red and white, the expressions of every passion by greater or less suffusions of colour in the one, preferable to that eternal monotony, which reigns in the countenances, that immoveable veil of black which covers all the emotions of the other race? Add to these, flowing hair, a more elegant symmetry of form, their own judgment in favour of the whites, declared by their preference of them...The circumstance of superior beauty, is thought worthy of attention in the propagation of our horses, dogs, and other domestic animals; why not in that of man?

Jefferson's message served as part of the great American brainwash campaign. It was coupled with other propaganda emphasizing that black was the standard color of evil, a blight from God, and the mark of Ham, Noah's cursed son.

African Americans, as the secondary audience of this campaign, were bombarded with images and words that stigmatized our appearance as the byproduct of a virulent disease. At the same time, the aesthetic superiority of white beauty—alabaster skin, sleek noses, sliver-thin lips, and straight, lustrous hair—was widely promoted as the absolute standard of beauty.

In the six decades since the Clark experiment, we have more images of African Americans than ever on television, in blockbuster films, and on the covers of popular magazines. Yet, even with the growth of these diverse media images, one constant remains—black beauty is still considered inferior to the "established" standard of beauty.

The idea that cultural norms defined during slavery still loom large in contemporary American society seems preposterous. "That was 150 years ago! What does it have to do with what's up, what's happening now?" some might say.

I would argue, almost everything.

Those Pretty, High-Yellow Girls

Being mixed, I knew that I was black but I don't necessarily look it. Men who only date white women see me as a prize, women who hate their brown skin want daughters that look like me. White men see me like an exotic car or something.
— Lisa, 36

Toni Morrison's 1970 novel *The Bluest Eye* tells the story of a black girl who desperately yearns for blonde hair and blue eyes. It speaks to light-skinned/dark-skinned racism *within* the African American community and paints portraits of those whose personal value (lessness) has been dictated to them from *without*.

For most of our history in the New World, we openly coveted light skin and straight hair. Today, the pinnacles of black female beauty remain almost white-looking. It is disturbingly telling that the long weave seems to be a prerequisite for black singers, actors, and models. Hip-hop videos feature light-skinned black, Latino, or Asian women—to the exclusion of darker-skinned black dancers. In these befuddled musical sketches of black life, blinged-out heroes surround themselves with lighter-skinned trophies. The darker women in such videos are rarely positioned as the Pedestal Prize—that place is usually reserved for the surrogate white girl.

Color-Struck Class Wars

The color grading and class stratification structure intensified under the plantation system. Division among slaves was aggravated by the privileges some slavemasters awarded to their light-skinned offspring. Even if the slaver didn't acknowledge his children, the known fact that they were spawns of the perceived superior race solidified, in some instances, skin color as an indicator of status on the plantation.

African Americans throughout the generations sought ways to lessen the stigma of inferiority. Mothers wistfully pinched the wide, broad noses of their children in a vain attempt to Europeanize them. The attempt to cover up our blackness started with bleaching creams, heavily advertised in the black press. Other blacks tell stories of parents who rubbed their faces with grapefruit or added a bit of Clorox to their bath in crude attempts to lighten skin color. Many a black child was warned not to drink coffee, or told to "get out of the sun, 'cause it will make you black." Many of these children grew up and repeated their parents' practices with their own children, albeit in perhaps less-abrasive forms.

Author and journalist asha bandele, who lives in a largely black, Caribbean neighborhood in Brooklyn, New York, recalled how her light-skinned, long-haired daughter was often the recipient of unbidden—and unwanted—gifts from strangers when she took the child shopping at the local knick-knack store:

> People would just buy something for my baby and hand it to me, saying, "She's just so beautiful. Look at her hair." Sometimes the person's own child would be standing there, gift-less—and brown.

The "color-struck" class war played out in black families, neighborhoods, social clubs, churches, colleges, fraternal organizations, and nearly every conceivable part of our culture. As the stigma progressed, class stratification within the black community became based, to a large degree, on the presence or absence of black features. It is a profound irony that the attractiveness rating was enhanced by the whiteness of hair, skin color, and facial features.

Sadly, that rating system continues today.

Pink & Pretty

When the Clarks conducted their original doll experiments, black women on the silver screen were stuck between two narrow standards of beauty—the servile, dark, kinky-haired prototype portrayed by actresses such as Hattie McDaniel, or long-haired, butterscotch beauties like Dorothy Dandridge or Lena Horne.

In a society designed by white male dictates, women in general have long abided hypocritical standards of beauty. Black women, however, had the double burden of adhering to images of loveliness that betrayed their natural features.

Madame C.J. Walker's hot comb, introduced and popularized in the early 1900s to straighten black women's hair, helped alter a prime physical symbol of shame. Walker was a brilliant marketer but, according to her biographer and kin, A'lelia Bundles, she too wrestled with the notion that she encouraged black women to emulate the standards of white beauty: "Right here let me correct the erroneous impression held by some that I claim to straighten hair," Walker told a reporter in 1918 after she had been called the "de-kink queen" by a white newspaper. *"I deplore such an impression because I have always held myself out as a hair culturist. I grow hair."*

Walker's intentions may have been misunderstood but her products helped black women—influenced by society's orders—to "straighten out" their natural beauty. In my neighborhood, little black girls attached long ribbons to their kinky braids and tossed their heads about, with the ribbons flowing down their backs, whisking across their faces, wildly imagining that they were long, silky, straight tresses.

Whoopi Goldberg memorably dramatized our hair hang-up when she created the character of a young black girl wearing a shirt on her head, pretending that it was beautiful hair cascading down her back and around her shoulders. All this acting out was the result of all-encompassing images of white beauty forced on the psyche of African Americans.

Black men may not be as obsessed over beauty standards as black women but we, too, have been psychologically influenced by a system that has deemed our natural look as something repulsive.

God Don't Like Ugly

heart throb, never, black and ugly as ever
however, I stay Gucci down to the socks
— Notorious B.I.G., "One More Chance"

As his lyrics seem to indicate, Biggie Smalls, aka Notorious B.I.G., was probably influenced by folks who looked like us. Like so many others, he probably heard blacks call one another ugly specifically because they were so black. After all, young, dark-skinned boys like Biggie had to notice older blacks fawning over lighter-skinned kids they considered pretty. These kids watched their own people compliment the fair-skinned kid's "nice complexion" (read: light-skinned), or enviously stroke their "good grade of hair" (read: naturally straight).

Positive white and negative black imagery affected all our young lives. As a child, I remember coming home after watching movies featuring stars like Cary Grant, Clark Gable, Roy Rogers, and Johnny "Tarzan" Weissmuller. I'd get in front of a mirror and attempt various forms of "tucking" in my lips, hoping to simulate the look of my heroes.

While women were using Madame Walker's products, black men suffered through caustic, lye-based "conks," popularized by athletes and entertainers like Sugar Ray Robinson, Nat "King" Cole, and numerous other black role models. Our hair had to be fried into flat and lifeless versions of its true form to be acceptable, even to ourselves.

In his autobiography, slain activist Malcolm X spoke to his once brainwashed condition that motivated his desire to "conk" his naturally red hair:

How ridiculous I was! Stupid enough to stand there simply lost in admiration of my hair now looking "white," reflected in the mirror...
I vowed that I'd never again be without a conk, and I never was for many years.

The uglified manifestations in men and boys are nowhere near as glaring as with women. Yet, there are indicators that black men still struggle with their share of absorbed misperceptions about their appearance. According to *Extreme Makeover*'s Dr. Anthony Griffin, a Beverly Hills plastic surgeon, the fastest growing increase in plastic surgery is among black men concened about their image. While we no longer have the spate of conks, we do still have the desire to tame our natural hairstyles. This is why stores still carry "S-Curl" and other perm products that help men "loosen their curls." Why else do school-age boys obsessively brush their short cuts in an attempt to "train" their hair into ocean waves?

The remnants of brainwashing linger and one of the strongest signs of its persistence is in black males who prefer women who look nothing like them.

The Message in the Medium

In early American literature, posters, and later, film, black males were caricatured as slow, slope-shouldered, slouchy, and sleepy. It's interesting to note that these images reveal an emphasis on looseness: loose head hanging from a horizontal neck; loose lips hanging from a downcast face; loose empty hands hanging from long, limp, simian-like arms; loose, tattered clothing, and loose shoes (if any); and loose, lazy, slurry speech.

White male figures, on the other hand, were generally projected as tight—majestically erect, stoic, intelligently involved, and totally in control of their world. In short order, both whites and blacks, exposed to the same negative images in books, plays, posters, postcards, salt and pepper shakers, "jolly nigger" banks, and other media products, totally embraced the mass-marketed standards of beauty.

Blacks, convinced that we were indeed grotesque, soon took over our own denigration. Whenever we fought or argued (which was often), our arsenal included creatively invective put-downs (which became known as "playing the dozens") and the most egregious slurs we could possibly hurl related to black physicality:

"Yo mama so black she's..."
"Yo mama so fat she's..."
"Yo mama so ugly she..."

There is no stronger social force, no greater mind-setter, no more-effective influencer than conventional media. Films, like all other forms of pop culture, reflect how the artist sees the world. Which images are in their work, however, demonstrates how artists see themselves. When we examine music videos produced by blacks that cast us as either pimps or whores but hardly ever as fully human, or movies that portray black women as fat, loud vulgarities, we recognize that we're still trapped in a perfect storm of self-hate. For centuries, the stigma associated with skin too dark, noses too broad, and hair too nappy hampered black self-esteem and the ability to raise black children who did not consider themselves black and ugly.

Black Pride: "Say it Loud!"

There was a brief moment of hope and collective transformation in the late 1960s, when the younger, less-tolerant progeny of the civil rights era birthed the Black Power movement. To be called black was no longer an insult, it was liberating. Suddenly, many of us sported dashikis, raised clenched fists, shouted "Black Power" and "Black Is Beautiful," and sang James Brown's "Say it Loud—I'm Black and I'm Proud."

This movement influenced every area of our culture and gave rise to the black arts movement. It wasn't just mainstream politics that changed, but education, music, fashion, and language shifted to reflect the demands of those who refused to go unheard.

We seemed to believe, at least for that moment, that black was the new beautiful. Afros emerged like black crowns, worn as a sign of liberation from shame and self-doubt. It was a demonstration of self-determination and self-love. It was a sign of hope and renewal of the spirit. Brown and ebony-skinned sisters were elevated to gorgeous sex symbols, visions of loveliness and grace. Black women

who had accepted the myth of inferiority and had all but given up on themselves, suddenly had role models like Pam Grier on movie screens kicking behinds and taking names. They could look at "bad" sisters like Kathleen Cleaver and Angela Davis and see themselves as not only beautiful but smart, strong, and politically conscious. Black women could see their whole selves reflected in the new *Essence* magazine (founded by long-time publisher and CEO Ed Lewis, with four partners in 1968).

Steeped in the symbolism of African artifacts, handshakes, slogans, songs, and self-affirming poetry, and the take-no-prisoners stance of black activism, we tried desperately to shake off centuries of negative indoctrination. In short we began slowly to love the whole of our black selves.

It is within this engaging environment that my firm, Burrell Communications Group, flourished—a time when our two largest clients, McDonald's and Coca-Cola, eagerly agreed with our strategy to inject more natural-looking black people in our ads.

Actually, I traveled a path blazed by another black advertising pioneer, Vince Cullers. In 1956, he founded Vince Cullers Advertising, Inc., the first black-owned advertising agency in the nation that expertly targeted the black consumer market. When Johnson Products hired him to advertise its black hair care product, Afro-Sheen, Cullers met the challenge with the proud tag line "Watu Wazuri," Swahili for "beautiful people." In that era of new-found pride, my firm had to challenge some of our clients and retrain employees who came to us from other agencies that were still clinging to entrenched standards of beauty. Fortunately, once provided with convincing information, most eagerly came on board and benefited from this newly liberated consumer base. It was indeed an electric time of unlimited possibility and an exciting time to own and operate an advertising agency specializing in the black consumer market.

The Empire Strikes Back

Unfortunately, the new movement lasted for less than a decade. Old folks, for the most part, never bought into it. When others referred to themselves as black or Afro-American, many elders insisted on keeping the "colored" or "Negro" brand, spouting defensive retorts that reflected the depth of the black inferiority complex conditioning: "I ain't black and I ain't never been to Africa."

By the late 1970s, many young people who were early enthusiasts of the "black is beautiful" concept gave in to the pervasive social pressure of fitting in with the mainstream. It was time, especially for college students who'd been in the forefront of the movement, to get jobs in government, in the nation's school systems, or in corporate America. Time to integrate and assimilate, fulfilling the dreams of generations past.

The 60s and 70s war on poverty got trumped by the '80s war on crime. Various social forces prevailed, led by popular culture and the media. As more formal and legal barriers to race fell, God-given hair styles were deemed not "professional" enough. Anything remotely approaching "natural"—'fros, cornrows, braids, dreadlocks—that offended or scared the heck out of white people in the workplace, became taboo. Black women, picking up on cues from their men as well as to attain good jobs, reverted to appearing less black, most by undergoing the process of Caucasianization of the hair. While still burdensome, it was much more doable than in the days of Madame C.J. Walker's "press and curl." Meanwhile, the hair-care industry relentlessly marketed new products, giving black men and women the soggy Jheri Curl look, followed by the '90s waterfall of weaves, extensions, and wigs of endless straight-hair variety for women.

As a response to the age of increasing American conservatism, a black college administrator dictated that no students in the business school would be allowed to wear African braids lest they disrupt the image of the proper businessperson. By 2007, a slide show presented by an unidentified *Glamour* magazine editor caused an uproar on the Internet. The presentation, "Dos and Don'ts of Corporate Fashion,"

shown at a prestigious law firm, basically forbade just about any "natural" black hairstyle in a corporate environment. *American Lawyer* magazine described parts of the slide show presentation:

> [First slide up]: ...an African American woman sporting an Afro—A real no-no, announced the Glamour editor to the 40 or so lawyers in the room. As for dreadlocks: How truly dreadful! The style maven said it was shocking that some people still think it appropriate to wear those hairstyles at the office. "No offense," she sniffed, but those "political" hairstyles really have to go.

According to Blackvoices.com the magazine quickly disavowed the editor's comments, saying that she in no way spoke for the publication. Whether she spoke for the magazine or not, the editor's comments were accurate. Tragically, imitating whiteness has once again became the new black look.

Back Where We Started

Today the hymn of "Black Is Beautiful" is something we occasionally utter and rarely believe. The signals, the cultural cues, the media messages, and charismatic public personalities all come together with a singular, consistent, resounding counter-theme: "Black Is Not Beautiful!" The hair and flair of lighter-skinned actresses and models in films and on magazine covers reinforce the notion that dark and lovely is fine for hair coloring products but indeed out of fashion in real life.

The preponderance of these images and messages sends clear signals to blacks, especially black children, that we are not pretty enough, not good enough. Consider the slogan "Perfection Made Easy," that SoftSheen Carson uses to promote its Dark and Lovely Kids Beautiful Beginnings Hair Care Systems. What messages are black children receiving when using these products to "relax" their hair? Most likely, they learn that black features don't fit the definition of perfection. What's disturbing is that the lessons don't always come from outsiders.

Consider the daughters of comedian Chris Rock. While promoting his 2009 film *Good Hair,* about the $9 billion black hair-care industry, Rock told interviewers that he was inspired to make the film by his two daughters, who didn't think they have "good hair." Rock's wife, Malaak Compton-Rock, added more detail to the story during the April 11, 2008 MSNBC "Conversation About Race" panel discussion. According to Compton-Rock, the couple's three-year-old daughter Zahra came home from school depressed because her hair was not as long as one of her non-black friends. Compton-Rock, told the MSNBC audience that she comforted Zahra by telling the child that she loved her hair's fluffiness and puffiness and that it did not detract from her unique beauty.

I wasn't the only one who caught the contradictions in Compton-Rock's heartfelt consolation. Thankfully, K. Danielle Edwards, a Nashville-based writer, addressed my concerns in "Mamas Wear Your Hair Natural," her BlackCommentator.com observations:

> Here was Compton-Rock, bemoaning her daughter's ambivalence about her own hair, seemingly befuddled and blaming society and the media, when she, herself, was donning at least 18 inches of silky straight weave!

In late September 2009, Oprah Winfrey interviewed a black mother whose three-year-old daughter, like the Rocks' child, also came home from school upset because her hair "was not pretty" and "wouldn't go down." With her husband and daughter by her side, the mother, Vanessa, described how she addressed her daughter's concern. She didn't just tell the child that her hair was perfectly acceptable. She showed her. Vanessa sheared her own locks that had been chemically relaxed since she herself was a child.

"I wanted to be a role model for our daughter to show her that straight is just one of the options we have as African American women. Now I'm wearing a teeny-weeny afro and I'm looking forward to it growing out and seeing what it teaches me about myself."

Again, I think Edwards, the Nashville writer summed up the situation better than I could when she stressed how daughters, in their formative years, "copy and mimic" everything their mothers do.

If we, as black women, go around looking like make-believe, pretend white women, playing a bad form of dress-up so common that we no longer see it for what it is, well, guess what? Our daughters will want to, too.

To deny that looking a certain way is not a huge factor in this society is to deny reality. The BI reprogramming process begins when we question why one image is consistently chosen over another; why one image is always counted "in," while the other, "dark and natural" image is too often counted out. We discover answers when we compare the uglified dynamics to the ugly lessons learned from slavery and race-based oppression.

Uglified: Connecting the Dots

Contemporary Manifestations	Historical Roots
White is right: Black beauty is the antithesis of white standards. The further we are from the European standard, the lower we find ourselves on the beauty scale.	Our historical odyssey is "proof" that our inferiority lay in our non-European characteristics: color, hair, facial features.
Get back black: In a color-coded society, many of us boast of additional "blood" (Indian, Irish, Italian) that boosts our value. On a sliding racial social scale, "lighter" or "whiter" is defined as "better."	During and after slavery, blacks understood that mixed racial heritage conferred greater status, and produced preferential treatment and labeled them more attractive. Hollywood and media affirmed the stigma. The consensus—that being of mixed race was more desirable than being "pure-bred black" prevailed.

Nappy? Not happy!: The obsession to alter black physicality and beauty standards is extraordinary. Our hair carries extraordinary psychodynamic ramifications and advertising weight. Blacks spend millions on hair care products to cover up or cure the scourge of blackness.	The coarse texture of our hair was used to "prove" our inferiority from the beginning. Conditioned to equate white hair as the epitome of "good" hair, we have strived to achieve it decade after decade. The conditioning was so successful that it has outlasted efforts to reclaim our own ethnic identities and standards of beauty.

At What Cost?

Along with intensive hair-care strategies, cosmetic surgical interventions designed to diminish the Africanized broad nose and other cultural inconveniences have become widely available. Though not as prevalent as hair procedures, it is increasingly an option for those who can afford it. Cosmetic surgery, with nearly a billion-dollar annual expenditure by African American men, women, and even some children, plays a large part in eliminating telltale signs of blackness.

We are bombarded with images of black women flinging, flipping, flicking copious mounds of weaves, extensions, wigs, falls, and relaxed hair. Dancers on music videos have "fine" (Caucasianized) features and "hair to spare." Advertisements for everything from cosmetics to automobiles ensure that today we are still fed ample, steady diets of white beauty standards via light-skinned black African Americans. Even among publications that regularly feature black celebrities, rarely will you find characteristically African features.

We can "go along to get along" with dominant society's dictates or we can start the analytical process by weighing the costs and benefits of our thoughts and actions.

Short-term Benefits

1. **Acceptance:** Why risk isolation, or losing employment or promotion, just to buck societal norms? It's easier to accept what's deemed normal and not make a fuss about our looks or our hair. If a nose job, weave, or perm will make me more attractive, so be it.

2. **Relieving the pain:** My child does not need to feel like an oddity. If their friends aren't wearing afros or hair puffs, why should I force it on my child? Sends an unnecessary message of rebellion and black identity to whites.

3. **Don't want any trouble:** Big afros, cornrows, and braids threaten white people. They immediately perceive these hairstyles as radical and me as rebellious. White people make and enforce the rules. Neither my child nor I need to be harassed, held back, or ostracized because of our hairstyles.

Long-term Costs

1. **Acceptance:** Accepting the status quo's definition of societal norms serves to sanction the conditioning of white superiority. As an evolving society that is becoming more and more global, it is incumbent on us to challenge what has been labeled "normal" by a narrow minority.

2. **Relieving the pain:** Discouraging your children's natural look simply because it defies popular imagery actually makes them an oddity. Future leaders need to feel proud of their unaltered look and must be discouraged from following the dictate of media messaging. Celebrating our unique look is not rebellious. Any effort to punish children comfortable in their natural look should be challenged aggressively.

3. **Don't want any trouble:** Altering our looks or hairstyles because whites feel threatened validates racist perceptions. Whites must learn that blacks with afros, cornrows, and braids can be just as professional, courteous, and creative as those with short or straightened hair. Yes, whites have more power than blacks to make and enforce rules. However, some rules—especially those influenced by a false sense of superiority—are made to be challenged and broken.

Centuries of propaganda created the perceptual aesthetic deficit. We will need powerful weapons to dis-enslave and reprogram how we see ourselves. To wage a winnable war, both internally and externally, we will need the proper ammunition.

Uglified—Positive Propaganda Cues

Look Past the Lie
We have to overcome the barrage of propaganda that tells us that European standards of beauty are the only valid ones.

Black Beauty—It's All Good
There is more than one way to be beautifully black. We come in all colors of the rainbow, and all shapes and sizes. Embrace who you are!

It's Yours to Define What It Means to be Fine
Whether you're perceived as beautiful or not depends largely on how you see yourself. If you feel beautiful, you will act beautiful, and you will be perceived as such.

Black Beauty Comes Naturally!
Let yourself be. Don't allow the propaganda to convince you that you need to be altered to be beautiful!

Black Beauty: No Alterations Necessary! (See above.)

Black Is Beautiful. Really!

The silver streak at the tip of her afro speaks to her maturity. She has dark skin and proud African features. She is beautiful. The photo accompanying the impressive bio of Xerox Corporation's Chief Executive Officer, Ursula M. Burns, exudes her outward and inner splendor. Women who look like Burns, who defy the popular Westernized definition of beauty, should be celebrated, not as the exception but as part of a diversified standard for African American beauty.

The so-called beauty norms must be altered and expanded to include women who are proud of their natural looks, like Burns. For our own and our children's sake, we must stop sending subliminal messages that our hair needs something extra to be okay or that our looks aren't acceptable—as is.

The Magic of the Moment

On November 4, 2008, a brown-skinned miracle—President-elect Barack Obama, accompanied by his beautiful, chocolate-colored South Side Chicago wife and their lovely young daughters—strode onto the Grant Park stage amid massive applause and thunderous chants of "Yes, we can!"

Although it will never be announced officially, the Obama family in the White House has already launched the biggest anti-BI campaign in the history of our nation. Obama may be of mixed heritage, but he looks like any other brother. How refreshing to see a black man with natural swagger defy negative stereotypes while professionally serving as the country's head of state.

How uplifting to also see a brilliant, strong-willed, dark-skinned First Lady serve with grandeur without a molecule of the stereotypical surly Sapphire or acquiescent Aunt Jemima–like baggage. And perhaps the greatest achievement is that Michelle Obama has never made the slightest attempt to be "whiter" than other first ladies.

In "The Power of the Fro," long-time Washington, DC hairstyle expert and journalism major Laquita Thomas-Banks wrote about the re-emergence of the afro and other natural hairstyles among today's young black models, singers, and entertainers, such as Angie Stone, Jill Scott, Tomiko Fraser, Marsha Hunt, Wakeema Hollis, Erykah Badu, and others. Thomas-Banks gave a nod to historic figures Angela Davis, Cicely Tyson, Pam Grier, and other women who classified the afro "as a symbol of black beauty, feminism, liberation, and cultural revolution that will be looked upon as such for years to come."

Those of us who know that long hair or light skin are not requisites to beauty must correct the record, beginning with our children, whose images of manhood and womanhood are, by our own hands, narrow, self-hating, and warped versions of the truth. The challenge is relevant today and our resolve must be firm. We must refuse to be consumers of black films and street lit that popularize negative black caricatures in ways worse than those of racially conditioned white filmmakers, cartoonists, and authors. If we have the courage to look at our own words and adopt new ways of speaking, we begin to stand as bulwarks against manipulated ignorance. If we never again say things like "He's so black..." in a way that makes *black* sound like a curse, a hated thing, we start reclaiming our minds and the minds of our children.

Terms like *ugly, and black bitch* are tentacles that strangle valuable bonds and connections. Adopting a new lexicon of supplemental terms such as *beautiful, beloved, brother,* and *sister,* not only builds positive consciousness, it may even reduce the reflexive need for negative racial epithets in times of anger and frustration.

Surveying how we see ourselves, talk about ourselves, and project ourselves, and then making meticulous, concerted efforts to redefine beauty by our own standards begins the ultimate journey in discovering our true proud, resilient, beautiful, and natural selves. Most important, perhaps, is the need to de-emphasize the reliance on "appearance" as the primary means of valuing people. Fortunately, the anti-brainwash campaign offers mechanisms created to help reprogram and empower blacks to reclaim their images and develop new, genuine standards of beauty.

Chapter 5

Homey-cide

Why Do We Keep Killing Each Other?

Look, you hear about people getting killed all the time:
little kids, teenagers, grown folks. Somewhere along the way,
you stop feeling surprised. "That's just black folks," you know?
You can't afford to get upset, 'cause that's just the way it is...
and I don't see it changing anytime soon. Do you?

— 'NETTE, 58, CHILD-CARE PROVIDER

Like spectators in a Roman coliseum, millions watched the horrific images, broadcast on news programs or streamed on the Internet. They saw what police described as an escalated dispute between two factions on the South Side of Chicago. There, in broad daylight, on a busy street, black teens were engaged in battle—cracking heads with railroad ties, smashing faces with balled fists, and denting bodies with well-aimed kicks.

As the gang-related melée came to an end, Derrion Albert, a 16-year-old honor student, lay on the sidewalk barely conscious. He had been struck repeatedly on his head with a torn up old plank. As Derrion crumpled to the ground and rolled in agony, several barbarous young men gleefully kicked and stomped him more.

Screaming teenage girls and grown women rushed to help the downed boy, car horns blared as the urban gladiators clashed, adrenaline-drunk boys ducked in and out of fist-throwing clusters,

some laughing as if engaged in a high school football game. Derrion was taken to a local hospital, where he was pronounced dead.

As news spread about Derrion's death, sympathizers placed teddy bears and flowers outside his family's home. Relatives and friends, some wearing T-shirts bearing the boy's photo, held a vigil to share their grief. The boy's grandfather, Joseph Walker, told a reporter he planned to pray for the boys who killed his grandson. Media pundits, authors, and commentators assumed predictable positions, blaming racism or race-baiters.

Days after the beating, police arrested and charged four teens, ages 14, 16, 18, and 19, for the murder. This was a case of swift justice and national outrage. Sadly, neither was due strictly to the fact that another black child died senselessly. Each year, thousands of black children die violent deaths in this country. The reaction to Derrion's death was mostly because millions watched the murder on the Internet. Overwhelming silence is the standard reaction to such senseless deaths. Why does it take live footage of a murder to get the coliseum to care?

Weusi Would Have Cared

It was 1986, during Detroit's so-called "summer of blood." Weusi Olusola, a 16-year-old high-school basketball All-Star, had just finished a hard shift at a neighborhood Hardee's restaurant. Plans to visit his girlfriend were altered forever when Weusi found himself caught in the middle of a shootout. One of four bullets that crashed into his body lodged in his spinal cord, leaving him paralyzed. Though confined to a wheelchair, Weusi rolled himself through Detroit's mean streets speaking to thousands of urban youth about the dangers of gun violence. Ten years after he was shot, he cofounded Pioneers for Peace, a volunteer antiviolence awareness group composed of people disabled by gun injuries. As president of the group, Weusi visited classrooms, auditoriums, and after-school programs, preaching the gospel of nonviolence and sharing the story of how his college hoop dreams ended in a nightmare created by yet another angry, young brother with a gun.

Serving as a visible reminder of senseless and deadly violence, Weusi joined Bill Cosby during a Detroit antiviolence rally in 2005 and participated in several other massive events, such as the Million Man and Million Mom Marches in Washington, D.C.

Yet in 2007, when the NAACP called for a mass protest, Weusi stayed home.

The rallying cry was in support of six black, Jena, Louisiana high school students charged with beating a white student. The incident was the culmination of several racially tense fracases that occurred after nooses were hung in the courtyard of Jena High School. Tens of thousands descended upon Jena to protest the perceived excessive and discriminatory punishment leveled against the black youth. Weusi couldn't quite wrap his head around the NAACP's priorities.

When comparing black folks' passionate response to white injustice and our collective silence with black-on-black violence, the response to the Jena Six case seemed like an overreaction. Weusi said, "I was amazed so many folks from here went down there. It made my heart weep. We can't even get parents to visit their kid's school. Can you imagine what it would be like if we could put that kind of energy into the gun-violence issue?"

That sort of energy would have been a refreshing change from some of today's traditional civil rights organizations. How many cities where young children were shot dead did the secular leaders fly over to get to Jena? More folks were moved to action by a case of white-on-black injustice than they were over black-on-black murder.

Simply put, it was another instance of symbolism over substance.

Weusi Olusola passed away in early 2009, after losing a courageous battle against bladder cancer. The major issue he fought so valiantly to eradicate since his own shooting still plagues America's urban communities. Almost worse than the senselessness of black-on-black violence is the cancer of silence that allows it to continue unabated.

Gates to Nowhere

Seven months after President Obama's inauguration, a once-cooled, hot-button issue—racial profiling—got pushed. It unleashed a relentless media circus. Passions and prognostications were at such a fevered pitch for weeks that, during a press conference, the first black president had to detour from questions about his healthcare reform initiative to address the issue.

On July 16, 2009, renowned Harvard professor Henry Louis Gates was arrested at his own home by a Cambridge police officer who had responded to a call about a possible break-in at Gates's premises. The reaction to the arrest mostly fell along racial lines, with most blacks convinced the case was another example of racial profiling and excessive policing of a black person. Many whites, on the other hand, insisted Gates's insolent attitude and abrasive accusations of racism accelerated the tension that led to his arrest.

While all this dead-end, back-and-forth debate consumed America's attention, an eight-year-old black Indianapolis boy's life ended tragically. On July 22, Jeremiah Williams was accidentally shot in the head while playing outside his apartment complex. Media reports stated that the 27-year-old suspect came to the area armed and ready to settle differences with an 18-year-old who was also shot but survived.

Three days after the boy's death, I typed "Gates," "police," and "Cambridge" into Google's news search engine and got almost 9,000 results. Moments later, I typed in "Jeremiah Williams," "Indianapolis," and "shot." How many results did I receive for the child? ONE!

Although the numbers would have surely increased had I used the regular search procedure that includes blogs and online commentaries, I'm reasonably certain the nine-thousand-to-one ratio would have remained a constant even with an expanded search.

Besides, I was interested in what was labeled "news," not online chatter. And it was clear that the incident involving Gates was newsworthy while little Jeremiah was not.

What happened to Professor Gates shouldn't have been labeled "news"—it's an everyday occurrence, part of being black in America.

If all racial profiling by police ended tomorrow, it still wouldn't change the "homey-cide" rate.

As Weusi Olusola observed, our priorities are drastically out of whack. How many young Jeremiah Williamses lost their lives while black folk wrestled with their emotions, passionately debated, and quietly fretted about Skip Gates?

News and No-News

Unlike high-profile cases of murdered children, such as six-year-old beauty queen JonBenet Ramsey in 1996 or two-year-old Caylee Anthony in 2008, the deaths of black children receive little to no media mention and limited nationwide black outrage. The skewed media attention doesn't just apply to black children. The deaths of white women receive far more media treatment than those of black females. Thousands of black lives, male and female, are snuffed out annually through violence, yet there are few call-outs for nationwide rallies to stem this form of American genocide.

Just weeks before the noose-hanging incident in Jena, Louisiana, a heinous murder in Atlanta of a Morehouse College student received scant mention on black radio and in the white media. Carlnell Walker, Jr., a 23-year-old junior, was beaten, tortured, stabbed, and then bound and stuffed in the trunk of his car and left to die. Four men accused of his murder were or had been "Morehouse men," a distinction thousands have worn with honor. According to the Associated Press, the police said they believed the killers were after a $3,000 insurance settlement check Carlnell was expecting.

Had young Carlnell been tortured by white supremacists, as with James Byrd, who was dragged to death behind a pickup truck in Jasper, Texas, in 1998, we can be assured there would be national indignation. Had Carlnell been shot by cops—as was Sean Bell, an unarmed 23-year-old New Yorker felled in a hail of 50 gunshots on the day he was to be married—Atlanta college students, as well as thousands of other African Americans would have taken their outrage to the streets and to the Internet.

My brief online experiment with Jeremiah Williams and Professor Gates illustrates the effectiveness of the BI brainwashing campaign. African Americans are stuck in deep denial about black-on-black killings. We buy into media diversions, like the Gates case, that keep us incessantly talking about white-instigated racial incidents, while black kids—sitting on front porches, lying in beds, or playing in front of homes—cease to exist due to random gun violence instigated by blacks.

It seems we are more consumed with how whites treat us and less concerned, or even numbed out, about how we treat each other. Could it be because many blacks are so convinced that white people are superior and therefore their opinions of us, and actions toward us, are more important than our actions and opinions of ourselves?

In the spirit of Weusi Olusola, we must consciously adjust our priorities and dedicate the necessary energy to the scourge of black homicide, violence, and disproportionate death. Here, we explore *why* African Americans kill and die at such unbalanced rates, and why most African Americans are still reluctant to speak up or take action in the face of a national epidemic.

Dynamics of Death

You have a subculture of young black men pretending to be men by killing each other...
— Jim Brown, founder of Amer-I-Can, from the documentary *Crips and Bloods: Made in America*

Blacks are just 13 percent of the population. Yet, according to a 2005 Bureau of Justice Statistics report from the U.S. Department of Justice, we account for about half of all the country's homicides. Recent statistics do indeed show the magnitude of the deaths but they don't fully detail the underlying forces that fuel these disproportionate rates.

Homey-cide Dynamics

Murdering minors: *Young people, gang-affiliated or not, who kill at astronomical rates.*

A 2007 Justice Department study confirmed that more than half of black murder victims (51 percent) were in their late teens and twenties. Comparatively, just over a third (37 percent) of whites murdered during the same period were between the ages of 17 and 29.

Death for respect: *Unplanned aggression that leads to death. Homicide for insignificant reasons, such as insults, arguments, or feelings of disrespect.*

The traffic altercation, the shoulder bump, the "you insulted me" therefore "you must die" madness prevails. For homicides involving black victims for whom the circumstances could be identified, 69 percent were not related to felonies. Of these, 56 percent involved arguments between the victim and the offender. In most cases, the instigating factors escalated from the emotional and artificial concept of RESPECT.

All in the family: *Spouses and intimate partners who kill; black men take the lead in homey-cide statistics as both victims and perpetrators.*

Our rate of domestic violence, where spouses and intimate partners kill each other, is far greater than that of any other ethnic group. Black males are not only the most likely victims of homicide; they dominate as killers, especially in taking the life of another black male.

See no evil: *Blacks often ignore or fail to address black-on-black violence; there is an increasing collective numbness to black violence and murder.*

Black-on-black violence has become the new norm in our communities. This apathy, or deadness, devalues black life and contributes to the skyrocketing rate of violence, especially among our young people.

These death dynamics, backed by national trends, present an ugly truth—African American lives are snuffed out at levels no sane, civilized community should tolerate. However, buried within this truth lies an unexplored link to America's "original sin" that put the madness in motion and keeps the BI addicts living up to predetermined expectations.

Roots of Violence

Every day, that's my diet: a spoonful of hatred. It's just a question of when is this going to erupt, and upon who is it going to erupt? Am I going to attack myself? Am I going to attack my brother?... Point is, I'm a walking time bomb: I'm gonna go off, someday, somewhere, on somebody. The question is, Upon whom?
— Kumasi, activist, former gang member, from the documentary *Crips and Bloods: Made in America*

The acclaimed *All God's Children*, by *New York Times* correspondent Fox Butterfield, should be mandatory reading for anyone seeking to understand how America's violent past has tainted future generations. Assigned to profile Willie Bosket, once considered the most violent prisoner in the New York prison system, Butterfield traced the man's family history back to the slave era, where he discovered a cycle of violence that was transmitted across generations. Butterfield's book details a black man's pathology not rooted in Africa but embedded in a legacy of Scotch-Irish violence that thrived around Edgefield, South

Carolina. Butterfield detailed a violent Southern code of honor in the Bosket family tree that included deadly duels over the smallest insult.

Mental health experts are in general agreement that persistent exposure to humiliation, brutality, and abuse, physical or emotional, can program people to humiliate, brutalize, and abuse others. Apart from the indigenous people of this country, no other ethnic group has been subjected to the centuries of abuse that Africans and their descendants have experienced.

In spite of this, most African Americans have never committed a violent crime. Since we were first brought to this country in chains, we have resisted, rebelled, and refused to be sucked in by the negative messaging designed to debase us both physically and mentally. That in and of itself is the great miracle, a testimony to the resilience of the human spirit to triumph over the most degrading of circumstances.

Still, vestiges of degradation remain very much alive, and our struggle to make amends with a twisted, physically and mentally debilitating past is far from over. Murder and savagery is as much a part of America's fabric as are its romanticized renditions of westward expansion and innovative economic and social revolutions. Blood has stained the lives of millions who migrated to the new country. In other words, we didn't create the violence. It created us.

The Badass Negro

If you ain't where I'm from, fuck you, that's just how it is where we from. That's the whole motto: Kill or be killed.
— Big Girch, gang member, from the documentary *Crips and Bloods: Made in America*

Historians tell us that not all slaves were compliant and docile. Some men and women refused to keep their anger and rage in check. The so-called "bad nigger," an iconic figure in African American folklore, has deep roots in slave society. Living in a world that did its best to break spirits, those known to be defiant, mean, and not to be messed with were treated as heroes by other slaves.

95

The "bad" black man's refusal to follow the rules, and willingness to fight back if provoked, was his badge of courage, even if it ultimately resulted in death. Eugene Genovese, in *Roll Jordan Roll: The World that the Slaves Made,* writes that the best of these men were "... the ones most dramatically saying 'No!' and reminding others that there are worse things than death. No people wholly lacking such an attitude can expect to survive. But the aim remains to live, not to die heroically."

Owners sometimes encouraged their slaves to be ferocious. The battle royal, a throwback to the gladiator fights of the Roman empire, was a popular form of white entertainment in which slaveowners would herd their strongest male slaves—blindfolded—into a ring and force them to fight each other until only one man was left standing. Observers placed bets on the projected winner and the victor's owner pocketed the winnings. The contest was a divisive sport designed to pit black men against one another and humiliate them further by forcing them to stumble blindly in front of jeering crowds as they beat themselves to bloody pulps.

The battle royal, graphically depicted in the opening chapter of Ralph Ellison's classic, *Invisible Man,* continued long after the abolishment of slavery and well into the 1930s. "Smokers" were common pre-events during major boxing matches. Even then, the pugilists in these spectacles were always black men. Blacks have maintained attitudes that helped us tolerate and endure slavery. Some of those adopted attitudes, however, such as black-on-black violence and stubborn, nihilistic posturing, serve no purpose in the 21st century. These days we kill because we've swallowed the BI campaign's messages: "We are inferior. We are less than. Black life has no value."

Baddest Man in the Whole Damn Town

Fear kept many blacks on the straight and narrow. As a substitute for confronting white power, many others turned to drinking, gambling, and ultimately fussing, fighting, maiming, and murdering each other. Indeed, the harshness, frequency, and high visibility of punishment under slavery and afterward created a climate in which being "bad" in white eyes, even to the extent of criminal behavior, carried no stigma. Slave and free black communities not only protected but also revered the rebel. It was an environment where the bad black man— mean, evil, thoroughly incorrigible—was nurtured and could flourish. It's impossible not to make the connection between the brutality in the outer world and the brutality that, for some, came to define their private lives.

Dr. Benjamin Mays, mentor to Dr. Martin Luther King, Jr., and the long-time president of Morehouse College, opens his autobiography, *Born to Rebel*, describing how the tyranny in the South Carolina town Ninety Six influenced blacks of that era:

> I believe to this day that Negroes in my county fought among themselves because they were taking out on other Negroes what they really wanted but feared to take out on whites. It was difficult, virtually impossible, to combine manhood and blackness under one skin in the days of my youth. To exercise manhood, as white men displayed it, was to invite disaster.

In *All God's Children*, Butterfield paints a compelling portrait of Willie Bosket's great-grandfather Pud, at the time the "baddest man" in Saluda Country, South Carolina, and just a few miles from where Benjamin Mays grew up. Pud never initiated a fight but, as a relative told Butterfield, "If you pushed him he had to beat you. Step on his foot at a dance or walking by, just brush him and there'd be a fight."

The "badass black man," as a musical theme, lilted through time. It was celebrated in blues ballads like "Bad, Bad Leroy Brown," and "Staggerlee," the 19th-century black pimp who killed a man in a bar as he begged for his life. The theme blasted loud in black 1970s films, such as *Superfly, Slaughter, Trouble Man,* and *Shaft*, which produced a song about one "bad mutha (shut yo' mouth)" black film detective.

Considering the adulation of the dangerous, ass-kicking Negro, is it any wonder why today's rapping prodigies, like 50 Cent, lyrically resurrect this deadly persona?

I make a 187 look easy
Fuck that, I lay my murder·game down
—50 Cent, "Curtis 187"

No Law, No Order

I know where yo kids and yo wife be, wife be
Bust a nigga head to the white meat, white meat
—Lil' Jon & the Eastside Boyz, "White Meat"

Through slavery, Reconstruction, and northern migration, the era of Jim Crow rule and legal segregation (and, many will argue, in these modern times), representatives of the law have been willing accomplices in containing, beating, oppressing, lynching, and murdering black people. Where law was adulterated, some blacks created their own system of order.

In the last quarter of the 19th century, sociologist W.E.B. Du Bois also observed that crime among blacks, once rare, had increased dramatically. A distinct black criminal class was emerging in the cities. Du Bois noted that some blacks preferred to live outside the law because they saw no point in living within the law. Many blacks came to regard the justice system as a structure of dualities. Influenced by white superiority, the system was crafted to punish blacks who committed crimes against whites more severely than those who committed crimes against fellow blacks.

Arguably, swift and often cruel punishment for blacks who murder whites serves as a deterrent. However, if one accepts that theory, then the flip side of the hypothesis may also apply, as authors Shaun L. Gabbidon and Helen Taylor Greene explored in their book, *Race, Crime and Justice:*

> To the extent that homicide is a preventable or deterrable crime, one must examine the role of law enforcement authorities in the genesis of black homicide…leniency in the treatment of black [intra-racial, or within the race] offenders may tend to encourage black-on-black aggression.

Dying for Respect

*Don't step on my reputation. My name is all I got, so I got to keep
it. I am a man of respect.*

The words of Willie Bosket's great-grandfather, Pud, reflect
the attitude of many young black men today. *Respect* represents
something worth protecting or risking your life (or another life) over.
For far too many young black men, to be dissed is considered a kill-
or-be-killed affront.

Slavery and the country's addiction to race-based violence is no
excuse for the murderous behavior of blacks today. However, to fix a
problem you have to understand its roots. Exploring antisocial mores
and values, as well as societal and legal injustices, helps us connect
the dots between the deadly "code of honor" of yesteryear and the
nihilistic "code of respect" defiantly practiced today.

Through slick propaganda, the criminal code of respect is referred
to as a "black thing." The message that black men are America's
demons is peddled relentlessly on the nightly news and crime shows,
and through entertainment media. These messages hit black boys
everywhere—on the basketball court, in the schoolyard, and when
they gather on the street. Negative media reinforcements not only
influence how cops, judges, employers, and others view black males,
they affect how young blacks view themselves.

The socialization process is the means by which children learn
societal and behavioral rules. It helps them determine and develop
sets of beliefs, values, and attitudes about themselves, culture, family,
society, and ethnic groups. Family and other institutions are "major
transmitters" in the social learning process. However, as Gordon L.
Berry stressed in his article on the media's effect on black youth, in
contemporary society, "the phenomenon of mass communication
competes with these traditional socializing institutions."

In other words, the media—television, films, video games, music
videos—are all major socializers. Television, in particular, has maximum
impact on child socialization, especially if the values or views recur; if
they're presented in dramatic form that evoke emotional reactions;

if they link with a child's needs and interests; and if no standard (friends, parents, environment) is supplied to counteract what's offered by television.

According to the National Institute on Media and the Family, exposure to media violence is positively related to "aggressive behavior, aggressive ideas, arousal, and anger." In 2001, Iowa State University researchers concluded that violent music lyrics increase "aggressive thoughts and hostile feelings," and that young people who play violent video games, even for short periods, are more likely to behave aggressively.

It's a known fact that blacks consume much more television than whites. Berry cited several studies indicating how black children use television to learn "new facts and information about life" and to learn how people "behave, talk, dress, and look." The scary reality is that black children perceive media-fed behaviors as true reflections of life.

In a society created to reinforce white superiority, the intended benefactors receive balanced messages of good and bad, destructive and constructive, real and unreal. For blacks, there are no filters that say, "This is pretend." Many of our children consider media messages and images as authentic reflections of who we are.

Black men are the descendents of a race that, due to skin color, has been systematically denied opportunity to meld into mainstream society. Therefore, for those with little self-esteem, who feel they have nothing else of worth, honor becomes everything. Without it, they would be spiritually bankrupt. Young black people have no idea how this warped mindset is dictated by a script drafted for their demise centuries before they were even born.

Prison: A Peculiar Institution

Part of the mechanics of oppressing people is to pervert them to the extent that they become the instrument of their own oppression.
— Kumasi, activist, former gang member, from the documentary *Crips and Bloods: Made in America*

No parent need be reminded that black boys suffer greater consequences for their missteps. They are incarcerated at higher rates and more frequently than whites who commit similar offenses. Of the 2.3 million people currently in the nation's prisons, 60 percent are racial and ethnic minorities. For black males in their twenties, one in every eight is in jail on any given day, according to The Sentencing Project.

In early 2009, Virginia Senator Jim Webb, a staunch proponent of radical prison reform, cited sobering statistics about the incarceration of African Americans. For instance, even though there's "little statistical difference among racial groups regarding actual drug use," blacks—who make up roughly 12 percent of the nation's population—account for 37 percent of those arrested on drug charges, 59 percent of those convicted, and 74 percent of all drug offenders sentenced to prison.

Thanks to a society structured to protect and expand white superiority, white teenage boys who get into trouble are far more likely to receive lighter sentences, treatment, and rehabilitation for their crimes. On the other hand, black boys more easily end up in jail or juvenile detention. In fact, as Marian Wright Edelman, founder of The Children's Defense Fund, noted, "more and more of those who enter the Prison Pipeline start with arrest records as young children."

Edelman questioned the sanity of a nation willing to spend more on prisons than on Head Start programs. She sounded an alarm about the disproportionate number of black boys who are heartlessly trapped in a "youth detention culture" permeated with cruelty, "where the focus is often on control and punishment instead of rehabilitation."

To illustrate her point, Edelman cited data from a 2003 U.S. Department of Justice investigation into conditions at Oakley and Columbia Juvenile Training Schools in Mississippi, where juveniles were "hog-tied with chains, physically assaulted by guards, sprayed with chemicals…forced to eat their own vomit and put in dark, solitary confinement cells after being stripped naked."

The Mississippi juvenile centers may be extreme cases. However, conditions at such sites reflect the results of a rapidly expanded prison system (a 500 per cent increase over the past thirty years, according to The Sentencing Project). It is a system clogged with the targets of

the nation's 25-plus-year failed "war on drugs" that in reality is more of an orchestrated war on poor, uneducated blacks and Latinos.

When examining the skyrocketing black homicide rate, we must consider how black boys learn to become hardened criminals through exposure to adult criminal mentors in prisons. We have to scrutinize a society that created a prison industrial system that spits out deadlier and more contemptuous offenders than went in. The nation's prison system is the modern-day equivalent of slave plantations—a system where poor blacks have no rights, no real justice, and are openly treated as animalistic, inferior human beings.

Killing Us Quietly

If for nothing else but survival, generations of blacks have been astute observers of the white power structure. This explains why many of us cringe when we hear news accounts of horrendous black-on-black crimes or hesitate to publicly condemn blacks who kill blacks. Deep down, we fear that whites, especially those seeking to validate their sense of white superiority, will judge us all by the negative actions of a few.

Black leaders and individuals are hesitant to endorse any stereotype that feeds into cemented racial perceptions. In our homes, churches, and among ourselves, some of us *do* talk about the senseless acts of violence. However, publicly we still wear the mask of duality, clinging to the ludicrous notion that we can keep our dirty laundry in the hamper.

We will, however, tsk-tsk, moan, and wail about a lost life in front of news cameras and dutifully deliver teddy bears to the porches of murdered children. We perpetuate the myth. If we expose the Founding Fathers' contribution to America's creation of the heartless monsters roaming 21st-century concrete jungles, we're afraid we might be dismissed as radical, paranoid, or "stuck in the past." What we won't do is recognize that, collectively, we have the inherent power and responsibility to address black-on-black violence.

We can't talk about change without first discussing America's "original sin" and the system that set this whole destructive cycle in motion. It's imperative that we retrace the tracks before boarding the solution train.

Homey-cide: Connecting the Dots

Contemporary Manifestations	Historical Roots
Murdering minors: Young people, gang-affiliated and not, who kill at astronomical rates.	Slaves were taught to devalue black life, and this is a "value" we passed down to our children. Personal oppression, generational poverty, illegal drug trafficking, gangs, and self-hatred created a kill or be killed "code of respect" among young people.
Death for respect: Unplanned aggression that leads to death. Homicide for insignificant reasons, such as insults, arguments, or feelings of disrespect.	Stripped of respectability and dignity through humiliation, ridicule, and physical and psychological trauma, we were left with shattered egos and pent-up rage. We became hypersensitive to any emotional trigger.
All in the family: Spouses and intimate partners who kill; black males are most homicide victims and most killers of other black males.	From the very beginning of our American experience there was a welling up of violent rage and self-hatred within us. The easiest target for black rage and self-hatred is those closest to us who cannot retaliate.
See no evil: Blacks who ignore or fail to address black-on-black violence; a collective numbness to black violence and homicide.	Black men and women have become immune to intra-racial violence. "Shutting down" is an effective psychic defense. The fact that all blacks are judged by the negative tendencies of a few forces many to repress public outrage.

All Cost, No Benefit

Analyzing the temporary benefits versus the long-term costs of homicide is a wasted exercise in this chapter. Frankly, there are no benefits to be derived from following the deadly code of respect, defying the law, or through the violent release of pent-up emotions. The costs, on the other hand, are overwhelming. There's no upside to living in communities where deadly violence rages out of control. We cannot keep burying our young. Our race will never heal as long as we allow or ignore senseless killing and violence.

Black-on-black violence must be denormalized—in real life and pretend life.

Look at almost any dramatic film targeting black audiences. Whether it's a "gritty urban drama," a script about a black couple or black family, or even a fluffy, inner-city dance movie, you can almost bet that, by the film's end, you will see a violent beat-down or a murder. And the same intense motif flows without censorship through rap lyrics, TV shows, and video games. Family violence, the murder of our youth, hair-trigger sadism, and apathy toward the disproportionate rates of violence—the major forces of homicide—are not insurmountable challenges. The cycle of self-destruction and violence can and must be broken.

What follows are tools that may help us meet these challenges.

Positive Propaganda Cues to Halt Homey-cide

Life: Because we're all worth it

All too often, we think that life is worthless and that we cannot recover from our pain. What we must realize is that it is worth sticking around because, with hope, we never know how far we can go. The first step toward saving others' lives is to appreciate the value of our own.

Turn a life in tension into a life intention
Part of what creates our stress and disconnection with humanity is that we do not feel we have a purpose in life. If we can take that negative energy (tension) and turn it into positive energy (intention), then there is a great chance for our recovery.

Diss-stress
We must get over the stress and anger that keep us killing one another and keep us from reaching our full potential as human beings.

Life is a prerequisite to everything else: Value it!
The finality of death precludes any hope for positive change. Stay alive so that you'll have a chance to truly live. It's as simple as that.

Futures, Not Funerals

Our silence must be broken, inaction must be reversed, and the value of every black life must be reinforced. Weusi Olusola may be gone but his organization, Pioneers for Peace, lives on. There are dozens of others across the nation working desperately to offer alternatives to the drug trade and gang violence. Seek them out, support their efforts.

Let's make a commitment to be just as loud and just as angry about death related to black-on-black violence as to white-on-black crime, even if it's not captured on video, as was young Derrion Albert's murder. We need to be just as vigilant and engaged about the murder of a black child by another black child as we were about a Harvard professor who was disrespected and inconvenienced by a white police officer.

To accomplish this new orientation, we need a black media machine (be it Internet- or cable-based) that overwhelms us with the faces, stories, and circumstances of every murdered child. If twenty young black people die in a week, imagine seeing twenty stories that week, stressing their value and the community's loss. Imagine passionate conversations about the unnecessary deaths of black children.

After violence in Chicago claimed the lives of 22 students (20 by gun violence) in the 2007–2008 school years, parents volunteered to provide safe passage to and from school for their children. High school students and school administrators took to the streets protesting the killings. Those of us freed from the shackles of helplessness and inferiority must multiply such efforts. Our mantra should match the rallying cry of those Chicago parents, students, and educators: "We want futures, not funerals!"

Chapter 6

Slow Suicide

Why Do We Neglect Body, Mind, and Spirit?

*I was so surprised when my mother called me from the hospital
to say doctors had found a tumor. It was inoperable cancer. My
mother had not been to a doctor for a checkup in more than five
years. If not for the consistent pain, she wouldn't have gone when
she did. If they had caught the cancer earlier, her doctor told us,
they could have treated it. Instead, she was told that she had
three months to live. Six weeks later, she was dead. I try not to be
angry with her...but she didn't have to die.*

— JANINE

Tragically, stories like Janine's are heard too often in black
communities.

According to James Macinko, lead author of the study "Black-White
Differences in Avoidable Mortality in the United States, 1980–2005,"
two-thirds of the differences between black and white mortality
rates are due to causes that could be "prevented or cured." Many
health disparities can be reduced with a renewed focus on prevention
ensuring good, quality health care for all Americans, Macinko said. The
uneven blow from the three major killers of African Americans—heart
disease, cancer, and stroke—plus other serious illnesses, may call for
something more drastic than public policies.

Let's consider the sobering data:

- Cardiovascular diseases rank as the number-one killer of
  African Americans, claiming the lives of over 37 percent of
  the more than 285,000 blacks who die each year.

- African American adults are 1.7 times more likely to have strokes than their white adult counterparts. Further, black men are 60 percent more likely to die from a stroke than white male adults.

- In 2009, among African Americans, it was reported that an estimated 150,090 new cases of invasive cancers would be diagnosed and about 63,360 blacks would die from cancer-related deaths.

- African Americans are 1.6 times more likely to have diabetes than white, non-Latino Americans and more than twice as likely to suffer its most debilitating consequences. About 2.7 million blacks (11.4 percent) over 20 have the disease.

- Black women are 40 percent more likely to die of breast cancer than are white women.

- In 2007, blacks accounted for 51 percent of the 42,655 new HIV/AIDS diagnoses (including children) and 48 percent of the 551,932 persons living with HIV/AIDS in 34 states.

- In 2005, blacks were 1.4 times as likely to be obese as non-Hispanic whites.

- Blacks suffer higher rates of depression (8 percent) than whites (4.8 percent).

:::

"Can I ask you this question, Mr. G? Have you ever had your colon checked, or anything like that?"

While his beefy, tattooed arm slid the clippers along the elderly man's head, barber Mel Sampson, Jr., peppered his patron with questions and comments about his health: "Now with your heart being weak like that, you don't think that smoking's gonna hurt you at any point, Mr. G?"

Sampson, the owner of Mel's Barber Shop in New Orleans, was one of 25 barber and salon shop owners who took part in a Tulane University health study. In 2009, the Prevention Research Center at Tulane trained hair stylists to remind customers about the importance of healthful lifestyles, getting regular checkups and health screenings. The Tulane program is one of many innovative medical approaches designed to address a national crisis—the disproportionate rates of black illness and death related to treatable diseases.

Between August 2008 and August 2009, the world lost several black talents, including soul singers Levi Stubbs of the Four Tops and Isaac Hayes, best-selling author E. Lynn Harris, and the world's first black supermodel, Naomi Sims. The leading causes of death among hundreds of thousands of blacks each year are heart disease, cancer, and stroke. Hayes died from a massive stroke, Harris succumbed to heart disease, complicated by high blood pressure, Sims passed away after a battle with breast cancer, and Stubbs suffered from a series of illnesses, including stroke and cancer. The four celebrities had something in common: they all died from illnesses medical practitioners label as "treatable and preventable."

Deathly Denial

Yeah, it ran in my family, but you often think that it's going to happen to someone else, never you.
— Randy Jackson, *American Idol* co-host

Even at around 350 pounds, Randy Jackson, New Orleans native and co-host of television's *American Idol*, never imagined he'd be stricken with diabetes. Even though his father suffered from the illness, Jackson was stunned to learn that he, too, had Type 2 diabetes. Jackson was lucky. After his diagnosis in 1999, he had gastric bypass surgery, drastically altered his Southern diet, and started exercising regularly. Today, he's kept the weight off and kept the condition at controllable

levels, and serves as a national spokesman for diabetes awareness. Many of us have not been so lucky. Despite the deaths attributed to our diets and lifestyles in our immediate families, we are still hesitant to address our healthcare dilemma.

Educator and author Dr. Jawanza Kunjufu provides a compelling example of this state of denial in his book, *Satan! I'm Taking Back My Health*. Kunjufu describes a church service where the names of all the sick and infirm parishioners are called out right before the announcement that pork chops, ham, and fried chicken will be served after the service. Kunjufu's humorous swipe speaks to two deadly serious issues—our diet and our silence about personal and community health issues.

The painful question that remains, however, is why we are so hesitant to face personal and community health issues even as the black health crisis swells.

She Didn't Have to Die

Another mystifying disparity exists within the number of blacks who, for various reasons, neglect their health more than whites. Often we won't seek medical treatment until a disease has progressed to an irreversible stage. Lack of health insurance leads many to forgo screenings for illnesses such as cancer until it's too late for effective treatment. Then there are those of us who don't trust the medical system or have resigned themselves to the fatalistic belief that good health and good care are simply not an option for black folk.

The African American health crisis has finally motivated researchers to consider what my firm concluded almost 40 years ago—"Black people are not dark-skinned white people." Our habits, customs, and motivators are influenced by unique history and social stimuli. The mechanisms we use to cope with physical pain and mental duress vary drastically. These factors, however, do not mitigate the crisis. Self-destructive behaviors, such as overeating, smoking, drug and alcohol addiction, irresponsible sexual activity, and other high-risk behaviors, amount to what Dr. Alvin Poussaint once declared to be "slow suicide."

Programs like Tulane University's will certainly help remind blacks that they need to address health concerns but, in many ways, it's like bringing a water gun to douse an inferno. Health reminders address the symptoms but they won't extinguish the embers that spark self-devaluation and encourage us to do harmful things to our bodies.

We Know Better

Just as drug use can be a response to low self-esteem that leads to depression, which in turn fuels lower self-esteem, compulsive overeating almost always starts as a "solution" that quickly becomes its own problem and makes other problems—like depression—even worse.
— Terrie M. Williams

In *Black Pain: It Just Looks Like We're Not Hurting,* former *Essence* editor Susan Taylor described readers' reactions in June 2006 after *Essence* featured an article by the book's author, Terrie M. Williams:

The moment that issue hit the stands, a tidal wave of responses began pouring into the *Essence* offices...thousands of men and women were moved to write to us not only to express their admiration of Terrie's courage but to break their silence...

Williams's book, which tackles the taboo subject of black depression, speaks volumes about the kind of people we tend to be. We have been conditioned to maintain Teflon exteriors even when confronting soul-crushing adversity.

Repression Depression

Fuck these skinny bitches...look at her shaking...bitch, cuz you hongry...get a motherfucking two-piece and a biscuit!"
— Mo'Nique, 2009 comedy show

Blacks endure in silence or engage in denial while our loved ones suffer or die every day from poor diets, smoking, depression, and sedentary lifestyles. In fact, we've developed defenses to validate obesity and a laundry list of fear-based reasons why we should *not* see a doctor.

We know we have poor eating habits—some of our most cherished dishes are laden with fat and salt. But we deny the damage with excuses like "this is the way black folk always ate." We aren't deaf or blind to media messages specifically created to prod us into consuming bad food and addictive products, such as malt liquor and menthol cigarettes. We tolerate these insults because the products help us cope with unknown feelings and undiagnosed anxieties.

These days, black grandmothers are becoming younger and younger (mostly because their daughters are having babies at earlier ages). Yet, what we see on sitcoms and movies are mostly roles of aged, ass-kicking, sassy, big-breasted, obese grandmas—as in the *Madea* series, *Big Mama's House, Hannah Montana, House of Payne, Norbit, The Nutty Professor, etc., etc.* It's like the proverbial chicken and egg question: does the stereotype portray reality or does reality dictate the stereotype? An examination of our attitudes indicates a definite correlation.

Slow Suicide Dynamics

1. **Deadly denial:** We die at unprecedented rates from cardiovascular disease, cancer, and stroke. Even though survival rates would drastically improve with better diets, preventive care, and early diagnosis, we

refuse to take the necessary steps to save ourselves. Since we have been historically devalued, we devalue ourselves and our health.

2. **Repression of depression:** The dilemma of unaddressed mental health issues and depression within the black community. We refuse to acknowledge the problem, label people "punks" and "crazy" if they choose to get help, and therefore cannot help ourselves.

3. **Glorification of unhealthy weight stereotypes and health-destroying lifestyles:** We have fetishized unhealthy behaviors, from "healthy-sized 'thick' women" to unhealthy food preparations and portions. Conversely, we criticize healthy people:

    "Don't nobody want a bone but a dog," or *"Oh, you one of those rabbit-food-eating folks?"* And the media glorification of alcohol and drug abuse: You are not having a good Friday night unless there's Cristal or Grey Goose on the scene, or a "blunt" to share with the homies.

4. **Chew-i-cide—killing ourselves with every bite:** Over-consumption of disease-producing food is slow suicide—especially when it is over-processed and chemically enhanced "food" with no nutritional value. Slow suicide by unconscious or compulsive eating is a reflection of our untreated trauma and depression.

5. **Death wish:** Profound ambivalence about the worth of our lives is masked as an unconscious death wish. We engage in numerous risky behaviors ranging from unsafe sex, and violence-provoking altercations, to addictions, to food, drugs, and alcohol. Due to various reasons (some real,

some imagined), we avoid going to doctors. It's only after symptoms become too severe that we seek treatment, and most times it is emergency room treatment.

Although our attitudes may fit Hollywood portrayals and racist depictions of us as irresponsible and incapable, the problem is far more nuanced, as are the solutions.

We cannot discount our history and the unresolved trauma that cue these destructive responses. Negative, distorted, self-critical, and self-hating attitudes branded into us for centuries, as well as our often distinctive and distorted rationalizations about weight, food, and body image, fuel many of our health disorders. Most important is the scant attention paid to the strategic and manipulative media messages that urge us to consume deadly products or engage in risky, life-threatening behavior.

Works Every Time

The first time I got drunk it was an accident, and I was about seven. I got into some apple Schnapps, and gulped down like half of it. The weird thing was, when my family found out, it was almost like I was a hero. They were laughing and joking: it was like I had done something cool.
— Eric, 41, financial advisor

Advertising agencies make fortunes gathering, analyzing, and manipulating the societal, historical, and economic factors that motivate consumer purchases. Since Burrell Communication claim to fame was our expertise with the black consumer market, in the mid-1970s we were hired by a major cigarette company to help boost their brands' penetration among black consumers. This was before we knew much about the product.

Through research, we found specific, concrete documentation that this tobacco company and others targeted black kids, to get them and keep them hooked on their deadly products. These campaigns were largely waged through the menthol brand, which blacks dominated. Even today, more than 80 percent of black smokers use menthol cigarettes.

Back in the 1970s they saturated the black market with free samples and hip and cool images that tapped into our sense of powerlessness, low self-esteem, and emasculated identities. Needless to say, my firm backed out of the contract.

It's no accident that actor Billy Dee Williams has resurfaced on billboards in predominantly urban areas across the country. On the signs, the actor holds a tall can of Colt 45 malt liquor next to the bold, colorful words: "Works every time." Williams, who represented the epitome of black cool in the mid-1970s, was also a spokesman for the brand in the 1980s.

Colt 45's logo features a bucking bronco, a nod to its extra kick derived from the sugar and other additives to boost the beverage's alcoholic strength. Like menthol cigarettes, blacks are the target for malt liquor in the United States. Although hip-hop artists have done their part to romanticize "da 40," Billy Dee obviously still has swaying power. Perhaps it's because marketers understand that black men identify with messages that emphasize cool, even if it's from a black movie star past his box-office prime.

The Food Fixers

What have we done in the United States? We've taken fat, sugar, and salt; we've put it on every corner. We made it available 24/7. We've made food into entertainment. We advertise it as something you'll want. I mean, walk into a food court and watch people eat. We're living, literally, in a food carnival.
— Dr. David Kessler

In an August 2009 *Democracy Now!* interview, Dr. David Kessler, author, pediatrician, educator, and former United States Food and Drug Administration commissioner, bluntly compared America's food industry with Big Tobacco. Kessler claimed that, as far as addicting

Americans to deadly products was concerned, the food industry was just as culpable. With the "emotional gloss of advertising," Kessler explained, the food industry's successful marketing of unhealthy food products has led to a "profound public-health epidemic" in this country.

Indeed, similar marketing techniques are used to sell all products, be they cigarettes, malt liquor, or potato chips. Food companies are intrinsically aware of the motivators that encourage blacks to eat, drink, and consume. They know our history, the foods that have sustained us for centuries, and the distorted, self-critical attitudes that have been branded into us. They market in ways that speak to our tainted self-image and tensions.

African American women have the highest rates of being overweight or obese when compared to other groups in this country. The industry is attentive to the disproportionate numbers of black women who are unpartnered. To emphasize it promotes emotional mood savers—sweet, fatty, self-indulgent, unhealthy products that contribute to obesity.

In 2005, the New York City Department of Health released findings from a study, "Women at Risk: The Health of Women in New York City." The study documented the disturbing relationship between the declining health of black and Hispanic women and the disproportionate number of negative, health-related advertisements found in magazines that target these women. The investigative team cited research based on a study of advertisements published in two popular black magazines with majority black female readerships. They discovered that nearly 50 percent of the ads in the publications were devoted to alcoholic beverages. Contrast those figures with the meager two percent of alcoholic ads found in white-oriented women's journals.

Women's magazines serve as key sources for information used for health-related decisions and purchases. The "Women at Risk" study found that readers of black and Hispanic magazines were "exposed to proportionally fewer health-promoting advertisements and more health-diminishing advertisements."

Children (black, white, or "other") are also fair game for the food industry's hired guns of advertising. An estimated 40,000 ads a year, on television alone, help boost obesity and poor nutrition among kids in the U.S., according to the American Academy of Pediatrics. Over the course of one year, the average 2-to-7-year-old child will be bombarded with nearly 30 hours and more than 4,400 food ads. African American children, ages 6 to 7, were 1.3 times as likely to be overweight as non-Hispanic whites, based on 2003-2004 data.

According to a 2006 study published in *Pediatrics & Adolescent Medicine*, more ads for fast food and sugary snacks appear on black-oriented children's channels than on channels with more general programming for children. The one-week study reviewed nearly 1,100 ads on the black-targeted cable channel, Black Entertainment Television (BET), and those that ran on the WB Network and Disney Channel. Of the ads reviewed, more than 50 percent were for fast food and sugary drinks. Of those, BET hosted about 66 percent of the fast-food ads, 82 percent of the sugary-drink ads, and 60 percent of the spots for snacks.

A BET spokesman and others representing fast food manufacturers disputed the findings, and the researchers acknowledge that more study must be conducted before any definitive conclusions are drawn. However, the studies clearly illustrate the media's disproportionate negative effect on black children's health.

The food industry is way ahead of the medical experts, fitness magazines, and health writers who have not explored black attitudes and loyalties regarding food consumption. Many of us are still reacting to hurt and humiliation from our past, clinging to old systems of survival that may have been useful back in the day, or essential to survival in the history of our grandparents and great-grandparents, but are self-destructive in the present.

The Hand That Feeds You

We had very bad eatin'. Bread, meat, water. And they fed it to us in a trough, jes' like the hogs. And ah went in may [sic] shirt till I was 16, nevah had no clothes. And the flo' in ouah cabin was dirt,

and at night we'd jes' take a blanket and lay down on the flo'. The dog was supe'ior to us; they would take him in the house.
— Richard Toler, former Virginia slave

Deprivation began the moment Africans were captured and enslaved. Slaveowners found that controlling the food supply was an effective way to command obedience and subservience.

Children born into slavery quickly learned where they stood in the pecking order. The black mother's milk was often diverted to the white child, leaving the black baby to be weaned on deprivation. Benny Dillard, a former Georgia slave, recalled how slavemasters "never let chillun have no meat till they was big enough to work in the fields." Children, Dillard said, often ate bread with milk and cornpone soaked with peas and "pot liquor" (the broth left from cooking greens) from wooden bowls, and used oyster or mussel shells for spoons. Archeological digs at slave quarters in recent years have unearthed evidence of the toll this abuse took on blacks. "Skeletal analysis reveals malnutrition, especially in young children," wrote researcher Anne Yentsch in her essay "Excavating African-American Food History."

One former slave, interviewed for the government's WPA slave narrative project, described how a black cook fed slave children by "… crumbling cornbread into a trough and pouring buttermilk over it… Sometimes that trough would be a sight, because us never stopped to wash our hands, and before us had been eating more than a minute or two what was in the trough would look like red mud what had come off our hands…" Feeding people in the manner one would feed a dog or horse is part of the dehumanizing process. If one is fed like an animal, it is easier to accept and adopt the status of livestock.

Putting the Soul in It

We were given the rejects, the leftovers and the garbage, but we made a cuisine of it that has won many accolades.
— Harris, a Virginia slave

Despite scourges of malnutrition and hunger, slaves endured. The majority not only survived, they improvised. Relying on fading memories of their homeland, they creatively transformed rubbish into meals that resembled something their palates considered food. Harris, a former slave, praised black cooks who incorporated African culinary methods in their "grilling, steaming, boiling, toasting, baking, and frying." The cooks, Harris said, used spices generously "to disguise spoiled meats and enhance flavors." Thus, they "helped us to survive with their ability to quite literally turn a sow's ear into something wonderful."

Variations on traditional African meals, such as "fufu," became the slave's standard vegetable-based soups and stews. Large amounts of readily available fat, sugar, and salt were used as seasoning. Salt was also an American mainstay not only as seasoning but as a preservative for meat before refrigeration. Blacks had also acquired a taste for fried foods, which was a southern tradition. Fried okra, sweet potato pie, and popular rice, bean, and okra-based dishes, such as gumbo and jambalaya, are intertwined with the history of the black American experience.

The Concrete Struggle

After Emancipation, some blacks who remained in the rural South who could plant or hunt their own food were, in some ways, better off than those who migrated north. In the cold North, many blacks relied on cheap dishes and recipes passed down from their ancestors. They fell back on meal-stretching ingredients, such as rice, beans, and cornmeal, to supersize meals for the entire family. Many found they could stretch their dollars by purchasing canned goods, potted meat, fruits, vegetables, and other provisions offered by big city stores.

Not only has the brutal and inhumane experience of slavery impacted black lives today, survival skills stood the test of time as well. Family history and fond memories of delectable dishes are also interwoven into the history of those tough times. And when times get tough, we turn to the food of those times, even when we can afford otherwise.

Lifestyles of the Poor
& Not-So-Famous

There is no dividing line between the past and present for Yejide Kmt of Homewood, Pittsburgh. Yejide is car-less and walks two miles past landfills, crackheads, and prostitutes, she said, just to get to the nearest food store. The impoverished 26-year-old mother of five has a daughter who has been repeatedly hospitalized for asthma and eczema. Yejide felt she doesn't have the luxury or the money to obtain healthy food on a regular basis. So she made do, often grappling with what was most healthy over what was most affordable—a seven-dollar salad or a filling snack that cost under a buck: "I'd get my child a 35-cent honeybun. I want my child to not be hungry, and that (honeybun) had the most calories."

The Center for Minority Health at the University of Pittsburgh presented Yejide's story in its May 2009 article, "Root of the Problem." Dr. Stephen Thomas, director of the center, said the lack of access to good food is only one of the major challenges low-income blacks and other minorities face. They must also overcome "ignorance and a constant barrage of billboards advertising unhealthy food in poor neighborhoods," Thomas said.

As If Poverty
Weren't Enough

Possible cancer symptoms, such as a persistent cough, are being missed because black patients tend to delay doctor visits. U.S. Census data shows that more than 19 percent of blacks in this country are uninsured as opposed to 10.8 percent of whites. Poor and uninsured people are more likely to be treated for various kinds of cancers at late stages. Blacks, even those with insurance, are more likely to receive substandard clinical care and services.

Black Enterprise.com reported that 7 percent of black women with breast cancer get no treatment and 35 percent do not receive radiation after mastectomy compared with 26 percent of white women who do not receive the treatment.

According to a study released in 2008 by the American Cancer Society (ACS), the widest disparities were noted in cancers, such as breast cancer, lung cancer, colon cancer, and melanoma, which could be detected early through standard screening and/or medical assessments. To illustrate the importance of early detection, the ACS points to the five-year survival rate of 93 percent of the patients who receive a diagnosis of Stage 1 colon cancer. That number plummets to 44 percent for diagnoses at Stage 3 and 8 percent for Stage 4 diagnoses. As if poverty, diet, and our propensity toward deadly illness weren't enough, researchers have also noted that racism and stress related to racism add to our healthcare woes.

Racism's Hidden Toll, by Arline T. Geronimus, a professor in the University of Michigan School of Public Health, revealed that the "stress of living in a racist society" causes African Americans to age faster, experience greater health problems, and die sooner than whites. These disparities, Geronimus argues, are a direct result of institutionalized, structural, and economic conditions.

Racism has a direct as well as indirect impact on blacks. ACS researchers found that the health disparity might also be caused by a lack of health literacy and an inadequate supply of providers in minority communities. It's clear that black people suffer from a litany of illnesses that kill us at drastic rates. This chapter underscores the fact that we arrived in the 21st century with 17th-century baggage that keeps us unhealthy and ill suited for longevity.

Slow Suicide: Connecting the Dots

Contemporary Manifestations	Historical Roots
Deadly denial: We die at unprecedented rates from preventable diseases like heart disease, cancer, and stroke.	Historically devalued, we are resigned to worst-case scenarios. We expect the scraps of America's healthcare system. We don't feel worthy of or connected to the basic human right of health care.
Repression of depression: Denial of and inability to cope with depression and mental health issues. Shaming and blaming individuals who try to get help. Undiagnosed mental health issues exacerbate problems and often lead to incarceration.	Slaves were forbidden to express the full spectrum of human emotions. We learned to repress our sadness and woes: restraint led to pent-up emotions, and finally to physical and mental overload and disease.
Glorification of the unhealthy: Glamorizing negative behaviors. Criticizing or putting down healthy people. Responding to media messages that glorify alcohol or drug use and equate irresponsible behavior with "good times."	The trauma of institutionalized slavery created an emotional black hole that demanded filling by whatever means possible, resulting in over-indulgent use of food, drink, and other excesses. To rationalize our pain, we were compelled to "make our excesses a good thing."

Chew-i-cide: The slow suicide resulting from over-consumption of nutrient-poor self-destructive, foods.	Food deprivation and expectation of eating the scraps from the slavemaster's table impacted our diets. Slaves were forced to eat and live unhealthily. Post-slavery and modern-day poverty and unemployment continued our dependence on cheap, unhealthy food. Food trauma is in our DNA. The pendulum swings from starvation to obesity.
Death-wish: Ambivalence about the value of our lives. Reckless engagement in risky behaviors—unsafe sex, unprovoked physical altercations, and addiction to alcohol, drugs, and food.	Black life has long been discounted and outside of our control since slavery. Trauma taught us that "life is not so great," and therefore dying didn't frighten us. We rationalized that doing whatever we wanted to do, no matter how self-destructive, was "no big thing."

Guinea Pig Woes

In my day, you were taught that you were brought here as a slave.
You heard about how pitiful you were...you heard about the most
heinous crimes in the world that were committed against you. You
begin to believe it... you are convincing yourself that it's not true,
you're not a "nigger," you know?
— Eric

Much of our reluctance to face up to our health issues is based on fear—historical race-based medical atrocities, fear of discovering a disease we can't afford to treat, or fear of what others might think if we

reveal that we suffer from certain diseases. These fears are legitimate. For example, time will never erase the horror of the Tuskegee Syphilis Experiment, where the government's public-health department conducted a 40-year (1932 to 1972) experiment on 399 black men in the late stages of syphilis that deprived them of treatment and led to premature death.

What may not be as widely known as the syphilis experiment are the cases of race-based atrocities detailed in Harriet A. Washington's book, *Medical Apartheid: The Dark History of Medical Experimentation on Black Americans from Colonial Times to the Present.*

Washington gives a painful 400-year account of the medical crimes committed against blacks that include colonial-era research to understand brain and body functions, the female reproductive system, and to test surgical procedures. She writes about the mind control experiments conducted on black inmates, mental patients, and misbehaving black boys (as young as five) who were forced to undergo "blind-cut lobotomies" between 1936 and 1960.

She draws comparisons to contemporary examples, such as the court-ordered sterilization of mostly black women and girls in Baltimore, and the New York City fenfluramine experiment (1992 to 1997), where up to 113 black boys were cherry-picked and given the drug (later found to cause heart problems) so researchers could gauge their predisposition toward violence.

Depressed? Not Me

Although the use of antidepressants has doubled in the United States from 13 million prescriptions in 1996 to 27.1 million prescriptions in 2005, blacks were the only socio-demographic group that showed no increase in usage of the drugs. This would probably seem like a positive indicator if not for the fact that blacks suffer higher rates of depression than whites and other ethnic groups. George Smith, a Chicago psychologist, listed lack of health insurance, misunderstanding of mental health issues, fear of medication, and the rejection of antidepressants "because of religious or personal beliefs" as some reasons blacks are reluctant to take depression-related drugs.

Fear also motivates many blacks not to talk about their problems, even when we're being examined by doctors. A 2009 study by University of North Carolina at Chapel Hill researchers found that black patients with high blood pressure have poorer communication with doctors than white patients with the same condition. Poor communication hampers follow-up treatment, which leads to worse disease outcomes. There are various reasons that explain why we're hesitant to address illness, but they pale when compared to the spiraling cost of our silence.

Many of the black-on-black homicides in our communities should really be classified as "second-hand suicides," said Pittsburgh's Dr. Stephen Thomas. Considering the "root causes of self-destructive behavior—including such mental health issues as anxiety and depression brought on by the stress of home life, lack of healthy self-esteem and a prevailing incidence of hopelessness among black males and youth," the homicide rate should come as no surprise.

For a people who have been labeled mentally inferior for centuries, it's tough to confess feelings of depression, mental fatigue, or instability. For many, such feelings betray our positive image as strong, resilient people who withstood unimaginable adversity. The image is real, as are the benefits derived from our ancestors who sacrificed so we wouldn't have to live as endangered second-class citizens. In other words, our ticket has been paid. We have the right to be equal...and healthy.

Keeping It Together
While Falling Apart

For many of us, the idea of appearing crazy...is enough to drive us mad. Our deep and insistent need to keep it together, even at the cost of our mental health, is a price worth paying for too many of us.
— Terrie M. Williams

Our other sets of fears are not easily dismissed either. *Knowing* we have an illness means we have to do something about it, which often opens a Pandora's box of concerns for black people, especially those surviving on little to nothing: What if they have no health insurance? Will they lose their jobs? Who will take care of their children if they are hospitalized? Denial about the realities of our health has been trivialized and institutionalized in our literature, sitcoms, movies, and in black music videos: Madea is obese but she doesn't have cardiovascular disease. Billy Dee pushes Colt 45 but never explains what "works every time" after drunken youth roam urban streets. Hip-hop artists encourage unbridled sex yet they rarely advocate condom usage or sing about the ravages of AIDS and other sexually transmitted diseases. While we place our health in God's hands only, laugh at obesity, drink to be merry, and dance to the tunes of sexual irresponsibility, the unnecessary casualties of death by slow suicide continue to keep funeral homes busy.

AIDS Is Killing Us

We know there are black gay rappers, black gay athletes, but they're all on the DL…If you're white, you can come out as an openly gay skier or actor or whatever. It might hurt you some, but it's not like if you're black and gay, because then it's like you've let down the whole black community, black women, black history, black pride.
— Rakeem, self-described "urban, black gay man on the DL"

Rakeem was one of several black gay men writer Benoit Denizet-Lewis interviewed for his stunning August 2003 *New York Times* article, "Double Lives on the Down Low."

While drawing readers into the mysterious world of the "DL" (slang used to describe the behavior of men who have sex with women but secretly have sex with men as well) Denizet-Lewis also offered a glimpse into "black culture that deems masculinity and fatherhood as a black man's primary responsibility—and homosexuality as a white man's perversion."

The article accentuates how, even in the face of the black AIDS crisis, honestly talking about the issue in black communities has proved "remarkably difficult, whether it be in black churches, in black organizations, or on inner-city playgrounds." The longer we remain silent, the larger the crisis grows and the more lives are impacted—lives like that of Marvelyn Brown, a black woman infected with HIV in 2003 at the age of 19 by a man she said knew he was HIV positive but did not tell her.

> I kept thinking to myself that he doesn't have a condom...but I thought, "This is my Prince Charming and I wouldn't mind being his baby's mother if this is the worst that could happen."

The rate for new HIV infections for black women is nearly 15 times that of white women. As with other black health crises, we simply cannot afford to ignore the multiple ways HIV/AIDS (needle sharing among drug addicts, unprotected risky sexual encounters, transmission from mother to baby at birth, etc.) is spreading throughout black communities.

Consider the growth of AIDS among black men in our nation's prisons. According to AVERT, an international HIV and AIDS charity group, black males stand about a one-in-three chance of serving time in prison during their lifetimes. The statistic is important because of the growth of HIV in the prison system. On its Web site, AVERT cites conclusions from a 2003 University of California at Berkeley study indicating that the increasing rate of HIV in heterosexuals, particularly women, closely follows the increased rates of incarcerations of black men during the 1980s and early 1990s.

Although the research indicates that black men became infected in jail and then went on to infect their female partners upon release, the CDC refutes the theory, claiming that the vast majority of black men are actually infected *before* incarceration. The HIV/AIDS epidemic will continue to rise unless we openly address the many ways in which blacks are infected with the disease. The first step, I believe, is analyzing our hesitancy to discuss the topic—period.

Benefit & Cost
of Slow Suicide

It's seriously way past time for us to rise above our fears (as legitimate as some may be) and stop dodging the subject of our disproportionate death and illness. A simple analysis of our delayed actions should compel the next needed steps.

Short-term Benefits

1. **Deadly denial:** What I don't know won't kill me any quicker. I know cardiovascular disease, cancer, and stroke kill many black people but maybe I'll be one of the lucky ones. When it's my time to go, it's my time. Diets are frustrating, preventative care is costly, and early diagnosis won't prevent the inevitable.

2. **Repression of depression:** Denial keeps a depressing reality at bay. Misdiagnosing or ignoring people with mental illness reinforces the delusion that we are immune to such maladies.

3. **Glorification of unhealthy behavior:** It's easier to glamorize unhealthy behavior than do the hard work to stay healthy. Criticizing healthy people relieves us of envying them or analyzing ourselves. Besides, based on media accounts, unhealthy behavior is normal.

4. **Chew-i-cide:** We eat what our parents and grandparents ate. Certain so-called "bad foods" are part of the black experience. To deny these dishes is to deny our culture.

BLACK INFERIORITY CAMPAIGN

Brainwashing, Branding, and Resistance

1619

First Africans landed in Jamestown, VA.

TO BE SOLD on board the Ship *Bance-Yland*, on tuesday the 6th of *May* next, at *Ashley-Ferry*; a choice cargo of about 250 fine healthy

NEGROES, just arrived from the Windward & Rice Coast. —The utmost care has already been taken, and shall be continued, to keep them free from the least danger of being infected with the SMALL-POX, no boat having been on board, and all other communication with people from *Charles-Town* prevented. *Austin, Laurens, & Appleby.*

N. B. Full one Half of the above Negroes have had the SMALL-POX in their own Country.

1776

Propaganda Masterpiece

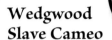

The Declaration of Independence — the first document of the new nation promoted and perpetuated slavery by ignoring it.

Wedgwood Slave Cameo

One of the few images designed to advance slave emancipation.

1620s

The first American "brands" were not products. They were slaves whom American landowners turned into commodities.

1600s   1700s

"All persons except Negroes are to be provided with guns and ammunitions or be fined at the pleasure of the Governor or council."

1630s, 1640s, 1650s

"Slaves for sale" posters became some of the first ads in America.

1650s

Slave Codes — Legal Brainwashing Begins

Laws were passed (Virginia) to legally separate Africans from white indentured servants and slaves. This propaganda maneuver legalized black inferiority and white superiority.

1781

Thomas Jefferson's *Notes on the State of Virginia*

Jefferson wrote blacks "are inferior . . . in the endowments both of body and mind" five years after he wrote "all men are created equal." This respected opinion justified and legitimized slavery.

Branding Jesus **White**

The image of a white Jesus is one of the clearest examples of the power of propaganda. Worshipping a blue-eyed, blond-haired Jesus reinforced the concept of black inferiority.

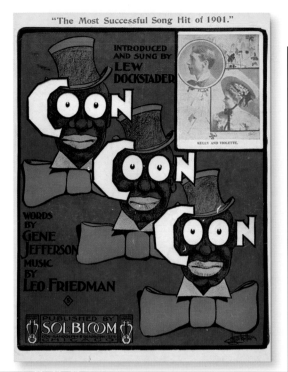

Brand Extensions:
Coons, Toms, Bucks, Mammies, Pickaninnies, and Jezebels

Once slaveholders succeeded in branding blacks inferior, they created sub-categories, each with its own "brand story." The Jim Crow brand stood for a happy-go-lucky field slave; the Zip Coon brand depicted a preening, ostentatious free black who pretended to be educated, but whose fractured diction betrayed his ignorance. Throughout American history these brands were updated for each generation.

1800s

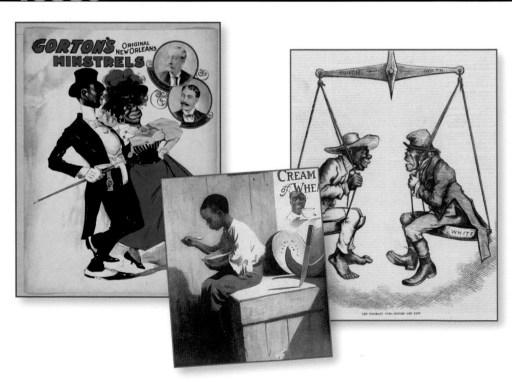

Resistance Leader

Many blacks refused to tolerate legal servitude or second-class citizenship. Frederick Douglass, former slave, abolitionist, and orator, helped to change the destiny of the nation.

1861
Civil War

The Emancipation Proclamation legally ended chattel slavery, but introduced a new era of oppression and legal segregation.

1861

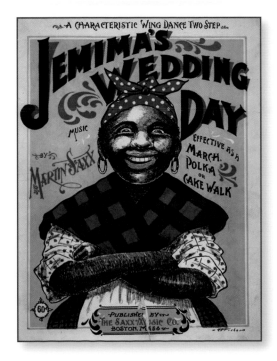

The Black Inferiority Marketing Strategy

As with any propaganda, the campaign against black America had clear goals:

Convince blacks that they were innately inferior to whites.

Convince whites that blacks were condemned by God and were destined to be their servants.

Convince whites that free black labor was necessary to build national and personal wealth.

The Black Inferiority Campaign Continues

Although not a part of traditional media, acts of unspeakable brutality, intimidation, and murder were also a part of the Black Inferiority propaganda campaign.

1915

The pro–Ku Klux Klan movie justified slavery, increased white fear of blacks, and helped fuel an epidemic of lynchings and backlash for decades to come.

1900s 1915 1927

Culture of Intimidation and Death

Photos of lynching and black men being burned alive (with happy white onlookers) were popular postcards.

Freedom Fighter

One of the many courageous black Americans who fought back, Ida B. Wells became a lifelong crusader against lynching and racism.

1927
Movie Black Magic

The first "talkie," *The Jazz Singer*, advanced movie-making, but set black Americans back once more.

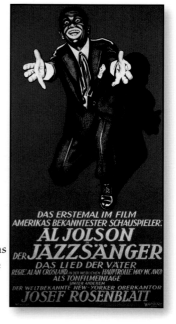

1939
Hollywood Plays Its Role

Movies like *Gone with the Wind* and *Casablanca* cast blacks in subservient, brutish, or buffoonish roles. Animators like Disney and Warner Brothers also perpetuated racist stereotypes.

1933   **1939**

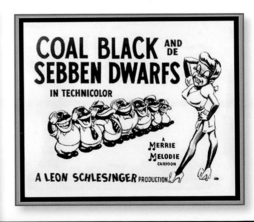

Freshening the Brand

Aunt Jemima has been peddling pancake mixes since she was first introduced at the Columbian Exposition in Chicago in 1893. Over the years, she has had numerous makeovers, reflecting changing politics and styles.

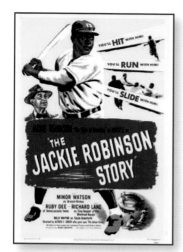

1947

The Late 60s — for One Brief, Shining Moment, Black Was Beautiful

Black Americans saw themselves as beautiful and unique. The world accepted their newfound pride, self-definition, and self-determination.

1963

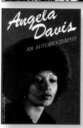

1940s 1950s 1960s

Muhammad Ali, Malcolm X

These leaders and others became iconic symbols of defiance, self-identity, and unapologetic blackness in the 1960s.

The 70s — New Images

Starting in the late 60s, a new type of advertising, created by black-owned ad agencies, began to promote positive, natural images.

Trailblazers

Black entertainers blazed new trails and gained mainstream audiences, but unmistakable barriers remained.

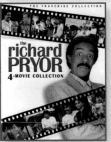

1970s

1990s

1972
Blaxploitation

Unfortunately, the period of black pride and defiant imagery was trumped by updated, exploitable stereotypes.

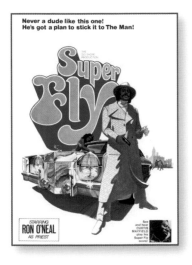

1994
O.J. Simpson

White America's one-time hero turned darker overnight.

1995
Million Man March

For the first time in modern history, an estimated one million black men gathered in Washington, DC to claim responsibility for their families, communities, and their destinies.

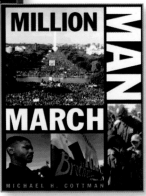

2000-2010

The Image Wars Continue

African Americans have gained unprecedented exposure, wealth, and power, especially in pop culture. But instead of using it to improve our image for ourselves and the world, many of our most successful stars and entertainers have only helped to extend the Black Inferiority brand.

For every positive image of black humanity, there are hundreds of media images and messages depicting stereotypical, one-dimensional figures.

5. **Death wish:** A little sin never hurt anyone. What's called a "death wish" is really just fun. Besides, if the lifestyle were so dangerous, the media wouldn't promote it as much and the government wouldn't sanction companies that willfully hurt people.

Long-term Costs

1. **Deadly denial:** What you don't know will, in fact, kill you quicker. Luck doesn't factor in with cardiovascular disease, cancer, or stroke. The diseases will kill you or someone you love. You may not be able to control when it's your time to go, but inaction certainly increases your odds of dying unnecessarily. Diet, preventive care, and early diagnosis may be frustrating, costly, and time-consuming, but the payoff is well worth the effort.

2. **Repression of depression:** Denial exacerbates the problem. If we shame or label people who choose to get help, we deny ourselves and our families the available knowledge and resources to address our conditions.

3. **Glorification of the unhealthy behavior:** Glamorizing negative behavior legitimizes unhealthy behavior. Our children will naturally shun healthy activities that we criticize or devalue. Adhering to media messages that glorify alcohol or drug usage is irresponsible behavior. Constant good times only serve to make us accomplices to our own destruction.

4. **Chew-i-cide:** Our slave ancestors had little choice in what they were given to eat. We do. Over-consumption of slave-era food amounts to the continuation of slave-era thinking. Eating what our

parents and grandparents ate is a rationale for self-destruction.

5. **Death wish**: Fun in moderation is the goal. No
   behavior, short of saving lives, is worth taking
   our own lives. No matter what messages are sent
   through the media, unsafe sex, addiction to alcohol
   and drugs, or other reckless behavior has profound
   and deadly consequences on our personal and
   communal lives.

The cost we're paying in wasted lives should compel us to move into action now! Despite our hang-ups, there's no reasonable excuse for inaction. After all, our children and the next generation also deserve the right to live long, happy, and healthy lives.

The Capitalist Game

It's not a part of my stubborn nature to wave the white flag in the face of opposition. I prefer to analyze and discover innovative ways to win against my adversaries. I know the strategies of the food and drug industries, marketers all too well. Let me rephrase that: I know *they know us* all too well. The marketers who push the poison that's killing us have mastered the art of exploiting our weaknesses. The media—through magazine articles and ads, and dumb, formulaic dramas and comedies—utilize cumulative, dulling techniques that distance us from critical thinking and make us detour to the refrigerator, to the liquor store, the club, or anywhere that allows us to fill the void with poison.

Still, there's a card we've yet to play—our cleansed, critical thinking minds. From a renewed perspective we can see the food industry for what it is—an engine that's in business to sell goods and services, and make profits for itself and its shareholders—period. It's a machine that operates so well, it even makes its transgressions seem benevolent.

Consider that America's corporate elite directs donations to civil rights organizations, hospitals, youth clubs, and other health-related charities and endeavors, in exchange for positive PR. With the right marketing pitch, they gain consumer trust and put forth the illusion that they are giving back almost as much as they're bringing in. The operative word here is *illusion*. Most often, the small percentage of donations is only a tiny fraction of the profit these companies derive from the problems they helped create. As I said, the poison pushers have mastered the art of exploiting our weaknesses. Now, it's time to play our unexpected card.

Playing the Trump Card

It's unreasonable to expect food and beverage companies that exploit critical unconsciousness to betray their economic interest. Such businesses merely exemplify a corporate model that is the American way of doing business.

If we grew our own food, lived healthy, less chemically enhanced lives, the food manufacturing, marketing, packaging, trucking, and even the medical and drug industries, would all take huge hits. My goal isn't to crash America's economy but to find a balanced and holistic way to live and let live—longer and healthier. Therefore, the healthier strategy is to engage individual and collective critical thinking: "You have a good mind, use it!"

We don't have to start from scratch. Founder of the Nation of Islam (NOI) and author of *How to Eat to Live*, Elijah Muhammad, taught his followers to avoid greasy meats like pork, eat more plants, grow their own vegetables, and process their own meats. Activist and health guru Dick Gregory introduced his Slim-Safe Bahamian Diet Drink Mix and a whole line of products, based on raw fruit and vegetables designed to battle obesity and improve health.

Bryant Terry, an "eco-chef" food justice activist, and author of *Vegan Soul Kitchen: Fresh, Healthy, and Creative African-American Cuisine*, works to illuminate the connections between poverty, malnutrition, institutional racism, and food insecurity. In 2002, Terry founded

"b-healthy" (Build Healthy Eating and Lifestyles to Help Youth), an initiative designed to encourage urban youth to think critically about food and nutrition and to empower them to create their own healthy, sustainable food systems.

Positive Propaganda Cues for Healthy Living

Self-empowered, critical consciousness will create new standards and discover innovative ways to balance fun with responsibility and good health. For those who are up to the challenge, I offer the following helpful tips:

Free of the big three
The words *treatable* and *preventable* should motivate us to tackle disproportionate death related to heart disease, cancer, and stroke. Learn more, get check-ups, speak up, speak out, and protect yourselves and your loved ones.

Don't live to eat, eat to live
What is food for? Think about it. Too often we use food just to make us feel good. In reality, healthy eating can make us feel good *and* live well for the long run.

Exercise—your rite to life
Commit to regular physical activity. Your body was made to move. It is your temple: Move it now so you can still use it later.

Diss-stress
Name the enemy. Stress, anxiety, and depression are catalysts for the major physical illnesses that plague our community. Stand up and seek professional help. There's no shame in learning how to diss-stress to combat long-term illness and disease.

Self-love is a healing thing

Before you can take care of others, you must take care of yourself. Respect yourself enough to recognize your own needs and don't postpone taking action to fulfill them.

What do you *really* crave?

On a conscious level, we may think we want that ice cream, that donut, that cigarette, or "da 40," but there's another hole we're really trying to fill. Have the courage to find out what it is, create a healing strategy, and prosper—for yourself and your family.

Health practitioners are beginning to understand that programs aimed at helping black people address the health crisis must be drafted with our history, paranoia, and unique culture in mind. For those who've recognized and are trying to move beyond the powerful influences of the BI Complex, *perspective* becomes a key resource in our arsenal of consciousness-raising tools. With proper perspective, we can reject any hidden shame related to our history and build on our tradition of survival and resilience.

Free minds don't glorify a food heritage that threatens to kill us. Free minds will question movies and media messages that perpetuate unhealthy stereotypes that we unconsciously internalize. We will look at the motives of corporate givebacks and recognize that nothing is ever "free." The costs are merely hidden.

These advances are within our control. Once we commit to seeing ourselves as the conscious creators of our own destinies, once we lovingly attend to our own minds, bodies, and souls, the dealers of death will quake and our slow suicides will be a thing of the past.

Chapter 7

Buy Now, Pay Later

Why Can't We Stop Shopping?

For the young kids, it's about having brand-new, white gym shoes. They are impoverished, but they are buying 200-dollar gym shoes, clothes that I can't afford...and I HAVE a good job, you know? Why aren't their families putting that money into savings, into a college fund? Why do they have a 300-dollar phone, but no computer?

— WILL, 40, TEACHER

It was a time of great optimism for four-time NBA All-Star Latrell Sprewell. The money was flowing at such an awesome pace during the 2004–05 season that the superstar was able to reject a three-year, $21-million extension to his already $14.6-million contract with the Minnesota Timberwolves.

Less than three years later, numerous news agencies reported the financial woes of Sprewell, who hadn't played pro ball since rejecting the offer. Apparently, the basketball player owed about $70,000 in unpaid taxes. His company, Sprewell Motorsports, had not paid credit card bills in months, his home was up for foreclosure and his million-dollar yacht was auctioned off to help pay what he owed on the boat.

Black kids who dream of living the glorious lives of basketball superstars should know, according to statistics cited by the NBA Players' Association, that about 60 percent of retired basketball players

go broke within five years after leaving the NBA. Since black players dominate professional basketball, it's safe to assume that a large proportion of that 60 percent are black. Sprewell is an appropriate example of the financial slam dunk NBA players face after the limelight dims. But basketball is not the only dominion where "black wealth" is often an intangible façade.

Before he passed away in June 2009, the King of Pop, Michael Jackson, lived way above his already over-extended means. According to *Newsweek*, Jackson's "history of bad management, excessive personal spending, and big legal bills left him, at his death, facing bankruptcy." Jackson ran up hundreds of millions in personal debt borrowed against his assets (*Newsweek* estimated his total borrowing may have exceeded $400 million).

Yet, during the 2003 documentary *Living with Michael Jackson*, Jackson took British journalist Martin Bashir and his camera crew on a lavish, multimillion-dollar Las Vegas shopping spree, purchasing elaborate vases, marble chess sets, 10-foot urns, and other expensive objects as if they were M&Ms. Even as Jackson's world was collapsing under debt, the media captured other spending exploits—in 2005, $150,000 blown in under 30 minutes at Harrods, a luxury London department store, and another impromptu midnight shopping spree in 2006 at London's trendy Topshop, on Oxford Street.

We can never know for sure, but it seems as if the extravagant purchases were the late entertainer's way of replacing the reality of insecurity and low self-esteem with the illusion of comfort and control. It's a reality shared by millions of emotionally fractured, but less fortunate, blacks.

Bravo cable television network's *Real Housewives of Atlanta* was promoted as a reality series showcasing the professional, social, and family lives of five suburban Atlanta women. Four of the five housewives are African American.

During the first season, the women were livin' large, showing off custom-built mansions, luxury cars, and designer clothes. Viewers tagged along as the women enjoyed private spa and BOTOX appointments, attended highbrow parties and fundraisers, and even an $18,000 birthday party one mom hosted for her 11-year-old daughter. Turns out, according to numerous media reports, three of the four black housewives were actually broke or struggling to hold on to what they had.

One of the women, who filed bankruptcy in 2007, was evicted from her multimillion-dollar Duluth, Georgia, mansion and faced a lawsuit from her ex-husband for defaulting on a $150,000 loan. The spouse of another housewife owed more than $100,000 in taxes. The couple's five-bedroom home, seen on the show, was actually rental property from which they were eventually evicted due to missed payments. News reports also noted that another cast member bounced a $346.00 check, had to sell her lavish home and, in 2008, was forced to take her children out of private school and enroll them in public school.

The women seem to have followed paths blazed by black notables whose fortunes were squandered due to personal flaws, lack of financial education, or a need to boost their self-esteem through spending.

The Atlanta housewives aren't the only ones who take cues from celebrities. Those of us who are getting by and those who are but one paycheck away from poverty like to live like the rich and famous, too. We wear the clothes they wear, consume the products they endorse, and try our damnedest to live the celebrity high life.

There's a historical timeline of black money madness that spans the eras of vaudeville, segregated baseball, and the black-entertainers-only chitlin circuit. Unfortunately, it's a negative timeline we still share today.

Lifestyles of the Rich & Not Famous

Our situation has the makings of a classic good news/bad news joke. First, the good news: We live in the richest consumer society on earth. Black collective buying power is almost $800 billion annually. The bad news? Because of our undisciplined, indiscriminate buying habits, African Americans are still America's poorest group.

The bad news affects blacks on all income levels. A study by Demos and the Institute for Assets and Social Policy, released in August of 2009, revealed that millions of middle-income-earning blacks—"from factory workers to bank tellers to white collar managers—are slipping toward destitution."

Although the recession threatens the elimination of the total black middle class, the study pointed out that 33 percent of this particular demographic was already in danger of falling out of middle class status before the economic downturn.

Just as low-income blacks were devastated by the subprime-mortgage catastrophe, so were middle- and upper-income African Americans. In fact, the Center for Responsible Lending reported that high-income blacks were almost twice as likely as low-income whites to receive high-interest subprime loans. Upper-income black and Hispanic homebuyers were more likely to face foreclosures due to high-cost subprime mortgage loans than whites, even though the groups had similar credit ratings. In the greater Boston area alone, noted Jim Campen, a University of Massachusetts economist, "70 percent of black and Hispanic borrowers with incomes between $92,000 and $152,000 received high-interest rate home loans, compared to 17 percent for whites."

According to Demos, black groups—upper, middle, and lower—experience disproportionate rates of financial risk due to abundant credit-card debt and high-interest purchases of depreciating items, such as cars, electronics, and fancy appliances. Low-income blacks, however, are the dominant supporters of the multibillion-dollar payday loan and rent-to-own entities that can charge triple-digit interest rates, and rent merchandise at sometimes more than 200 percent above the manufacturer's suggested retail price.

Mad Money

My nieces and nephews all live at home, and are either unemployed or underemployed. Yet, they are rocking Airforce Ones and Apple Bottom jeans, and they can keep a bottle of Grey Goose under

the bed. They look like they have something going, but really they
don't—a complete consumer mentality with no income!
— Toni, 36, elder-care worker

We start addressing our failure to stay on par with other ethnic groups who increase their wealth by honestly answering a few true or false questions:

True or False: Blacks often purchase because it makes them feel better.
True or False: Blacks purchase high-priced liquor, designer clothes, and fancy cars simply because these items represent "the best."
True or False: Blacks place more value on what's in the garage or closet than what's in their bank accounts or stock portfolios.
True or False: Blacks distrust financial institutions. Many of those who do save, sock their money away at home or other places deemed "safer."

Your answers reveal the deep dynamics of the buy now, pay later syndrome.

Buy Now, Pay Later Dynamics

1. **Livin' large while feeling low:** African Americans have a tendency to overcompensate through material brazenness. We seek the best to prove we are the best, using our dollars as defense mechanisms to "show them" that we are worthy. Blacks have a strange loyalty to the "best brand" because subpar products remind us of our perceived subpar status.

2. **Gotta have it now:** This is the intergenerational, instant-gratification component to our spending and saving habits. As uninformed consumers, we are susceptible to marketing pleas to "have it now," as opposed to saving, investing, or putting off unaffordable purchases.

3. **Paying the black tax:** We expect and willingly pay more for products at what are often astronomical interest rates. We endure a wide range of financial penalties due to our uncontrolled desire to "live large" and "have it now."

4. **Eat, drink, and be merry:** For many of us, life is, and has always been, considered fragile and unpredictable. Since tomorrow is never promised, we must have desired products now—at any and all cost. This attitude also explains why we hesitate to risk our hard-earned money in financial institutions or the stock market.

5. **Dollars and sense:** Blacks have been systematically excluded (and we've excluded ourselves) from learning the economic ABC's of American life. This has not only turned us into easily seduced buyers but also handicapped builders of personal and communal wealth.

These dynamics accentuate the mystery of why we lag behind others who have amassed generational wealth through financial acuity. To reverse this pattern, we must first understand how our consumer and saving patterns link to our psychological need to salve 400-year-old wounds.

Take My Money, Please!

When I was a kid, we had a three-year cycle: We'd have the flashy cars, the big TVs, my mother would rock the furs and the diamond rings. Then, we would either go bankrupt, or my father would get arrested. There was no temperance, no middle road for us. We were either sky high, or had our faces in the dirt. You get used to that kind of stuff.
— Alan, 49, internet salesman

The buy buy, now now sales pitches are all around. We are flooded with offers to purchase every day and every minute. Messages are in magazines, and on billboards, radio, TV, the Internet, bus kiosks, T-shirts, taxi roofs, tote bags, blimps, and stuffed in envelopes with the bills for the stuff we've already bought. It's difficult for any American to resist the relentless marketing barrage and gain a modicum of a financial foothold. But I believe the cues to incessantly buy resonate differently with a race that had to secure the right to be treated as humans and force white businesses to treat them like any other American consumer.

Unlike whites, we were denied the basic right to be free-willed consumers. Restrictive, but legal, covenants excluded African Americans from purchasing homes in neighborhoods considered white. We could not patronize white-only diners, theaters, clubs, and colleges or shop in many stores. For centuries, spending money "jes' like white folk" was not even a possibility. That all changed after we fought for the right to force our money upon whites.

I Am Somebody!

How did this financial and emotional rejection, supported by the incessant, centuries-long black inferiority campaign, affect us? Consider the sit-ins that accelerated the civil rights movement. Black Americans (and their white supporters) risked life and limb to force Southern lunch counters, restaurants, and stores to accept our business. In fact, much of the movement was about gaining the right to consume like whites—whether patronizing restaurants and hotels, or buying clothes, cars, televisions, or homes.

We were in survival mode, flexing our equal rights muscles while forsaking our economic education heads. Not to downplay the dismantling of legalized segregation, but the major thrust of the civil rights movement included the demand that whites allow us to consume their products and utilize their services. The profound irony of the movement was that it clogged arteries that recirculated hard-

earned cash back into black communities and businesses. Instead, the flow was rerouted to benefit white power brokers and businesses.

During slavery, blacks had little to no control over their lives and fates. This seeded a sense of "living in the now" in our psyches. In a society where rank is determined by material wealth, we are still seeking to buy lost status, only this time through mindless, unbridled consumption.

Shopping for Status & Respect

Get a good look at me, dummy
I said I look, I feel, I smell like money...
—Three 6 Mafia, "Like Money"

Prevalent socio-economic conditions, combined with historic prejudices, have resulted in a case of low self-esteem, or low "race esteem," that has affected our purchasing behavior. I myself haven't exactly been immune to these feelings of inadequacy. I was raised during a time when blacks seemed grateful that car dealers wanted their money. "I may be discriminated against, but General Motors will sell me anything I want," we'd say.

Years ago, as a fledgling executive, I obtained a charge account at an exclusive store—initially, I think, just to demonstrate to my white co-workers that I, too, could have an account. It most certainly wasn't because my salary justified my shopping there!

That fall day remains with me. The temperature suddenly dropped and I ducked into this particularly elite store looking for gloves. I waited at the counter while two sales clerks carried on a clearly personal conversation. Finally, one of them acknowledged me with a disdainful look and snipped, "Do you want something?"

Instead of leaving, I found myself—despite the unprofessional treatment—buying a pair of gloves, priced far beyond what I could afford, just to show them that they'd underestimated me.

There were also times when I've been in high-end stores and felt self-conscious about asking about the price of an item. The mere question seemed like an indictment against my social status. This sentiment is probably shared by other upwardly mobile African Americans who believe that asking a store clerk, especially a *white* store clerk, about a product's cost somehow implies an inability to afford the merchandise.

Acquiring expensive commodities—this conspicuous consumption—is our way of telling the world, "We have arrived. We are good enough." Meanwhile, as we send these expensive communiqués as signals of our worth, manufacturers of all the stuff are in on the joke, chuckling their way to the bank.

Champagne Taste and a Beer Budget

Our history of feeling inferior fuels the propensity for African Americans to buy name brands we perceive to be the best. Knowing that we have been considered "less than"—less smart, less capable, less clean, less law-abiding, less generous, less worthy, less, less, less—spawned a reflexive need to demonstrate that we are equally (if not more) worthy.

The 2005 Yankelovich Monitor Multicultural Marketing Study, in collaboration with Burrell Communications, revealed that brand choice is far more an emotional decision for blacks, in terms of what it says about us, than it is for whites. African Americans in this study agreed with the following statements:

- The brand you buy tells a lot about the type of person you are (47 percent black vs. 35 percent other)

- I like to buy brands that make me feel I've made it (46 percent black vs. 30 percent other)

- Brands give me a level of emotional satisfaction (67 percent black vs. 43 percent other)

Everyone but us seems to be aware of our consumer clout and buying habits. During a July 2009 conversation on the Branding Strategy Insider blog, frequent contributor Mark Ritson discussed gender, age, and ethnic loyalty to luxury brands:

> I personally believe that the face of luxury...people who lead that market, are, for me, for the most part, African American. It would be a mistake to see, for example, the hip-hop community as being not consistent with the luxury brands. If anyone has grasped the true meaning and heritage of luxury brands, it is that African American community.

This emotional void drives the hip-hop generation's insatiable hunger for blingier bling, shinier cars, pricier liquor, and premium-priced products. According to the 2008 study, "Young Urban Consumer Market in the U.S.," conducted by *Report Buyer,* an online source for business news and trends, hip-hop artists set the trends for the $594 billion young urban consumer market. The brands that are "spontaneously embraced" and experience "significant sales" in this young demographic are those that appear to be "genuinely used" by hip-hop artists and featured in their lyrics or videos.

Young black fans paying ludicrously high prices for brand-name items may be influenced by hip-hop artists, but in reality they're continuing a trend established long before their births.

Evolution of Slave-based Economics

It was in the slaveholder's best interest to keep slaves in such despair that they could concentrate only on servitude and survival. Deprived and beaten down emotionally, slaves had little left that inspired them to even imagine a future. For hundreds of years, survival was our sole focus. Slavery, oppression, vicious Jim Crow laws, and the government's failure to assure our rights and safety, solidified and legitimized levels of extreme insecurity. Life's uncertainty and cruelty conditioned us to grab whatever pleasures we could, the best and quickest way possible.

Harvesting Hopelessness

Under the post-Emancipation sharecropping system, whites deliberately saw to it that black farmers never got ahead. No matter how diligently they farmed, they fell deeper in debt to the landowner or storekeeper who supplied land, fertilizer, seed, mules, equipment, or whatever else was needed. Debt peonage replaced the chains of slavery. Whites still kept black sharecroppers impoverished and reliant on generally high interest commissary credit advanced against the following year's crop.

It's important to remember that this system, too, became an integral part of promoting the next brainwashing campaign. It birthed the concept that somehow the bad situation was the fault of the black sharecropper who didn't harvest enough to cover the debt. Thus, the lender was able to cast himself as the good guy who helped the black family survive rough times.

Migration Miseries

During the great migration, between 1910 and 1970, more than six million black men, women, and children flooded the northern urban centers of America. The promise of better education and job opportunities "up north" outweighed the realities of brutal racism. While many blacks received educational and job opportunities in meatpacking, steel, automobile, and other industrial and unionized industries, they also encountered a system of northern racial oppression that was equally damaging to their well-being.

Racial segregation, in the form of mortgage discrimination and redlining, insured that blacks were kept out of white neighborhoods and confined to overcrowded, inner-city slums where rent gouging was common. Whites were able to buy homes thanks to federal government initiatives, such as the 1934 National Housing Act. That measure, which helped kick off the postwar suburban housing boom, severely limited lending in African American neighborhoods.

Stylin' & Profilin'

I didn't pay my student loans for the longest time. I bought a BMW, rented a penthouse with a Jacuzzi, bought out the bar for strangers. I needed to look like a big shot, like "Hey, I've made it!"
— Alan, 49, Internet sales

For generations, we've been engaged in an effort to regain a sense of "somebodiness" through our material possessions and the way we dress. The slaveowning family dressed nicely when they went to church or greeted guests or attended functions. The fine attire of whites contrasted sharply with the worn apparel of most slaves. The way we dressed became a source of tension between the lowly field servant and the often respectably clothed house slave.

After bondage was no longer legal, the stigma of second-class lowliness shadowed blacks as they migrated north. Be it in Memphis or Harlem, on Friday and Saturday nights, blacks adorned the best to feel like the best. The joint, or neighborhood drinking establishment, was the place where common laborers could get a quick shot of status. Once they "hit the joint," blacks were able to mingle and be "somebody." The mad-money dynamic in all of this esteem-based spending was that blacks not only spent disproportionately to look sharp, they'd often blow a day's or week's pay showing off, buying drinks, or participating in other costly nightlife sprees.

The non-club-hopping crowd gained equal satisfaction on Sunday mornings. The one good suit, the fancy dresses, and elaborate hats worn to church contradicted the sense of lowliness the weekday uniform or daily work clothes represented. For the black generations up until the 1960s, said Gail Lowe, creator of the 2000 Smithsonian exhibit on African American faith, the way we dressed for service was our way of honoring the church and satisfying our "hunger for beauty and for self-respect."

During my high school years, I worked all kinds of jobs to raise enough money to buy Brooks Brothers suits. For me and a couple of my buddies, it wasn't education or religion that kept us coming to school or church—it was all about "showing up sharp!"

The Exceptions to the Rule

The opportunity to earn a dollar in a factory just now is worth more than the opportunity to spend a dollar in an opera house.
— Booker T. Washington

Although educator Booker T. Washington was criticized for urging blacks to amass social capital through education and manual labor only, he was still among the pioneers of the "do-for-self" economic responsibility movement.

The founder of the Universal Negro Improvement Association (UNIA), Marcus Mosiah Garvey, took the message to an unprecedented level. In the 1920s, Garvey focused on teaching blacks how to own and operate their own factories, grocery stores, restaurants, publishing houses, and international shipping companies.

For those who lived in what was known as the "capital of black economic independence"—Tulsa, Oklahoma, particularly the affluent black Greenwood area—economic independence was a way of life. Before a deadly race riot decimated Greenwood in 1921, the region hosted 28 black townships, more than 40 black municipalities, and a host of independently owned and operated businesses.

After Elijah Muhammad became the leader of the Nation of Islam in 1934, he centered the organization's mission on self-determination, racial separation, cultural pride, and economic independence.

Some of these attempts to build strong, self-sustaining economic foundations were fraught with failure due to government manipulation, disunity, misplaced loyalty, and distracting, counter-productive ideologies. Still, these examples illustrate that, since Emancipation, there were black leaders who thought seriously about the way we created, conserved, and invested our money.

There was a brief attitude of self-determination after the enactment of civil rights legislation. During the 1960s, '70s, and even into the '80s, there was an inspiring rallying cry for race-based solidarity, self-determination, and an intense drive to play a bigger role in the economic arena. Unfortunately, the promise of prosperity through social integration, like migration's promise, proved to be another frustrating shell game. With fractured identities, we still attempt to buy respectability and status. We are still emotional spenders and vulnerable pawns of high-priced vendors and predatory lenders.

What We Drive &
What We're Driving

A fascination with luxury cars has been another big thing for many blacks. On a psychological level, expensive cars represent fulfillable dreams. Next to homes, they are the most expensive item (thanks to available credit) the average African American can own. Cars, for men especially, are phallic symbols of power and control. In the black male psyche, they compensate for feelings of social emasculation. You can't park a house in front of a church or nightclub, but arriving in a flashy car garners instant admiration. For blacks, cars serve as mobile billboards that say "I have arrived!"

From Sharecropping to Payday Lending

We are a people conditioned to put our faith in the future, live in the now, and respond to promises of quick prosperity. From a marketing perspective, you couldn't ask for a better demographic. If a consumer group believes social status can be achieved through consumerism, why not make millions exploiting that perception?

Many credit card companies operate the most vicious kinds of predatory lending scams, and young African Americans give them particular delight. Before they even get jobs or establish credit histories, blacks are among the young demographic high-interest credit card companies target. The majority of young black credit card holders, however, don't have the options of some whites, whose parents will bail them out of debt or who are able to move into well-paying jobs.

At young ages, blacks who bought things they couldn't afford are introduced to an inescapable high-interest, credit-damaging cycle. The worse they feel about themselves, the more they buy (on credit) to feel better. No matter how deep they sink, credit card companies and other greedy, manipulative lenders are always there to help out with more stuff, albeit at inflated prices and interest rates.

Listen closely to the payday loan industry's spokesmen and you might recognize the resemblance to the sales pitch used by lenders of the sharecropping era. Their ads sympathetically explain how "everybody falls behind every now and then" and they, the payday lenders, are there to offer assistance. According to the Consumer Federation of America, the interest alone on payday loans, in some states, can be as high as 780 percent.

Used car salesmen promise to finance anybody, no matter how bad their credit. Rent-to-own dealers tell customers they can take furniture, appliances, and electronic equipment home today without worrying about credit checks.

It's no coincidence that high-interest credit card companies, payday lenders, rent-to-own companies, and used car dealerships are overrepresented in low-income black and Latino neighborhoods.

There could be no better territory than ones filled with the permanently underemployed and unemployed who have been generationally excluded from economic prosperity.

Like the landowning lenders of old, today's pitchmen swear they're helping these "risky" consumers reestablish good credit. What they fail to disclose is how they grossly inflate prices and demand interest rates so jacked up that uninformed, cash-strapped consumers wind up further damaging their already damaged credit.

Payday lending customers are allowed to take out additional loans to cover defaults. Risky car buyers can always get another "ride" and rent-to-own defaulters are courted by even sleazier competition. The mentally conditioned can still get their immediate "stuff," even after repossession, as long as they're willing to pay the "black tax"—higher prices at much higher interest rates.

Thus, as in the post–Civil War days, many blacks wind up trapped in a cycle of never-ending debt and a state of economic slavery. Worse yet, they're conditioned to believe their situations are their own fault. Meanwhile, the "good guys"—those with the resources to hire lobbyists to thwart regulatory opposition—exploit an exploitable demographic and make out like benevolent bandits.

We Gotta Have It

Even with less disposable income, we lead the general population in satisfying immediate desires. According to the Selig Center for Economic Growth, blacks allocate a disproportionate share of their spending to telephone service, apparel, television, radio, sound equipment, and personal care products and services.

Our spending habits are closely tracked by marketers of everything from Aamco to Ziebart. In 2003, we spent about $6.5 billion on personal items and services, $131 billion on housing, $56 billion on food, $33 billion on motor vehicles, and $23 billion on clothing, according to Target Market News. Yet the amount we spend on what goes in our hair and on our bodies is far greater than what we spend on what goes *in* our heads or into our bank accounts. We spent almost

$120 billion on hair care products, cars, clothes, and food, and only about $40.5 billion on health care, insurance, education, and books.

Faced with such a glaring imbalance in our spending priorities, perhaps it makes more sense to put a little less into a "do" and a lot more into education and earning a college diploma that will allow us to be more competitive in the 21st century.

Ripple Effect

There's an even more depressing image on the flipside of the black inferiority coin—the lack of economic self-determination and relative dearth of successful black enterprises. Our hunger for respect from whites has not only turned us into easy marks for the products they manufacture, inferiority conditioning has us so discombobulated, we're resistant to supporting black businesses.

Ironically, the group that bucks this trend seems to be hip-hop artists who have introduced clothing and product lines that are enthusiastically supported by black and white youth alike. Where once Kangol, Pro-Keds, Adidas, Timberland, and other white-owned companies dominated the hip-hop fashion world, Russell Simmons's Phat Farm, Sean "Diddy" Combs's Sean John, Nelly's Apple Bottom, Jay-Z's Rocawear, and 50 Cent's G-Unit reign supreme.

From a marketing perspective, it would be a mistake to dismiss hip-hop artists' ability to promote their version of black culture to international markets. Some have been savvy enough to not only be the profitable product but to be producers of the product. However, in most cases, they romanticize black dysfunction, which only amplifies the "buy now, pay later" dynamic. Also, it's yet to be seen if their individual accomplishments have made any contribution to true economic empowerment or reversed our fears about saving and investing, or tackled any of our other counterproductive mad money ways.

Matter of Trust

The present economic crisis, especially the drastic rate of unemployment, further reminds us that no matter what our circumstances are, they can get worse. The Bureau of Labor Statistics reported that the unemployment rate for African Americans, as of August 2009, was at 14.9 percent compared to 8.6 percent for whites. For far too many low- to no-income blacks, saving for a "rainy day" remains a foreign concept. Every day it rains!

We must also consider that our reluctance to invest, save, or prepare for financial downturns stem, in part, from betrayals by insurance companies and other financial institutions. I recall neighbors who were denied insurance benefits after the death of the policyholder who paid weekly premiums for years. The experience, sadly, was all too common for blacks back then.

In 2002, the Life Insurance Company of Georgia agreed to pay $55 million to settle allegations that it charged blacks higher premiums than it did whites for life insurance policies for more than 30 years. John Hancock Life Insurance Company, in 2009, agreed to settle a class-action suit for a reported $24.4 million. That lawsuit alleged that, prior to 1959, the company routinely sold lower grade policies to African Americans while it offered full range policies to whites.

Additionally, we were confronted with inequities in financial services. Anecdotes abound of blacks who failed to read the teeny-tiny fine print on credit contracts, or didn't understand complicated payout formulas when they invested with financial institutions. Distrust, fueled by exaggerated and repeated accounts of negative experiences at the hands of these institutions, are what keep many of us from even educating ourselves about the benefits of investing and savings. Thus, we effectively deny ourselves the needed parachute in case of sudden financial instability or disaster.

In short, most of us have been brainwashed to believe that preparing for the worst, saving, investing, or building wealth are luxuries for white people only.

Linking the Past, Understanding the Present

One of the major intentions of this book is to emphasize that our problems don't exist in isolation. They are part of our past history and present reality. Here, we identify the origins of our buying, spending, and saving habits, and the links to a tragic past:

Buy Now, Pay Later: Connecting the Dots

Contemporary Manifestations	Historical Roots
Livin' large while feeling low: The tendency to overcompensate; to seek the "best" brands to prove we are the best; to use our dollars to validate our worth and thwart perceptions of subpar status.	Dehumanization for slaves meant that they could not claim any status whatsoever. In America, status was defined by material possessions. Thus blacks have long sought to buy personhood and we've been trying by buying ever since.
Gotta have it now: The instant gratification component to our spending and savings habits; blacks are susceptible to marketing pleas to "have it now," as opposed to saving, investing, or delaying unaffordable purchases.	One thing that slavery taught us was that, "tomorrow is not promised." Due to our precarious existence and uncertain future, blacks learned to squeeze whatever joy was attainable in the moment.

Paying the black tax: We are willing to pay more at higher prices and interest rates, and endure a wide range of financial penalties.	Designated second-class citizens, we were taught that we deserved to get less, to pay more, and to be taken advantage of. Learned helplessness meant that there was nothing we could do about it anyway, so we believed that we deserved humiliation and harm.
Dollars and sense: Systematic exclusion from economic fundamentals of American life. Blacks are easily seduced into buying and are handicapped as builders of personal and communal wealth.	Enslaved blacks were denied the opportunity to learn about money because they were forced to work without pay. Without the benefit of financial literacy, blacks only saw the consumption side of the equation, not the money management side.

Mad Money Dynamics, Now & Then

Education has always been key to self-improvement and financial stability. During and after slavery, we were denied education and opportunities to fully immerse ourselves in the culture of money management and growth. Because of the psychic deficit caused by a race-based self-esteem deficiency, we are sitting ducks for mass media's version of consumer education: Buy, buy, buy. Buy now, pay later! Just as we believed in the promise of freedom, and the promise of equality, we also respond to commercial promises of self-worth through consumerism. We will continue thinking we can overcompensate for our blackness if we drive certain cars, wear certain outfits, or drink certain expensive liquors.

Until we break free of the conditioning, we will proceed as programmed.

Pulling the Programming Plug

We keep a bankroll, wallet full of credit cards
Cup full of Cristal, box full of cigars...
— Lil Scrappy, "Money in the Bank"

Now it's time to unplug from the forces that fuel the buy now, pay later madness. The process begins by examining the benefits and costs of our habits.

Short-term Benefits

1. **Overcompensation:** Gives us feelings of equality and worth.

2. **Name brand and expensive product loyalty:** Tempers feelings of inferiority; puts us on par with the quality of the product and allows us to project a false front and garner immediate attention.

3. **Willingness to pay higher prices at higher interest rates:** We get our stuff *now*!

4. **Resistance to saving or investing:** Counteracts fear of losing or being cheated out of our money or investments, and gives us a sense of security.

Long-term Costs

1. **Overcompensation:** False sense of value and worth based on unpredictable, external forces. Overcompensation strengthens a system designed to benefit from our poor money habits.

2. **Name brand and expensive product loyalty:** Money wasted to gain temporary feelings of high status; makes manufacturers richer while depleting individual and community resources.

3. **Willingness to pay higher prices at higher interest rates:** Depreciable products have no long-term value; continues the cycle of personal debt and guarantees consumers have no money to save, invest, or pass on.

4. **Hesitancy to save or invest:** Fuels paranoia and false sense of security; undermines long-term personal, family, and community security; predisposes us to financial mis-education, and inability to set and achieve financial goals.

Hopefully, we are now conscious that overspending, creating unnecessary debt, and failing to save and invest our money has dire personal and communal consequences. Hopefully, we are now ready for change.

A Disciplined, Long-term Strategy

I'm trying to change things, for myself and for my children. I no longer use credit cards unless I'm going to pay it back immediately. I'm paying down my student loans and other debt. Most importantly, I talk about money and finances with my kids. We have an account that we keep for special things. My kids get to watch the savings grow, and share in anticipation of what we are saving for. It's not about instant gratification. It's about long-term goals.
— Toni, 36, elder-care worker

Former Los Angeles Lakers player Magic Johnson is not among the percentage of professional basketball players who went broke after leaving the NBA. Johnson, CEO of Magic Johnson Enterprises, a Los Angeles–based company with a net worth of over $700 million, has generated millions while revitalizing urban areas with full-service retail outlets. In his book *32 Ways to Be a Champion in Business*, Johnson talks about financial literacy, discipline, money management, and striking a balance that benefits the business, his family, and the extended community. Johnson's attitude is worth emulating. Getting our minds and financial houses in order will not only benefit us individually but have a profound impact on the broader community.

Just as the idea of our inferiority was marketed and sold, it must be unsold. As in the days of old, marketing, promotion, and the power of positive propaganda are the keys to real, long-lasting solutions.

Buy Now, Pay Later
Positive Propaganda Cues

Put the "why?" in buy!
- When you make a purchase, ask yourself, "Why am I buying this? Am I buying because I actually need it, or because it makes me feel better?"

- Does buying the more expensive/high end brand make you feel important, or increase your self-esteem?

- Do you think about the consequences to your future when you overspend or accrue debt today?

Stuff is not enough
- How do you define the term *well-off*? Is it by what's in your garage and closet, or by what's in your bank account and stock portfolio?

Thou shalt not commit I-dollar-try
- We have a preoccupation with instant gratification through materialism. It needs to be our mission to put it in its place. Reclaim your total self: you are more than the label you wear!

We survived the worst. Now we need to prepare for the best life has to offer.

Pay It Forward

Scrutinizing the motivators, consciously changing our conversations about money, and becoming financially literate are prerequisites to change. We must also remember our history and thirst for education once blacks were emancipated. Teachers didn't need a degree to teach during the post-slavery era. As soon as a student became literate that student became a teacher.

Consumer education is an essential part of a comprehensive education. As soon as one of us becomes economically literate, it should be our duty to pay it forward. This is why I applaud black churches, organizations, and individuals that are attempting to normalize the mysteries of finance.

Consider the National Black Church Initiative's 16,000 affiliate churches' saving, education, and investment campaign. The initiative, supported by major financial institutions, seeks to teach low-income blacks how to save, invest, and benefit from long-term financial planning. On a smaller scale, Reverend Thurman Evans works with his young congregants, encouraging them to enhance their financial literacy and invest in home ownership rather than lavish weddings.

Investment clubs, like the one created by the Bossette family of Beaumont, Texas, also provide valuable grassroots lessons. In the early 1990s, 18 Bossette family members contributed a minimum of $40 per month after starting the Organization Investment Club (OIC). By 2000, the family amassed a portfolio in the upper six figures, according to *Black Enterprise* magazine.

With $750 billion in buying power, we can also create our own positive propaganda arsenal. To add balance to stories about reckless black celebrities, we can promote down-to-earth, penny-wise heroes, like Oseola McCarty of Hattiesburg, Mississippi. A lifelong, self-proclaimed washerwoman, McCarty, a 6th grade dropout, followed her mother's advice to always save money. Upon her death, McCarty bequeathed an estimated $150,000 of her life savings toward college scholarships for deserving but disadvantaged students.

Savvy celebrities need not be excluded as teachers either. In a 2009 interview with an online magazine, singer Beyoncé Knowles explained why she hadn't bought many luxury items with her estimated $80 million in earnings:

> Honestly, I'm very frugal. I haven't bought a car since I was 16 or any diamonds since I was 17. I have a lot of property. I've invested my money and I don't have to make any more. Thank God, because I'm set, I'm now able really to be free.

Empowerment Through In-Dolla-Ment!

It's up to reprogrammed thinkers like Sheryl Ridley-Dorsey, a certified public accountant from Lumberton, New Jersey, to help the next generation break free from black inferiority conditioning. Concerned that the average high school student doesn't possess basic skills in money management, Ridley-Dorsey created Black $treet Investment Club (B$IC) to teach children investment and business topics, ranging from personal finance and stock market techniques to operating their own businesses.

Our sheer numbers are all that's needed to promote a positive propaganda campaign consisting of encouraging examples, doable investment strategies, and other creative programs that take the mystery out of money management and investment. Nay-sayers will point to failed attempts in the past. The BI campaign has many convinced that we are forever doomed to live lives of financial inferiority. But this is a different time and a different era. We have more examples of success and more tech-savvy ways to help willing financial teachers teach.

This movement will be fostered by individuals prepared to break free from the psychological grip of the destructive BI Complex. Individuals with renewed minds will be prepared for unprecedented success—mentally armed and ready to reclaim our finances, our fortunes, and our future.

Chapter 8

D's Will Do

Why Do We Expect So Little of Each Other— and Ourselves?

Government programs alone won't get our children to the Promised Land. We need a new mindset, a new set of attitudes— because one of the most durable and destructive legacies of discrimination is the way that we have internalized a sense of limitation; how so many in our community have come to expect so little of ourselves.

— PRESIDENT BARACK OBAMA SPEAKING AT THE NAACP'S 2009 CENTENNIAL CELEBRATION

"There goes another statistic."

Pam Thompson, 35, a Chicago elementary school teacher, hated herself when she had such thoughts about one of her students. She wasn't really upset with the child. The comment was more of an indictment against the student's parent.

Pam called the student's mother, asking that she come to school after class. The student, a rather bright child, had received D's in reading and math. Not an insurmountable problem, Pam thought, especially with a little teacher/parent intervention. Pam developed an outline and asked the mother to come by so they could discuss activities the child could do at home to improve her grades.

The mother arrived at the meeting, defensive and in a huff.

"'Well, how many F's do you see on her report card?'" Pam recalled the mother asking. "Clearly, she was not giving her child any grief about those grades. She was pretty much asking, 'What's wrong with a D?'—as if D's were good enough."

"If only it were that one child," Pam remarked during our interview for this book. She had retained another student she couldn't, in good conscience, pass to the next grade level. The child could read low-level books, Pam said, but couldn't read the required chapter books. The child's mother questioned Pam's decision: "Are you telling me that the reading grade is based on how well she can read?" Pam said, "She was upset because I wanted her child to be able to read beyond 'I have a cat.'"

In recent years, Pam has encountered black parents who insisted their children should receive good grades just for showing up at class. She's met parents who celebrate after learning their child received only three or four F's instead of the usual five or six.

"A lot of parents say things like 'All I want to know is if my child is passing.' Not, 'Is my child excelling, is she living up to her potential?' Just 'Is she passing?'"

Pam, who had enjoyed success in the private business sector, decided to switch careers and pursue her passion for teaching. In the mid-1990s, she accepted a position with a new "laboratory school" created to specifically address the city's deteriorating educational system. Within two years, she said, teaching was replaced with policing. She had to deal with constant disruption. During one violent clash between students, Pam was so badly injured she was off work for weeks. Even with the drama, Pam remains a dedicated teacher who insists on academic excellence. She says that she hasn't dedicated more than 20 years of her life to teaching to wind up willfully allowing kids to slip through the cracks.

Still, it troubles Pam deeply to know that far too many students, based largely on the low expectations of their parents, will no doubt wind up as statistics.

Dancing the D Dance

My niece went from speaking proper English to speaking ebonics to the 9th degree. She did it to fit in with her peers. One time, I tried to correct her language. Her mother got extremely defensive

and said, "She talks that way because she's a black girl." Whoa!
So, if you are black, you don't have to speak proper English? Yet
the American workforce requires that you be able to communicate.
There is a cultural enabling of this subpar behavior. We are
enabling our kids to fail.
— Toni, elder-care worker, 36

In education, D's will do. Too many black parents make excuses for their children's poor performance, with some actually doing the "D Dance" over mediocre grades. Some parents are content when their children receive the "I showed up" award, without challenging them to show up prepared for accomplishment.

Perhaps in no other area has the African American story seen so many twists, dead ends, and sinkholes than in the dominion of education. More important, perhaps, no other discussion makes African Americans as uncomfortable as the topic of why our children lag so far behind the children of other races.

Consider the 160,000 African American high school seniors in the class of 2007 who took the SAT. Just 1,176 scored over 700 on the verbal portion—the well-established standard for academic superiority. Compare this to the performance of Hispanics and Asians, who had similar numbers taking the test—2,671 Hispanics scored over 700 on verbal, while 11,630 Asians achieved that distinction. If we go back 12 years to 1995, the number was even worse for blacks: that year, only 164 scored over 700.

Although it has been attacked for decades as culturally biased, the much-maligned SAT test is still one of the most widely used measuring tools and predictors for student potential in college. In spite of the skepticism and charges of bias, in a society in which we all must function, the SAT scores of black children should be troubling to all of us.

The educational gap between black and white students may put many of us on edge, but as DIVERSE: Issues in Higher Education noted, the obstinate achievement gap persists, "despite economic and civil-rights gains for racial and ethnic minorities (that) range from the low expectations of educators, to watered-down academic offerings, to disinterest by the students and their families in their schooling."

For several decades, educators, policymakers, and parents alike have posited theories, initiated programs, clamored for funding, leveled charges of racism, and blamed parents and teachers, blamed the schools, blamed poverty, fatherlessness, or rap music.

Meanwhile, the numbers haven't budged.

Numbers Don't Lie

We institutionalized lower expectations. We're all guilty.
— Jack O'Connell, San Francisco school superintendent

We have to face the facts: African Americans are the worst students in the country. On every measure used to assess student performance, statistical and anecdotal, the level of black underachievement is stunning. Equally grim statistics were reported by DIVERSE, citing data from the National Assessment of Educational Progress (NAEP) that showed:

> Reading scores for 17-year-olds narrowed dramatically for black and Hispanic students between 1975 and 1988. From 1990 to 1999, however, gaps in reading and mathematics remained constant or grew slightly, and little progress has been made since. More alarmingly, black and Hispanic students' skills in English, math, and science are about four years behind those of white students, according to the NAEP data, also known as the Nation's Report Card.

The poverty excuse offers little solace. The performance gap is even greater between middle-class blacks and middle-class whites than it is between low-income blacks and low-income whites. As a federal clearinghouse on educational research noted, what's now known is that there's an even greater gap in student achievement in schools in suburban middle-income communities than in inner cities, particularly at the higher achievement levels (College Board, 1999).

The achievement gap also exists in the early school years. In 2006, Bruce Fuller, a University of California at Berkeley researcher, said that, on average, black students in fourth grade read about as well as white students in second grade

According to the Education Trust, a mere 12 percent of African American fourth graders reach proficient or advanced levels in reading, while a heartbreaking 61 percent have not been taught at even basic levels. The Education Trust also noted that, after years of gains in education, black students have begun slipping further behind at all levels of schooling:

> The patterns for mathematics achievement look very similar, with significant gap-closing until the early 90s, then a gradual reversal of those gains. In fact, the white-black gaps are approximately 10 points wider, about a year's worth of learning, than they were a decade ago...By the end of high school, African American students have math and reading skills that are virtually the same as those of eighth grade white students...In the last 20 years, the college enrollment rates of African Americans have steadily increased... [now African Americans] go to college at about the same rates as white students. However, African American college completion rates have not increased at the same pace, and a gap in college attainment remains.

Black and minority children are born with severe educational disadvantages, said Geoffrey Canada, director of the Harlem Children's Zone in New York: "The science on this is clear. We know poor families are less likely to have good health care. They're less likely to get the kind of good baby checks that you need during pregnancy...by the time this child is three years old, there's a gap of about 800-words difference between the two groups. And that gap just increases every year after that."

Because it led the state in high school dropout, crime, gang, and incarceration rates, "it was expected that children in Harlem would end up at the bottom of every important, positive indicator in New York State," Canada said.

The negative expectations go far beyond Harlem. An internalized sense of limitation embedded in the psyches of black parents and

sewn into the fabric of white society, I maintain, keeps black kids in a disadvantaged state.

D's Will Do—Dynamics

What feeds the black underachievement that plagues our communities?

1. **Fear of failure:** Out of fear or their own sense of inadequacy, parents too often stifle a child's urge to attempt academic success. Fear of failure promotes a "why even try?" attitude and detours promising youth onto pathways of mediocrity and underachievement.

2. **Misguided protection:** Black parents, who want their kids to feel good about themselves, rebel against having them stigmatized as "failures." Parents become unreasonably protective and defensive, defending both their children and themselves from feelings of inferiority.

3. **Success neurosis:** Black children are discouraged from moving ahead of "the group." Smart kids are ostracized as "stuck up" or accused of "acting white." Black parents often don't recognize the importance of providing kids with the tools necessary to handle negative attitudes and destructive trends.

4. **The "best black" syndrome:** To compensate for centuries of discrimination and exclusion, and to protect blacks' sense of self-worth, segregated categories for black achievement and accomplishments have been established. A black student isn't the "best engineer" but lands in the default position of being the best "black engineer."

In his NAACP speech, President Obama called for "a new mindset, a new set of attitudes" to reverse the crisis of black underachievement.

I agree—a new, reprogrammed mindset is in order. To get to that point, however, the urgent precursor is to thoroughly understand how the "can't do" mindset was first created and enforced.

The Best Black!

When it comes to black film festivals, it's not a question of quality, per se. I know that some of the films we have here are not that good. It does not really matter if the quality is up to par, what matters is that we get more black films out there, give more black filmmakers a chance to get their work out and seen.
— Frank, filmmaker

In many ways, African Americans have romanticized and institutionalized low expectations. Often our goal is not to be "the best" but to be "the best black"—as in "best black business" or "best black doctor" or "best black college." Inherent in these labels is a subliminal acceptance that our "best" is somehow naturally inferior or somehow different from the white "best."

Burrell Communications was often cited as the number one advertising and marketing firm among black agencies. This was a bittersweet acknowledgment. I'd have happily swapped the number one firm rating among black agencies for the number 24 rating among *all* agencies. Why? It's far more important to be rated on a level playing field for the entire industry than to be a winner in an inferior category. Besides, all black firms combined didn't bring in the equivalent billings of even one medium-sized, successful white agency.

To counter historical attempts to mute our accomplishments, we've created exclusive categories aimed at boosting our self-worth. We note the businesses that make *Black Enterprise* magazine's "100 largest black-owned companies" list. We celebrate black learning institutions like Spelman College, Howard University, Morehouse, and other schools on the "Top Black Colleges" listings.

These black businesses and schools rank high in the restricted zone of "blackness" but are often invisible on Fortune 500's "Top American

Corporations" or Forbes's "America's Best Colleges" list, which includes universities such as Harvard and Yale. Rarely do we question why the black entities are either positioned at the low end or not ranked at all on these prestigious "best" lists. For many of us, black success is all we can reasonably expect.

Proud to Be Dumb

As a young black man, I can't even recall how many times I heard "nerd" or "geek" or "college boy" or "You sound like a white boy" used as an insult. It's not about "white," it's about education and power. They didn't want me to have either.
— James, writer

James's comment speaks to another challenge black children face as they hobble toward adulthood without positive support or reinforcement. Astonishingly, there are still some of us who make light of academic achievement, assigning such leanings to something *not* related to "blackness."

Pittsburgh Steelers coach Mike Tomlin is all too familiar with this oddity. Tomlin, described by the *New York Times* as a "reluctant intellectual," worked hard to hide his brimming intellect even after becoming a member of the National Honor Society while attending Denbigh High in Newport News, Virginia. "He didn't want anybody to know he was smart or making good grades," Tomlin's mother, Julia Copeland, recalled. "He wanted to be a regular old Joe football player like the rest of the kids so they wouldn't call him a nerd." Most poor black kids don't have the community reinforcement that encourages them to sincerely believe they can become engineers, surgeons, or scientists. Hollywood has filled this void with characters that make underachievement acceptable and attractive.

Digging at the Root

Most experts believe that helping children understand they *can* achieve will go a long way to convince them that they can be anything they want to be in life. They ignore the reality that we live in the nation that birthed the BI campaign and that has, for so long, convinced black kids, their parents, and their ancestors that they *could not* be anything they wanted in this society.

The claim that African Americans lack intelligence was first voiced upon our arrival in Jamestown in 1619. The initial attempt to deny our humanity by denying our intellect has grown more insidious over the centuries. Since our society is built on the theory of white superiority and black inferiority, simply trying to convince a black child that he or she "can achieve anything" reminds me of the wise words of Dr. Martin Luther King, Jr.: "The job of arousing manhood within a people that have been taught for so many centuries that they are nobody is not easy."

An Educated Slave Is a Dangerous Slave

A piece of property or a dumb animal doesn't need a book!

Such was the reasoning of slaveowners who not only saw no profit in slaves who could read or write, but considered the very concept a threat to their livelihoods.

Frederick Douglass made it clear why an educated slave was a dangerous slave: "The more I read, the more I was led to abhor and detest my enslavers."

A literate slave might challenge the very rationale for bondage. Interpreting the Bible may have led the slave to discount the white preacher's lessons about obliging his master. It may have exposed slaves to Jesus's true lessons of equality and humanity that contradicted the slaveowner's decree of black inferiority. Bible stories about "righteous" men who vanquished "sinners" might have inspired the slave to righteous rebellion.

If Southern states were unified on one goal before Emancipation, it was prohibiting slaves from being educated. As W.E.B. Du Bois observed, "The laws on this point were explicit and severe." These laws were made even stronger after Nat Turner and the dozens of slaves he recruited killed about 60 whites in 1831. Slavery's protectors recognized the incendiary correlation between education and insurrection. After all, Turner—smart and charismatic—read, preached, and drew followers based on his interpretation of the Christian Bible.

Unlearning Helplessness

Even in the midst of heightened suspicion, determined slaves found ways to learn, as Heather Andrea Williams, a University of North Carolina professor, detailed in *Self-Taught: African American Education in Slavery and Freedom*. In a 2005 interview Williams said:

> Many former slaves told of learning to read from a slave mistress who believed it her Christian duty to teach a slave to read the Bible. Some, especially in the early periods, joined churches because they knew that ministers would sometimes teach them so that they could read the catechism. These enslaved people often had a copy of Webster's Spelling Book and would get people to teach them to identify the letters of the alphabet. Then, the next stage was to start teaching other slaves themselves, which many of them did.

After centuries of brutality and degradation, the majority of freed blacks came out of slavery infused with the certainty that "book learning" was the key to salvation.

In a narrative that former Virginia slave John Washington wrote after the Civil War, blacks put reading and writing "near the top of the list of the most sought after fruits of liberty, alongside family reconstitution and land ownership."

Before the Southern states were brought back into the Union following the Civil War, Northern states gave blacks a succession of new rights, including the right to vote. During this period, known as

Reconstruction, 22 blacks were elected to Congress and others took control of legislatures in states with black majorities, such as Alabama, Mississippi, and South Carolina.

One of the most significant developments of this period was the establishment of the public school system in the South. Most historians agree that it came about because of the fierce resolve of former slaves to be educated. In fact, one of the few points both W.E.B. Du Bois and Booker T. Washington actually agreed on was the former slave's inexorable thirst for learning. Du Bois wrote: "The very feeling of inferiority which slavery forced upon them fathered an intense desire to rise out of their condition by means of education."

Booker T. Washington said the deep desire for education amounted to a whole race intent on going to school: "Few were too young, and none too old, to make the attempt to learn. As fast as any kind of teachers could be secured, not only were day-schools filled, but night-schools as well..."

Du Bois noted that from 1866 to 1870, former slaves contributed the astounding amount of $785,700 to establish their own schools. This was more understandable than astonishing, wrote Heather Williams:

> It made perfect sense that someone who had climbed into a hole in the woods to attend school would, in freedom, sacrifice time and money to build a schoolhouse. It rang true that people who waited up until ten o'clock at night to sneak off to classes on the plantation would want to establish schools in the open as soon as they possibly could.

Blacks, for the most part, had a shared mission and vision. Education was widely perceived as the only viable road to freedom and equality. Reconstruction-era legislation gave them an opportunity to finally pave that road to glory.

What happened? How did mediocrity overpower such certainty? What powerful force caused many of us, even now, to revert to the slavemaster's dictate? Answers can be traced back to the fear of an educated slave and the resulting mental chaos from an orchestrated, blatant, and later, clandestine 18th-century agenda.

Lessons of Inferiority

The national debate surrounding the status of slaves before, during, and after the Civil War provides a stark picture of the contempt for blacks held by whites in the South *and* the North—even by those whom American lore now describes as "friendly to the Negro."

Countless historians have touted Abraham Lincoln's egalitarianism. Not surprisingly, most fail to mention that the president who freed the slaves maintained that blacks were and would always be inferior to whites. Consider Lincoln's words in 1858, on the eve of the Civil War, in a debate with Stephen A. Douglas:

> I will say then that I am not, nor ever have been in favor of bringing about in any way the social and political equality of the white and black races. That I am not nor ever have been in favor of making voters or jurors of Negroes, nor of qualifying them to hold office, nor to intermarry with white people, and I will say in addition to this that there is a physical difference between the black and white races which I believe will forever forbid the two races living together on terms of social and political equality. And inasmuch as they cannot so live, while they do remain together there must be the position of superior and inferior, and I as much as any other man am in favor of having the superior position assigned to the white race.

At the time, Lincoln articulated beliefs that had been propagated for some 200 years. John Caldwell Calhoun, the South Carolina slaveowner and vice president under John Quincy Adams, insisted that Africans were innately inferior to Europeans. Calhoun, affectionately known as the symbol of the "Old South," publicly labeled the institution of slavery "a positive good."

The inherent inferiority of blacks was a sentiment also shared by prominent authors, school reformers, and scholars of Lincoln's day, such as renowned Harvard zoologist Louis Agassiz who, in 1847, said: "The brain of the Negro is that of the imperfect brain of a 7 month's infant in the womb of a white."

Mis-Educating the Negro

The foundation for black failure was laid long before the U.S. Supreme Court, in 1896, ruled that racially separate facilities were constitutional. The common-school system, which served as the model for black schools, was thoroughly skewed to support and foster white superiority, as Harvard scholar Dr. Carter G. Woodson stressed in his landmark thesis, *The Mis-Education of the Negro*:

> The so-called modern education, with all its defects, however, does others so much more good than it does the Negro, because it has been worked out in conformity to the needs of those who have enslaved and oppressed weaker peoples.

Each generation after the 17th century produced crops of white scholars who specialized in the theory of black inferiority and legitimized warped hypotheses that circulated through the country's most elite institutions of higher learning. In a 2007 academic brief calling for a "Free Standing Africana Studies Major Program at Ramapo College of New Jersey," professors Dr. Karl Johnson and Dr. David Lewis-Colman gave a history of "institutionalized racism" in learning institutions.

> Until the 1960s, for example, most U.S. historians taught that southern states had been forced to adopt Jim Crow in response to African American corruption and incompetence during Reconstruction. For the first three decades of the 20th century, scientific racism defined much of social science and natural science scholarship. Many prominent biologists, sociologists, psychologists, and anthropologists dedicated their scholarly lives to proving the moral and intellectual inferiority of Africans and their descendents to justify the racism endemic in U.S. institutions.

Though most segregated schools were woefully underfunded and incompatible with white schools, they were, at least, located in segregated black neighborhoods and largely influenced by black administrators, teachers, and parents. Within the area of their own

control, blacks had the opportunity to learn and adapt from trial and error. However, this brief educational experiment ended abruptly in 1954 when the Supreme Court offered blacks a better alternative.

Separate but Reaffirmed

The hope placed in the establishment of independent black learning institutions shifted drastically after the U.S. Supreme Court ruled that racial separation in schools was wrong and fostered feelings of inferiority in black children. Fortified with the belief that white schools offered better opportunities for their children, Southern blacks boldly confronted vicious mobs intent on keeping their kids out of historically white learning institutions.

Perhaps the most memorable of these clashes was the September 1957 showdown in Little Rock, Arkansas, when nine black students, known as the "Little Rock Nine," integrated Central High School with the help of armed federal guards.

Yet, 50 years after legal desegregation, Central High and other schools across the country still struggle with segregation, inequality, and underachieving black youth.

Government-mandated integration, as noted by Dr. Terrence Roberts, one of the Little Rock Nine students, just wasn't enough to counteract the legacy of racism.

> [I]f you do something for 335 years, no matter what it is, you don't come to a screeching halt in 1954, whether it's the Supreme Court or any other court.

After *Brown v. Board of Education*, black schools were either shuttered or further deprived of resources. Millions of black kids throughout the country were bused out of their neighborhoods into white school districts. Black teachers, principals, parents, and students abandoned neighborhoods and headed for suburbia seeking the promise of superior education. Many black kids were cast from protective environments and placed in schools where they weren't wanted, weren't understood, and weren't treated as able or equal. In her book *Walking in Circles: The Black Struggle for School Reform* (published posthumously in 2007), legendary educator Barbara Sizemore bluntly wrote that the *Brown* decision "led us down a dangerous path, which began when we agreed to say anything all black was all bad."

Integrated Inferiority

Although integration was sold as the necessary step toward black academic excellence, in reality it was a plunge into the quicksand of failure. As Carter G. Woodson stressed almost 80 years ago, blacks had integrated into a system that "...inspires and stimulates the oppressor with the thought that he is everything and has accomplished everything worthwhile, depresses and crushes at the same time the spark of genius in the Negro by making him feel that his race does not amount to much and never will measure up to the standards of other peoples."

The promise of black achievement had been intricately intertwined with a system in which blacks had no control. Julian Weissglass, director of the National Coalition for Equity in Education, described how educational institutions, powered by people conditioned to, "consciously or unconsciously," act and react in certain ways, has caused tremendous harm:

> I contend that although no one is born prejudiced, many of the assumptions, values, and practices of people and institutions hinder the learning of students of color and students from low socioeconomic classes. Race and class biases in particular are major causes of differential success.

Subtle, blatant, conscious, or unconscious attitudes lead educators to expect less of black and Latino students than of whites. It impacts curriculum, policies, and how funds are allocated to public schools. These attitudes, as Weissglass noted, factor into the popular practice of "tracking"—where disproportionate numbers of black and Latino

students are relegated to low tracks, most often with less experienced teachers. Children consigned to these tracking programs are rarely reclassified, even after they've shown improvement.

Educational theorists and scholars, eager to escape the implications of the past, are unaware of the BI campaign. They compare black achievement with students who have not been permanently typecast as "less than." Asian students, for example, have not internalized the stigma that they are "less intelligent" than whites. Children may not be able to identify the subtleties of institutionalized racism, but they are aware of how teachers and policies make them feel. Unable to comprehend the feeling that they are less intelligent or worthwhile than whites, many young people simply give up hope, rejecting the negativity and the school system itself.

Our History Lesson

A historical comparison of the present-day "D's will do" dynamic aligns with our trek from slavery to *Brown v. Board of Education*. It illustrates the complexity of our dilemma and the overwhelming success of the BI campaign.

D's Will Do: Connecting the Dots

Contemporary Manifestations	Historical Roots
Fear of failure: Parents attempt to avoid expectations of failure. Out of fear, they stifle a child's urge to attempt academic success.	During slavery, it was best to blend in rather than stand out, particularly in the area of intelligence or literacy. There was hell to pay for independent thinking.

Misguided protection: Defensive parents want to protect black kids and themselves from feelings of inferiority. Parents want their kids to feel good about themselves and not be stigmatized as failures.	We were brainwashed as slaves to believe in our inherent inferiority and that we were predestined for failure. Attempts at bettering ourselves were often met with violence and defeat.
Success neurosis: Discouraging black children from moving ahead of the group without challenging them to buck negative attitudes and trends.	Slaves believed they were weak and mentally inferior. Such people need to be coddled and protected from their deficiencies.
The "best black" syndrome: Fear of failure has led blacks to compensate by redefining success on so-called realistic terms. To protect our sense of worth, we've created segregated categories for black achievement.	Brainwashing subordinated and segregated blacks and black life into separate categories—black food, black clothes. Indeed all things black were substandard. In self-defense, we internalized our difference and defended against all who used it to harm us.

Identifying our historical links is but the first stage in addressing the "D's will do" dynamic. The real challenge is to come up with a collective way to help black parents and their kids become their own saviors.

Back to Africa Education

At the age of 14, Don Luther Lee was an angry, disillusioned teen, barely surviving in the ghetto of Detroit, Michigan. His father had abandoned the family. Later in life, Lee described his mother as resigned to work in the "sex trade." Still, she was the one who encouraged him to read. Lee recalled his feelings that day in the late 1950s when his mother sent him to the public library to check out Richard Wright's novel *Black Boy*:

I didn't want to go to a white librarian and ask for a black book. I didn't want to check out anything black...I hated myself. I had been taught to hate myself. All of the commercials and the American institutions taught white supremacy...Finally, I went to the library, found the book and sat down and started reading. For the first time, I was reading something that sounded like me, that looked like me.

Lee, better known today as Haki Madhubuti—poet, author, intellectual, and founder of Third World Press—has often described how Wright's book changed his life:

For the first time in my 14 years on Earth, I was reading literature that was not an insult to my own personhood and that was the beginning of this journey that I've been on for the last 45, 50 years...I stopped feeling sorry for myself. I stopped feeling inferior.

In 1969, Madhubuti cofounded the Institute of Positive Education, which, in 1972, opened the New Concept Development Center, an elementary school designed to educate kids while steering them away from "white enculturation." He started the school during the pinnacle of the "black power" movement, when a thirst for self-expression and exploration of authentic black culture was at its peak. It was a time when educators, activists, and college students championed the cause for racially inclusive curricula and African-centered approaches to education.

Although some schools focusing strictly on African-centered education have excelled in closing the achievement gap, others started in the '60s and '70s fizzled. Most of the schools were established to right a wrong, to be anti-white, to inspire black children with stories of black achievement and embellished accounts of black superiority. So intent were idealists to create the "best black" institutions, some fell into the trap of low expectations, failing to prepare kids to succeed outside the cocoon of blackness. Like schools established after the periods of Emancipation, Reconstruction, and legalized integration, most of the African-centered educational models turned out to be promising experiments cut short by the overwhelming power of a BI Complex–influenced nation.

Success from Within

Today, 55 years after the *Brown v. Board of Education* ruling, a perfect storm of factors has scuttled African American student achievement: economic isolation of the poor in high-crime neighborhoods; re-segregation that re-created all-black, under-resourced schools; concentration of the system's worst and most overworked teachers in these learning institutions; the waning of the nation's industrial economy; the erosion of the black extended family and value systems; the deadly drug trade; gun proliferation; and, most damaging, media that celebrates violence, materialism, and underachievement.

Yet when it comes to the question of control, there are two distinct categories: people who either take responsibility for what happens in their lives or those who credit outside forces—luck, God, relationships, education, jobs, and so forth. Noted psychologist Julian Rotter identified these behavioral types as "externals" and "internals." People with an external view attribute their experiences to outside forces. People with an internal orientation believe they control their own destinies.

Due to our historical state of "powerlessness," too many of us believe that our destinies are dictated by the whim of outside (read "white") forces, which dovetails conveniently with a system that reinforces black inferiority. Consider recent research conducted by Dr. David Williams of the University of Michigan that illustrates how a large number of whites still views blacks negatively:

- 29 percent think blacks are unintelligent
- 45 percent believe blacks are lazy
- Less than one in five thinks blacks are hard-working
- 56 percent of whites feel blacks would rather live on welfare than work

Common sense should alert us to the likelihood that many who harbor such feelings are interacting with black students—either as policymakers, administrators, or teachers. How can anyone who consciously or subconsciously adheres to the principles of black

inferiority help black kids see themselves as not inferior? How can such individuals possibly motivate kids to connect the rewards of education with the possible rewards of communities they have been conditioned to disrespect and disregard?

Superficial black history reminders won't be enough. Black kids need an anti-brainwashing curriculum aimed at demonstrating to them that the negativity in their lives has nothing to do with any kind of inherent deficiency or inability to achieve. With a narrative of white superiority actively in play and a large percentage of whites who still doubt black potential, I sincerely question their ability or willingness to invest in increasing race-based self-esteem in black youth.

Whatsamatta with You?

For decades, scholars, educators, politicians, and media pundits have approached the black educational achievement gap from an outsider's position, pointing accusatory fingers at black parents and children without exploring the toxic and counterproductive environment in which they are expected to succeed. Instead of asking "What's wrong with kids?" we should determine what's so utterly wrong with the "D's will do" dynamic.

Short-term Benefits

1. **Fear of failure:** If a child's desire to succeed is discouraged, the parents and the child never have to worry about failing to meet expectations. They are protected from disappointment.

2. **Misguided protection:** Prevents a biased society from messing with the minds of black kids. By setting low goals and keeping expectations to a minimum, no one gets hurt.

3. **Success neurosis:** Insures black children are part of the group. They aren't ostracized or made to feel like

outsiders by underachievers. They can fit in and be popular without stress.

4. **The "best black" syndrome:** By having a separate category of black achievement, children can accomplish achievable goals without worrying about whites who are at an advantage due to centuries of societal, economic, and educational preference.

Long-term Costs

1. **Fear of failure:** Human beings learn from mistakes. Stifling children's ability out of fear of failure increases the chances that they will fail. Efforts to avoid expectations of failure are fruitless. The children grow up to give up and retreat when faced with possibility.

2. **Misguided protection:** Actually endorses the doctrine of black inferiority. Instead of protecting kids from a biased society, parents actually make them vulnerable within that society. Setting low goals and keeping low expectations stifles children's ability to be the best they can be.

3. **Success neurosis:** Limiting children's achievement so they can fit in with underachievers guarantees that they will be underachievers for life. They are also denied the challenge of becoming comfortable with their unique selves and their ability to excel academically.

4. **The "best black" syndrome:** Creating separate categories of black achievement gives children an artificial sense of accomplishment. It also encourages the belief that whites are superior and can't be challenged.

Of course, black parents must play a crucial role, but the role must be redefined. Just as being the "best black" is inadequate, performing on the same level as whites is not good enough, either. Working to achieve superior performance in an inferior system isn't enough to prepare black children to improve so they see themselves as viable players or change agents in the global marketplace. Three important endeavors will help get us where we need to be—reprogram young minds, develop a new approach to African American education, and create a portfolio of positive propaganda tools to promote, protect, and reinforce a new education system.

Empowered to Empower

Once we're rid of the idea that we are "less than," we can begin to empower our children. We no longer tolerate friends, family members, or our children's peers who ridicule or put them down because they excel academically. We can celebrate our children's attempts to go beyond academic mediocrity and persuade them that they can aim for goals worthy of anybody.

D's Won't Do—
Positive Propoganda Cues

Wise up about dumbing down
It's *not* cool to not know.

Nerds: From ridiculed to really cool
You don't have to hide your books, your smarts, or your scholarship. Say it loud, "I'm smart and I'm proud!"

Wanna get over? Raise the bar!
Real success comes with extra effort and genuine accomplishment.

Good enough is *not* good enough!
In any area of your life, don't settle for mediocrity. Try to do the most you're capable of.

Improper Crisis/ Proper Procedure

Education experts are keeping an eye on the Afrikan Centered Education Collegium Campus (ACECC) in Kansas City, Missouri. The 40-acre campus, which opened in 2007, serves mostly black pre-kindergarten through 12th grade students. Teachers stress cultural pride and "expected greatness" as students strive for academic excellence. In 2007, all the schools on the campus met the Average Yearly Progress (AYP) standard mandated by the national "No Child Left Behind" Act.

The schools are the brainchild of educator Audrey Bullard, who worked as a teacher in Liberia for 18 months more than 30 years ago. In 1991, Bullard led a grassroots effort with other educators and parents to transform J.S. Chick Elementary in Kansas City into a school with an African-centered curriculum. The school has consistently scored as one of the top schools in the school district, with 48 percent of its students scoring at the proficient or advanced levels on the Missouri Assessment Program (MAP) fourth-grade math test in 2005. Comparatively, only 24 percent of black students and 36 percent of white students statewide scored as high that year. Although the approach relies heavily on parental involvement and an innovative curriculum, it offers another important component: students are taught to see themselves as contributors, leaders, potential entrepreneurs, and valuable parts of their communities.

The Betty Shabazz International Charter School in Chicago, founded by Madhubuti and his wife Safisha, is an institution that teaches black children that *they* control their lives and futures. It's a crucial factor, Madhubuti said:

You can't minimize the importance of cultural knowledge…you cannot build a healthy child—most certainly, he or she will not have a healthy world view—if he or she does not see himself or herself involved creatively in the development of civilization, culture, industry, science.

In 2006, the school ranked first in composite test scores among 10 public schools in the Greater Grand Crossing area, where Shabazz is the only charter. Sixty-seven percent of the school's students met the state's educational standards. When teaching science, for example, Makita Kheperu, principal at Shabazz, explained how the school makes the subject relevant to a student's environment: "In science, they examine what kinds of decisions scientists make…and they learn the scientific method by exploring culturally relevant questions like: Why is diabetes more prevalent among African Americans than the general population?"

According to Illinois State data, Shabazz and Woodlawn Community School—another African-centered Chicago school—outperformed several neighboring schools on the 2006 Illinois Standard Achievement Test, with about 68 percent of Woodland's students meeting the state's standards.

These schools reflect the unfinished business of educational experiments started after Emancipation with the likes of Booker T. Washington, W.E.B. Du Bois, and the dreamers who sought to establish independent black schools before they were sidetracked by the promise of better education in white schools. These institutions offer templates for educational reform that can reprogram parents and students to help close the achievement gap, and open bold new pathways to unlimited possibility.

Chapter 9

Bred to Be Led

Why Do We So Willingly Give Up Control of Our Lives?

Now, we're not really giving knowledge, and we're not giving educational information. What we're doing is teaching people how to "fly in the spirit"…"Oh, the Spirit did it, Oh, I'm waiting on God, Oh, the Lord will do it!"…The Church is trying to hide behind spirituality, when God is saying; "I've given you power, now you've got to get wisdom!"

— JUANITA BYNUM

Speaking in Atlanta, Georgia, before a group of clergy at the 2007 Gospel Baptist Conference, Juanita Bynum, internationally known Pentecostal televangelist, author, and gospel singer, confessed she planned to deliver a hard message: instead of providing knowledge, educational information, and directing church members to realize that they have inherent God-given power, churches are still encouraging parishioners to simply wait on the Lord to solve their problems. Bynum preached:

> Now, there's been a switch: the people that are in the pews have got themselves together, and the people in the pulpit (are) playing games! We cannot keep coming to the body of Christ, preaching baby messages, and babysitting the people of God! The church has got to get up: It's time to go!

I'm not sure how deeply Bynum has explored the subject. Her sermon was aimed at church leaders, not at the "people in the pews" who enable the ministers she chastised. Either way, she provides a serendipitous segue into our next topic: transferred responsibility. Somewhere in our American odyssey, we have turned over control of our lives and destinies, not only to the church, the original leaders of the African American community, but also to the leaders of civil rights and secular organizations. These selected emissaries articulate our frustrations and concerns, and tackle racial and social injustices in our name. African Americans have been conditioned to turn their personal power over to men and women who encourage them to "wait on God" or depend on external forces.

The Danger of Dependency

If implicitly, we teach people victimhood as their core self-identification, we are not teaching self-responsibility. We are teaching dependency and impotence. The danger is that they will feel "somebody has to do something, and that if the rescuer does not come, they are doomed."
— Nathaniel Branden

We will look into the origin of the black church and how it provided the template of leadership for today's black secular organizations. But we first need to underscore the psychological rewards and costs when one keeps or gives up control of one's life.

In our chapter on the African American achievement gap, we briefly touched on Dr. Julian Rotter's 1966 internal-external "locus of control" studies. Rotter basically developed a means to determine high or low levels of control by rating individual beliefs. If someone thinks their life circumstances are under the control of outside forces, they have a low level of control. If, on the other hand, a person believes things happen based primarily on their own behavior and resources, or "inside forces," they have a high level of control.

Those who recognize the power of the "inside force" are believed to be more psychologically adjusted, have higher self-esteem and influence over others, and accomplish more because they believe they have more control over their lives than those who believe their lives are under the control of "outside forces."

Pull of the Pulpit

In the church, and through the minister, you can find all the answers. In fact, they are all written down for you. You don't even have to think your way through the Bible: that's the minister's job.
— David, coach, 36

What I find compelling about the black church is that embodied within its structure are all the key elements of a classic marketing/ advertising campaign: objective, strategy, and tactics. The stated objective is to spread the gospel and offer solace and salvation. The tactics are multifaceted, ranging from street-corner ministries to stadium-sized, megachurch services. The pervasive messaging includes books, Web sites, speaking tours, televised revivals, and more. There's plenty of merchandise to reinforce the brand, including books, videos, and everything else, from holy water to holy hankies.

If there's any doubt about the institution's marketing power, watch a megachurch worshiping gala on Sunday morning cable. You will see loyal parishioners packed in spacious auditoriums, mass choirs, professional bands, video visuals, praise dancers, praise teams, and a high-tech emotional revival that would compete with any Super Bowl halftime show.

This form of church worship has become a master media marketer, delivering influential messages enhanced with holy glitz and pious passion. What may go undetected, however, is another form of the black inferiority marketing campaign. As it pertains to the church, it's God-mandated inferiority.

Come, All Ye Sinners

*The implications are there: We are sinners. We can't help it; it is
in our nature. So the only medicine, the only way to get "right" is
to go to church every week, and get your weekly dose.*
— Delores, 45, teacher

Mainstream Christianity programmed us to accept and embrace
suffering and oppression. Although it's a general religious precept
that we are all "sinners," blacks were taught that their skin color and
servile position in life were heavenly markers of earthly damnation. The
black sinners' BI programming was so convincing that we ourselves
adopted and perpetrated the conviction. Our religious leaders teach
the Christian ideal of redemptive suffering as personified in the form
of Jesus. We suffer here. We gain salvation in heaven. We suffered
enslavement and apartheid dehumanization *for our own good.* We
continue to suffer *for our own good.*

Tom Krattenmaker, an expert on religion and member of *USA
Today*'s board of contributors, noted that the concept of God standing
"with the dispossessed against the scourge of dehumanizing racism" is
deeply embedded in black religious history. These experts of theological
propaganda have an inside track with blacks whose identity is tightly
wound around perceptions of inferiority, poverty, and helplessness.
The subtle but inescapable conclusion: should we no longer qualify
as oppressed and downtrodden, we would no longer be part of the
Christian community. This concept can be traced all the way back to
our Christian indoctrination beneath the yoke of enslavement.

Bred to Be Led Dynamics

The following Bred to Be Led dynamics reflect our dependence on
the hereafter, on black ministers, and black leaders. They reveal how
and why, in this day and age, blacks are still such loyally conditioned
followers.

- **Religious resignation:** Que sera, sera...I accept God's will without question. I will "Wait on God!" I will not reach beyond what is given.

- **Addicted to suffering:** Wretchedness is my natural state and my birthright. If I suffer gladly now, my reward will be in heaven.

- **Makes me wanna holla:** The need for preachers or leaders who connect to our emotional vulnerability, then give us hope and lead us through our challenges and troubles. They relieve us of the burden of responsibility.

- **Prosperity gospel:** Attachment to ministers who teach and preach the "need for greed." We willingly allow them to take congregants' money without benefit for the flock.

- **Leadership dependency:** The expectation that organized secular groups will speak and act in our behalf. The sense of helplessness if the organizational leaders do not offer direction or marching orders.

The introduction of plantation-style Christianity and the black preacher; the formation of the black church and its extension into the civil rights movement; our acquiescence to church and political leaders—all are, unfortunately, branches of a tree rooted in 17th-century soil. But before examining the modern-day black church's offshoots and extensions, we must focus on the genesis of the first, most powerful black force—religion.

Upon This Rock

This battle is not yours
It's the Lord's, not yours...
— Yolanda Adams, "The Battle Is Not Yours"

What do Nannie Helen Burroughs, Adam Clayton Powell, Jr., Martin Luther King, Jr., former Congressman Walter Fauntroy, and former executive director of the NAACP Benjamin Hooks have in common? All were or are active in the arena of social justice and all have roots in the black church. The transition from the church to civil rights leadership is a natural one. The most organized black struggle was birthed in the black church. The same theme of oppression and hierarchal redress runs through the arteries of both entities. Like ministers, secular leaders are at the ready to ferret out and confront acts of transgression on behalf of the flock. Like churches, our major civil rights organizations are funded to act for us, not to encourage individual responsibility.

In the post–civil rights era, some organizations have attempted to correct educational and economic disadvantage. They attack racial and economic disparities, and other important and worthwhile issues. But that's akin to treating the symptoms and ignoring the disease.

In the 21st century, the problem for African Americans has less to do with blatant racism than with its imprint on our psyches. We've been brainwashed to internalize the myth of inferiority and have not yet wrested our image from the original mythmakers. The Massa's gift of religion wasn't to empower but to contain, to keep the slave's attention heavenward. The term "black leader" is a throwback to a time when the slavemaster designated one slave as his spokesman, or spy.

Do We Have to Go There?

Is it possible that these seminal African American institutions also play a part in the brainwashing process? To many, the very suggestion is tantamount to attacking the church and civil rights organizations, and all of their considerable contributions. It's one of those "don't go there" subjects. We have been programmed to be so defensive about all things black, the mere topic threatens to become another zero-sum game: you're either for it or against it, pro-religion or anti-religion, pro-black or a sellout. Even so, I maintain that it would be a disservice to our people if we did not examine the complicit role of churches and secular organizations in the BI campaign.

It would also be an incomplete exploration if we ignored how those roots, over the years, have grown a branch of what Minister Claudette A. Copeland calls "toxic churches," in which "pastoral care has come to mean care of the pastor with no guarantees of care by the pastor."

This chapter is an attempt to dig up the soil to examine the roots, to replant and fertilize the crop for a bumper yield. The black church and secular institutions have been and continue to be major forces of great power and influence. But, as the old saying goes, "With great power, comes great responsibility."

God-Sanctioned Servitude

Seems like niggers jus' got to pray. Half they life am in prayin'. Some nigger take turn 'bout to watch and see if Marse Tom anyways 'bout, then they circle theyselves on the floor in the cabin and pray. They git to moanin' low and gentle, "Some day, some day, some day, this yoke gwine be lifted offen our shoulders."
— William Moore, WPA Slave Narrative Project

To keep his property under control, the slavemaster routinely stamped out any sign of emerging leadership. Thus, he was able to train slave leaders who fit his agenda and destroy those who did not, wrote leading black psychologist Dr. Na'im Akbar in his essay, "Breaking the Chains of Psychological Slavery." Most slaveowners, however, relied on another popular means of control—religion.

Here, it's important to state the obvious: Slaves were taught to worship a white savior. Even though the literal Biblical description is of Jesus as a swarthy Middle Easterner, most available images present him as Nordic, Germanic, blue-eyed, blond—unambiguously white. With this slanted depiction is the assumption that Jesus's father, God, shares his son's pigmentation. Slaves were taught from both testaments of the Bible that a vengeful God created them to be perpetual servants of His superior white children.

This reliance on religion as a controlling force introduced what historian John Hope Franklin described as the "third strand braided between our enslavement and our liberation":

> Once the planters were convinced that conversion did not have the effect of setting their slaves free they sought to use the church as an agency for maintaining the institution of slavery. Ministers were encouraged to instruct the slaves along the lines of obedience and subserviency.

With subtle manipulation, slaveowners and preachers used Bible passages, such as Colossians 3:22, to validate the wretchedness of the enslaved:

> Servants, obey in all things your masters according to the flesh; not with eyeservice, as menpleasers; but in singleness of heart, fearing God.

By the beginning of the 19th century, the strange "braid" of African American Christianity was clearly established: a liberating impulse entwined with an enslaving constriction. Noah's Curse, or "the curse of Ham," central to slave Christian teaching, was but one convenient contrivance used to drive home the message of eternal black servitude. Though nothing in the passage states or even remotely suggests skin color, from medieval times forward, the passage was used to explain that dark-skinned people were the result of a curse from God for licentious behavior.

Christianization of slaves boomed after the religious revival movement, known as the First and Second Great Awakenings, swept through the South in the late 1700s. The enthusiastic form of worship—singing, shouting, dancing, handclapping—and the teaching that blacks, like whites, could receive personal salvation, appealed to slaves. Large numbers adopted the predominant religion of the slavemaster—the Methodist and Baptist faiths.

Still, blacks openly accepted the premise that God allowed their enslavement so that they could gain the benefits of Christian salvation. Of course, black abolitionists and some black preachers railed against this notion. Nevertheless, even when rejecting a racist God and using Christianity to promote liberation, a seed of self-loathing remained—the idea of blacks as uncivilized lesser beings in need of the white savior.

The Lovable, Dependable Black Preacher

The concept is simple, and it reads like this: We're so far gone that we need to have this preacher tell us HIS interpretation of the Bible, and tell us how to get closer to God. These things are, in essence, things that we should and could do for ourselves.
— Delores

Slave rebellions led by Gabriel Prosser in 1800 in Virginia and Denmark Vesey in South Carolina in 1822 panicked slaveholders into strictly regulating religious practices. Although the plantation preacher was most often white, some slaveowners allowed black slaves to preach a limited form of Gospel. Although they were "coerced into publicly parroting a version of Christianity compatible with the slave order," author William Banks wrote in *Black Intellectuals: Race and Responsibility in American Life*, slave ministers found ways to frame the Christian message differently.

In Massa's presence, he emphasized obedience and heavenly rewards. Behind his back, within the invisible church (slave galleries in white churches or the slave quarters), many black preachers reworked their sermons, passed along vital information among separated slave families and, at times, even helped plot escapes. Roles as trusted, cunning intermediaries between slavery and spiritual salvation earned the black preacher an enduring, cherished place among the enslaved and their descendants.

The Colored Way:
Black Organizations

According to what was issued out in the Bible, there was a time
for slavery, people had to be punished for their sin, and then there
was a time for it not to be, and the Lord had opened a good view
to Mr. Lincoln, and he promoted a good idea.
— Charlie Aarons, former slave

After slavery, many black religious leaders ventured beyond the parameters of church matters. The Free African Society, the precursor to the African Methodist Episcopal church, for example, was such an organization. Established in 1787 by ex-slaves as a nondenominational mutual aid society, the agency set out to tackle a full range of issues and needs that, according to its mission statement, "were not addressed in the regular church gatherings and social opportunities of Philadelphia."

In 1905, a group of 32 determined, freethinking black men met on the Canadian side of Niagara Falls to contemplate strategies and solutions to address racist barriers "people of color" faced mostly in the South. The group, known as The Niagara Movement, struggled financially and eventually disbanded in 1910. Before doing so, three whites had become members. Those whites were still members when the Niagara Movement morphed into the National Association for the Advancement of Colored People (NAACP), founded in 1909.

Considering the times, perhaps it was a good strategy to tone down the drastic platform of the Niagara Movement and create a more racially inclusive NAACP. Or perhaps it was a way to ensure that the solicitations sent out to 60 prominent Americans were returned with a monetary endorsement. What is known is that when the NAACP incorporated in 1911, it was a predominantly white agency with only one black executive board member, W.E.B. Du Bois.

Alliances with powerful whites exposed black organizations to influences from the dominant culture. For instance, Evelyn Brooks

Higginbotham, author of *Righteous Discontent: The Women's Movement in the Black Baptist Church, 1880–1920*, detailed the double-edged ramifications of the alliances between Southern black women and Northern white women in their Southern missionary efforts. The black groups often adopted the prevailing Victorian notion that black immorality was the true cause of discrimination. Black women, working with white women's societies, urged blacks to prove themselves worthy by mirroring white society.

Just as the slavemaster chose leadership that didn't threaten his rule and helped contain unpredictable, possibly radical blacks, prominent African Americans, once freed, adhered to similar agendas. Black organizations in the early 20th century, including the NAACP, turned to whites not only to fund their efforts but also to help set the tone and agenda for acceptable practices.

Such alliances tend to temper individual acts that whites may consider too radical. One has to wonder if the leaders of these organizations were in a position to take a stand as firm as the one taken by Warmoth T. Gibbs in 1960. At the time, black students at North Carolina Agricultural and Technical University in Greensboro, North Carolina, had begun lunch counter sit-ins at the local Woolworth and street protests aimed at ending segregation. Local white Greensboro officials and business owners went to Gibbs, the newly appointed president emeritus of the university, and strongly urged him to use his authority to reign in the unruly young demonstrators. Gibbs declined, offering a response one doesn't hear often from today's black clerics or civil rights leaders: "We teach our students how to think, not what to think."

Lost in Transition

> *We are a very black organization, but we ain't just a black organization, y'all: we're a human rights organization! We're a civil rights organization, and we fight for the dignity of all people in this country!*
> — NAACP president Ben Jealous

Speaking before a crowd during the NAACP's 100th Anniversary Convention, the organization's newly elected president, 36-year-old Rhodes Scholar Ben Jealous, made the announcement that the NAACP was strong and the agency was "winning!"

Jealous went on to list a number of NAACP accomplishments, including helping to redirect millions of dollars in stimulus money toward public schools; removing a "Confederate swastika [flag]" from state grounds in South Carolina; and delivering "the first woman of color [Judge Sonia Sotomayor] to a seat on the Supreme Court!"

Of all the accomplishments Jealous claimed for the NAACP, he failed to note that the organization didn't close the black achievement gap, didn't lower black-on-black crime, or help millions of blacks rise from poverty and unemployment, and the NAACP didn't create wholesome families or self-sustaining communities. Helping to direct federal money toward public schools, removing a racist symbol, and supporting a Hispanic Supreme Court judge are all worthwhile. But the word "winning," as far as I'm concerned, represents a disconnect between some esteemed secular organizations and the people they seek to serve.

Consider the results of a 2006 *Washington Post* survey in which black men were asked about the greatest problems facing their communities. In their responses, "racial discrimination" ranked 20 percentage points behind "black men not taking their educations seriously enough" and "too many black men becoming involved with crime." These findings indicate that the general population understands the important issues more than the leadership.

In early 2007, Bruce Gordon, then NAACP president, announced that he was stepping down after a brief tenure. He stated that he wanted the NAACP to expand its mission to include social service. Julian Bond, NAACP board chairperson at the time, stated: "Our mission is to fight discrimination and provide social justice. Social service organizations deal with the effects of racial discrimination. We deal with the beast itself."

We interviewed Gordon in preparation for this book. It seems the retired president of Verizon's retail markets division met some resistance in his attempt to steer the NAACP in a different direction:

"The big debate that I finally realized that I was not going to win was my desire to get us to be more accountable for our situation, and to stop thinking and acting as though the only way to do civil rights is to do it from a victim's point of view."

The NAACP, Gordon added, hadn't accepted the concept of advocating within black communities: "We don't need to spend all of our time getting white folks to do for us...we need to advocate within our own houses, our own families, our own communities. So I was clearly on a path to push for accountability...and they just were not hearing it.

"Old-school social change organizations are just that, 'old-school,'" he said, "and if they don't reinvent themselves, they will continue to decline in importance."

What some dismissed as divergent leadership styles within the NAACP was really an example of the ineffective leadership of some top secular organizations. Yes, they have done remarkable work in toppling legal and institutional race barriers. They've mastered the art of battling "the beast"—the external forces of racism. They have not, however, developed a means to maim the internal beast that's devouring our minds, lives, and communities.

Civil Rights in the Corporate Era

I'm not the one who's confused. You don't even know who you are.
— Rafika

When it comes to attacking the inner beast—the self-hatred, low self-esteem, and helplessness that fuels the nation's disproportionately high black dropout, crime, and poverty rates—traditional black organizations seem woefully stuck in an antiquated model. Furthermore, the sustainability of many of these black organizations depends on multiracial, well-endowed external sources, which limits their scope and their influence. One long-established civil rights organization recently listed seven corporations that donated $1,000,000 or more, and nine that donated between $500,000 and $1,000,000.

Having spent my life in corporate advertising, I can say with absolute certainty that corporations do not give money away for nothing. They give with the expectation of getting something in return. At its most benevolent, that something is good will. At its most pernicious, it is to be inoculated from criticism, and given support when criticism arises.

Most of the leading black organizations' donors include corporations with some of the most controversial business models in America—non-union retailers, large pharmaceutical companies, and insurance giants. These companies have nothing to gain from black groups that promote independent thinking. Critical thought encourages people to follow the money to find answers to burning social questions. It may compel them to support black competitors or withdraw support from companies whose practices are considered predatory or otherwise harmful to minority consumers.

A corporation also has to consider its public image. Mythmakers have done an admirable job of flipping the race debate on its ear. In the so-called "post-racial" environment, self-empowering black agendas are now widely dismissed as "separatist" or "racist." It's hard to imagine corporate money flowing to black organizations that start programs designed to expose and reverse a campaign that has warped our self-image and reinforced our sense of inferiority.

To be fair, major black organizations are forced to depend on corporate sponsorship. Since blacks have been conditioned to rely on outside forces, they tolerate these alliances. Companies pay a form of race penance in exchange for the positive PR that derives from being associated with an organization committed to uplifting blacks.

Double-helixed into our cultural DNA, it seems, is this paradoxical habit of depending on outsiders to save our race. Slavery is not totally dead. It's just been sanitized, modified, and modernized. We still look to the "master" for approval, guidance, and support. We reason that since we have no power, we need to be saved by somebody else—usually white corporate businesses or organizations. The social service organization is therefore tethered on a leash of learned helplessness that guarantees it will never, ever bite the hand that feeds it.

A History of Holy Dependence

Reviewing the history of the black church and its expansion into the civil rights arena reveals how the Bred to Be Led dynamics were and are still such a powerful force.

Bred to Be Led: Connecting the Dots

Contemporary Manifestations	Historical Roots
Religious resignation: I will "Wait on God!" and accept whatever is His will. I will not reach beyond what is given.	Slaves could escape and risk their lives, go mad, or learn to live without the freedom to control their own destiny. In most cases, we chose delusion over madness and/or death. We replaced hope in the present with hope in God and the hereafter.
Addicted to suffering: Wretchedness is my natural state and my birthright. If I suffer gladly now, my reward will be greater in heaven.	Government-sanctioned slavery relied upon the religious principle of redemptive suffering. Slaves' wretchedness and suffering were God's will. Blacks accepted the promise of heavenly rewards and worshipped a white God to gain a passport to eternity.
Makes me wanna holla: Preachers or leaders who tap into our emotional vulnerability through powerful oratory that relieves our pain, gives us hope, and leads us through our challenges and troubles. They also relieve us of the burden of responsibility.	The master-appointed slave preacher and the black church played a critical role in relieving the burden of oppression. Unquestioning dependence on religion and religious leaders for guidance squelched independent thought. Brainwashing elevated emotional responses over thought and manipulated our faith in outside forces.

199

Prosperity gospel: Ministers teach and preach the "need for greed." We willingly allow them to take congregants' money without creating true benefits for the flock.	We learned to accept our innate status as "inferior." Only men and women of God were supernaturally superior. Our need for salvation is so ingrained that we are willing to pay any cost to the gifted deliverer of emotional salvation.
Leadership dependency: The expectation that organized community groups will speak and act on our behalf. Sense of helplessness rooted in the belief that organization leaders will direct us or issue marching orders.	Illiteracy and oppression made many slaves believe that they were incapable of functioning without strong leadership. Leaders are designated as "superior" to think, speak for, and lead us.

Starting to Do Good/ Continuing to Do Well

There is a self-serving aspect that the race card has helped a lot of people. It's been the fallback position in lieu of critical thinking. You just whip it out. It's similar to "the devil you know is better than the devil you don't know." We know how to play that card. We have not a clue of what hand we'll wind up with if we give that up.
— Reverend Carrie Jackson, minister, New York

Years ago, I joined a newly formed black organization dedicated to promoting black business development. A major, white Fortune 100 corporation allowed us to hold our meetings at its headquarters. The firm always had a host to meet and greet us and sit in on our meetings.

One time, company officials told us there was a scheduling conflict and the facilities we used would not be available. Minor panic set in. Organizers fretted about what to do. Somewhat sarcastically, I suggested that perhaps we, as business owners, could have the meetings at one of our companies. We could even buy our own coffee and sweet rolls and, for once, hold a meeting without corporate oversight.

Surprisingly, it was an "aha" moment. Apparently, it hadn't occurred to my colleagues that we could actually function without outside help. Part of the "learned helplessness" conditioning requires that we buy into the idea that organizations cannot survive without outside interests funding their very survival. From my perspective, it's better to meet in a church basement and eat on our own dime than to gather at Four Seasons and dine on gourmet meals, compliments of white benefactors.

Some black organizations are now so large and venerable that self-preservation and organizational growth are their principal concerns. Without disease and illness, we wouldn't need doctors and the healthcare system; without criminals and crime, police officers and the prison industrial complex would serve very little purpose. Likewise, without overt racism, there would be little purpose for black leaders or organizations with constricted race-based agendas. With no other bucket to cast down, it may be in their best interest to maintain—not solve—the race problem.

Passing the Plate for Truth

The need for radical change becomes more urgent when we weigh the temporary benefits of supporting outmoded institutions against the long-term costs of promoting collective obsolescence.

Short-term Benefits

1. **Religious resignation:** Accepting whatever God has willed and waiting on heavenly rewards remove the burden to individually draft our own fortunes and futures, and makes us feel better about bad situations that we can't control.

2. **Addicted to suffering:** Provides a biblical rationale for our perceived wretchedness. If it's our natural state and birthright, then we can tolerate suffering with the hope of heavenly reward.

3. **Makes me wanna holla:** Hope is a valuable commodity. We gain immediate gratification from ministers who lead us through challenges and relief from the personal burden of actually doing something.

4. **Prosperity gospel:** Our value and self-worth are demonstrated through our minister's fame and material achievements. Surely someone who preaches prosperity must look prosperous. Congregants must invest in the blessed messenger in the hope of prospering.

5. **Leadership dependency:** Since we feel unqualified and incapable, it's best to wait on guidance from respected leaders. Following individuals already identified as our leaders, who have the proper connections and clout, simply makes sense.

Long-term Costs

1. **Religious resignation:** Believing that God has willed misfortune upon you reinforces a sense of innate unworthiness. Waiting on heavenly rewards robs you and your family from exploring and finding rewards right here on Earth.

2. **Addicted to suffering:** Perception of divine wretchedness becomes a self-fulfilling prophecy. Believing it is your natural birthright to suffer allows you to unconsciously tolerate or even seek suffering.

3. **Makes me wanna holla:** Seeking external avenues of hope and transferring the burden of responsibility keeps a person in a childlike position while elevating another human being to a Godlike status. Seeking personal gratification through God's minister is like a drug addiction. It can only provide temporary escape.

4. **Prosperity gospel:** Seeing our value and self-worth through the fame and opulence of a religious figure ultimately only benefits the religious figure. You have just as much right to prosperity as the deliverer of the message and a better chance of achieving it through your own initiative.

5. **Leadership dependency:** Waiting on the guidance or actions of a respected leader or organized group robs us of the rewards of individual action. It also reinforces feelings of personal inadequacy. Sometimes the leader with the impressive connections and perceived clout is beholden to the agenda of the agent who granted such privilege.

In *The Mis-Education of the Negro,* Carter G. Woodson urged blacks to seek and demand new levels of leadership. Seek not leaders who ask "what others can do for him," Woodson said. "Seek those who will do for himself."

Bred to Be Led
Positive Propaganda Cues:

In the spirit of creating self-appointed leaders, I offer these positive propaganda cues.

Fellowship not followship
Become a member of a fellowship, a group of people who exchange ideas and openness, rather than a

followship that mindlessly trudges after those who may lead you somewhere you don't want to go.

Don't take *know* for an answer
Question the whole idea of certainty. Be able to recognize the difference between *believing* and *knowing*.

Look for the leader in you
We need to re-orient ourselves to understand our innate strengths and the ability to find, define, and develop our best self.

Forging a New Kind of Leadership

Reverend Johnny Ray Youngblood of Brooklyn's St. Paul Community Baptist Church once saw his church described in the *New York Times* as "one of God's Alcatrazes" because of the depressing, crime-filled surrounding area. Ten years after he became pastor, St. Paul's parishioners have transformed the neighborhood. The church built a school on its property and turned abandoned homes and houses of ill repute into family-owned homes and businesses. Youngblood and his church also played instrumental roles in the construction of some 2,300 single-family homes in Brooklyn.

Part of Youngblood's appeal, wrote Maura Sheehy in the *Christian Science Monitor,* is his ability to "connect the church and spirituality" to the daily lives of his congregation.

"He eschews the more traditional wait-for-deliverance-in-the-promised-land brand of rhetoric for an approach committed to change in the present," Sheehy wrote.

Youngblood's interest in connecting the dots between slavery and its present-day manifestations led to the creation of the annual Commemoration of the MAAFA, "a psychosocial dramatic depiction of the horror of the trans-Atlantic slave trade [that] pays tribute to the millions of men, women, and children who were lost in the government-sanctioned, multi-continent sale of humans."

In 2000, the A.M.E. Church elected Vashti Murphy McKenzie, a former journalist, as its first woman bishop. McKenzie not only broke what she called the stained-glass ceiling, as pastor of Payne Memorial A.M.E. Church in Baltimore, Maryland, she emphasized her management and community-building skills to increase property value from $1.6 to $5.6 million.

McKenzie launched 25 innovative ministries and initiatives, ranging from welfare-to-work programs, to senior-citizen computer classes, to high school job fairs, and to establishing companies, such as a catering service for former welfare recipients. McKenzie expanded her influence by presiding over the A.M.E. Church's 18th Episcopal District, with 200 churches and 10,000 members in Botswana, Mozambique, and Lesotho. I've yet to see McKenzie, who gives new meaning to the phrase "prosperity gospel," on Sunday morning cable trying to convince congregants to buy her a mansion or lease a Bentley.

Initiatives like those of Reverend Youngblood and Bishop McKenzie are representative of ministers who don't oversee celebrity churches. Instead, they use their gift of influence to empower communities. Even if we aren't perfectly aligned with their specific religious beliefs and/or political associations, their do-for-self "best practices" should be studied, adapted, and adopted. Such religious and secular leaders operate outside the maze controlled by powerful benefactors whose gifts are rarely free.

Although we have been conditioned by a lifetime of destructive images and messages, this learned helplessness and unconscious dependency has outlived its usefulness. Reversing this negative inheritance will be difficult—extraordinarily so. As Bruce Gordon said during our interview: "We may not have all of the power we want but we do have all of the power we need." It's time to claim it!

Once we reverse the mind game, once we understand that we need not depend on leaders or any external force for guidance, once we recognize that we are all potential agents of change, it is then—and only then—that we become an empowered people, prepared to think critically and fully engage in self-advocacy.

Chapter 10

Diss-Unity

Why Can't We Stick Together?

All the time they want to take your place
the backstabbers—backstabbers

—THE O'JAYS

The racially ugly tone of the 2007/2008 presidential campaign should have come as no surprise once Barack Obama officially declared his intention to become president of the United States. All 43 men who held the office before him were white. With a viable African American candidate in the race, of course racial paranoia would escalate and be exploited. What did come as a surprise were the derisive, verbal bombs launched by high profile blacks, some of whom, many thought, should have known better. Former United Nations Ambassador and civil rights icon Andrew Young comes to mind. During an Atlanta urban media forum in late 2007, Young decided to wade into the area of heredity and sexual prowess when comparing Obama to former President Bill Clinton, the husband of Hillary Clinton, another candidate in the race. "Bill is every bit as black as Barack," Young quipped, adding, "He's probably gone with more black women than Barack." Young quickly told the audience he was "clowning."

But even when listing Obama's possible strong points if he had to deal with America's biggest threats—China and Islam—Young adopted a condescending and demeaning tone: "He had a Chinese half-sister, his mother married an African first, then she went to Indonesia and married a Chinese. So he grew up in a Chinese family. He went to Islamic schools in Indonesia."

At least Young didn't use the black drug-dealer stereotype. That was Bob Johnson, the founder of BET. In a state of exaggerated hubris in 2008, Johnson went after Obama and his staffers for criticizing remarks made by his chosen candidate, Hillary Clinton, saying, "I am frankly insulted that the Obama campaign would imply that we are so stupid that we would think Hillary and Bill Clinton, who have been deeply and emotionally involved in black issues since Barack Obama was doing something in the neighborhood—and I won't say what he was doing, but he said it in the book—when they have been involved."

Johnson didn't have to spell out that "something." In *Dreams from My Father*, Obama wrote about his youthful alcohol and illegal drug use. As if the not-so-veiled swipe wasn't enough, Johnson, during the same speech, managed to twist the knife further. He compared Obama to the character played by Sidney Poitier in *Guess Who's Coming to Dinner*, a film about a white elderly couple whose world was rocked when their daughter brought her black beau home for dinner. ". . . this ain't a movie, Sidney. This is real life," Johnson snapped. Johnson later issued a statement claiming that his comment at the South Carolina Clinton rally was in reference to Obama's early life as a community organizer in Chicago. I'm not sure which was more insulting—the comment or the explanation.

As a candidate, Obama was fair game for criticism. But Young and Johnson could have campaigned on behalf of Clinton without going personal, without dragging Obama through the mud, without the use of not-authentically-black, drug-abusing, socially coded threats that have been used for centuries to negatively define and divide blacks. In short, the brothers were crabbin' and backstabbin'. In defense of Hillary Clinton, the loyalists initiated personal attacks to keep Obama from winning the nomination.

Crabbin' and backstabbin' are as much a part of our everyday conversations as they are fixtures in our comedy routines. This is far more than just a verbal put-down. It's the full impact of the reflex that many blacks expect the worst from one another, harbor intense jealousy, and go to great lengths to sabotage their own. Just ask yourself: How many times have you encountered a black supervisor who was harder on black employees than his white charges, or was more disrespectful to blacks than any white boss? How often have you been sabotaged on the job by a black co-worker? Has a black friend or relative ever announced that they had to find a white lawyer, doctor, or plumber because they didn't trust blacks in those professions?

Crabbin' and backstabbin' are but a symptom of a much more sinister infirmity—disunity or, as we will often refer to it in this discussion, "diss-unity." In the civil rights and political arenas, crabbin' and backstabbin' are as old as the categories themselves. Some of our history's most impressive, far-reaching agendas have been nullified due to black backbiting and orchestrated disruption. Killing each other is not limited to young brothers on the streets. There are black-on-black drive-bys in the political, entertainment, civic, and business arenas.

This chapter examines how we have subconsciously accepted mistrust and powerlessness. Diss-unity is the handicap that hampers our ability to merge around almost anything, from job-related tasks to progressive, all-encompassing agendas. It is the biggest reason that blacks, as a whole, stay frozen on the lowest rung of society's ladder. Diss-unity is the modern-day manifestation of BI propaganda designed to keep us imprisoned in unconscious states of inferiority and hopelessness.

Disunited and It Feels So Bad

> There is a saying in the black community that blacks cannot improve as a people because, like crabs in a barrel, whenever one tries to climb out of the barrel the other ones will pull him back down.
> — The Disputed Truth blog

A crabbin' and backstabbin' moment in my early career involved a major account in which our ad agency had been significantly undercompensated for the work performed. After much finagling, we gained an audience with both the company's senior vice president, who was white, and a vice president, who was black. The senior VP listened to our concerns and concurred that we deserved more money. He threw out a higher number. We immediately agreed to the suggested amount. Upon seeing where things were headed, the black exec chimed in, blurting, "No, no, no, they don't need that much!" He then recommended a significantly lower amount.

Unfortunately, his boss felt he had no choice but to agree. The original higher number that our client suggested was obviously fair. It's not in any client's best interest to overpay a vendor. But why did the black executive counter his white superior's number? Why did he believe that we didn't "need" (or was it "deserve") that much? Did he think his stature would increase within the company if he demonstrated that he would keep a black-owned agency in its place? Or did he feel that we, as a black-owned agency, simply deserved less than a white-owned firm doing comparable work?

I have replayed that episode over the years and pondered the black executive's motivations. Today, I understand that he was but another victim of the powerful BI campaign. But was he an exception or the norm?

Of all the brainwashing techniques, disunity may be the most pervasive. It directly led to the all-too-prevalent notion that the "white man's ice is colder." It has historically branded black products, services, businesses, and people as inferior, substandard, not good enough. We are so disunited from our authentic selves that we find comfort in artificial boundaries. The East Coast/West Coast rap wars serve as a perfect example of diss-unity gone too far. What started as a new, creative expression of black artistry quickly spiraled downward into gun-toting rivalries between young rappers unable to separate myth from music.

At one time rap was defined by the sugary, benign fun stuff, like "Rappers Delight" by the Sugarhill Gang and "Summertime" by DJ Jazzy Jeff & the Fresh Prince, and tracks by other rappers like Kris Kross and MC Hammer. Politically conscious rap, following the 70s tradition of the Last Poets and Gil Scott-Heron, paved the way for Public Enemy. Somewhere along the line producers of hip-hop came to realize that the real money, the real avenues to fortune and fame, came via music about sex, drugs, and violence: how they "made it" on the carcasses of those who trespassed on their turf—either in the streets or in the industry.

Along the line, powerful forces realized there was gold in black music divisions.

As in a relay race, whites carried the 17th-century baton of black inferiority for centuries and, amazingly, in the 20th and 21st centuries they have been able to pass it off to blacks so they could finish the race—literally.

> *Everything white people don't like about black people,*
> *black people* REALLY *don't like about black people!*
> — Chris Rock, 1997

Chris Rock's routine was funny because we all know obnoxious or self-destructive people. What's not so hilarious is the unrecognized conditioning that feeds such humor. Rock's comment, "Everything white people don't like about black people, black people really don't like about black people," underscores the fact that we have been duped. Today we are proudly repeating the negative sentiments and stereotypes that many whites hold about us.

It's become fashionable for us to disrespect each other and assume that certain blacks will function like modern-day minstrels. We pretend we have the luxury of categorizing ourselves as "niggas" and "blacks" when it's always been a fuzzy distinction many whites use to rationalize discrimination. Numerous business and personal encounters have revealed the deep layers of division in our race. Perhaps, if you consider the following modern dynamics of diss-unity, you, too, will recognize a familiar pattern.

Diss-Unity Dynamics

1. **Crabbin':** Complaining about blacks who have moved ahead of you. If I crab enough, maybe others will share my discontent and keep that person in their proper place.

2. **Backstabbin':** Sabotaging successful blacks due to envy, jealousy, or hatred.

3. **Lack of coalescence:** Refusal to support and unify with other blacks. Fear that if another black person rises to your level, your job or upward mobility will be threatened. Inability to form strong coalitions. Rather than uniting to gain the power to influence, black groups function at a low level and can't seem to get traction.

4. **Lack of support/mistrust of black goods and services:** "The white man's ice is colder." A genuine belief that any goods or services created or distributed by blacks are inherently inferior. Therefore, we sometimes go out of our way to not support them.

5. **Exceptionalism:** The belief that you are the exception to the "inferior black" rule. You are special because you are the only black at the corporate management level or invited to the country club. Whites say you are different than other blacks, you're special, and you like it that way.

Diss-Unity for Sale

It has now become the vogue to expose our intraracial divisions through TV dramas, social commentary, and comedy shows. Black conservative pundits, such as John McWhorter and Shelby Steele, have made comfortable livings as media experts on black dysfunction.

By contrast, the era of Obama is the showcase for the "exceptional black." This character has been a Hollywood fixture since the 1920s in films featuring a protective, black female housekeeper shooing a biscuit-stealing black driver or house servant out of Massa's kitchen. Today, the tradition continues with the feuds between Tracy Jordan (comedian Tracy Morgan) and James "Toofer" Spurlock (actor Keith Powell) on the NBC comedy show *30 Rock.*

Toofer is the Harvard-educated defender of everything black who takes Tracy to task for his buffoonish ways and his tendency to play to the stereotype. Tracy is the foul-mouthed, N-word hurling, late-for-work, ghetto-ized party guy who gives Toofer a hard time for being too nerdy and straitlaced. The white leading characters, actors Tina Fey and Alec Baldwin, are just as goofy, but they serve as referees who patiently help the black characters navigate their differences. Fans of the show will no doubt fall back on the "it's only a comedy" defense. As funny as they may be, TV shows like *30 Rock* do not educate. They humiliate.

It Began with a Boat

It's little wonder that many of us instinctively doubt and mistrust those of our own hue. For generations we've been deluged through print and digital media, and literary, scholarly, artistic, and marketing imagery of disunited, disconnected, and uncivilized Africans and African Americans.

Our history offers a legitimate reason why other minorities have come to this country and surpassed African Americans in the areas of business development, and educational and cultural advancement. There's a valid explanation why whites, who may disagree on everything, can still coalesce and execute agendas that benefit their families, friends, and personal fortunes.

There may be legitimate justification but there will be no significant and sustainable progress until we explore why we are more comfortable supporting whites than blacks, why we cling to individualism over collectivism, why our wounded egos prohibit us

from coalescing and pooling our skills, and why we maintain rigid lower-class versus upper-class, light skin versus dark skin, highly educated versus uneducated divisions.

We can crack the code that explains our inability to unify and our compulsion to disrespect and undermine one another. To do so, however, we have to go back—way back—to another time and another continent, when a strange boat arrived on West African shores.

From Many Tribes to One

In my experience, black people hate on each other more than any other race will hate on us. We are the most critical of each other, we insult each other's looks. We're more racist toward blacks than they are!
— Junior, 35, restaurant worker

In many ways, blacks brought to America were predisposed to division.

The largest number of African slaves from the 16th through the 18th centuries came from the interior of West Africa. Dutch and Portuguese traders encountered a plethora of divergent cultures, warring factions, and sophisticated, archaic, or migrating societies. The soon-to-be slaves spoke different languages, worshipped different gods, and participated in innovative or complex forms of government. Captives were herded onto ships, many unable to communicate with the new slave next to them. Together these diverse and culturally divided people set out on a journey of thousands of miles—each as an individual island.

That Extra-Special Slave

After arriving in the New World, the next cruelty was to auction slaves to the highest bidder with no regard for family or tribal connections. Slaveowners practiced numerous techniques to kindle distrust and keep blacks afraid to unify. To maintain control, sometimes whole slave communities were punished for one troublemaking slave's transgression, real or imagined. This form of brainwashing divided the slaves' loyalties and convinced some that it was in their best interest to distance themselves from rebels or attempt to thwart their efforts:

> *Marster would tell me, "Loosanna, if you keep yo' ears open an' tell me what de darkies talk 'bout, dey'll be somp'n' good in it for you." (He meant for me to listen when dey'd talk 'bout runnin' off an' such.) I'd stay 'roun' de old folks an' make lak I was a-playin'. All de time I'd be a-listenin'. Den I'd go an tell Marster what I heard...I'd say "bring me some goobers, or a doll, or some stick candy, or anything." An' you can bet yo' bottom dollar he'd always bring me somp'n'.*
> — Anna Baker, former slave

It was not bad luck or timing that sabotaged Denmark Vesey's famous attempted insurrection in 1822. It was betrayal by fellow slaves. Similar betrayals are also believed to have stopped many of the estimated 250 Southern slave uprisings documented by historians. Informing on rebellious slaves was one of the few ways blacks could seek reward from slaveowners. The snitches, Dr. Naim Akbar explained, having demonstrated their loyalty, became the slaveowner's "grafted leader"—"a slave body and a master's head."

Slave-on-Slave Violence

Slaveowners employed overseers and drivers to manage their farms and plantations, and to drive the slaves, like cattle, to work. Most often, these supervisors were poorer-class white men but, as noted by Charles Joyner, author of *Down by the Riverside: A South Carolina Slave Community*, blacks occasionally served as overseers and drivers. For about three years, Thomas Jefferson, who at the time owned 118 slaves on his Monticello plantation, relied on Great George, his trusted black overseer. When George died in 1797, Jefferson hired a white overseer with a reputation for keeping the slaves in line by withholding supplies or whipping them, even if they were sick. The ability to extract the maximum amount of labor and obedience from slaves was a prerequisite for overseers and drivers, black or white. In *Crafting the Overseer's Image*, author William E. Wiethoff detailed how slaveowners relied on enslaved blacks to apply the "dispassionate instrument of plantation discipline." The author recounts the narrative of a former slave, William Curtis, whose master used colored overseers to administer whippings "with ferocity unmatched by white overseers." In the first part of the book *Clotel: Or, The President's Daughter: A Narrative of Slave Life in the United States,* published in 1853, author and former slave William Wells Brown described his reaction at the age of 10 when he heard his own mother being whipped by a "Negro driver":

> "Oh, pray! Oh, pray! Oh, pray!" These are the words which slaves generally utter when imploring mercy at the hands of their oppressors. The son heard it, though he was some way off. He heard the crack of the whip and the groans of his poor mother. The cold chill ran over him, and he wept aloud; but he was a slave like his mother, and could render her no assistance.

Imagine the rage and contempt that boiled in the mind of slaves who'd been pushed beyond exhaustion or whose backs had been ripped to shreds by a cat-o'-nine-tails–wielding black overseer. Did the driver feel "special" or above the slaves he brutalized? Did he loathe himself or justify his actions in the name of survival? Such states of existence must have driven some slaves insane. This probably explains why 27-year-old Clyde Manning, a black slave who had no idea Emancipation had occurred some 56 years earlier, helped his master kill 11 of his friends and fellow slaves.

The Color of Dissent

> Often black people in such settings collude in their own shaming
> and humiliation because they have been socialized by internalized
> racism to feel "chosen," better than other black people.
> — bell hooks

Another damaging aspect of enslavement was the "field slave
versus house slave" class system, with rewards and punishments that
helped solidify color-coded division. In her legal dissertation, Shades
of Brown: The Law of Skin Color, Trina Jones of Duke University
examined the historical roots and contemporary significance of
prejudicial treatment practiced by individuals of the same race.
Distinctions based upon mixed-racial heritage became routine early
on. Some whites fervently embraced the theory that light-skinned
blacks were intellectually superior because of the white blood in
their veins, Jones wrote. Many mulatto slaves attracted higher prices
on the slave market and received coveted indoor assignments on
plantations. Some traveled with the slavemaster and, because of their
close association with the slaveowner and his family, learned how to
read and write. Many hard-working field slaves, not benefiting
from the master's favors, regarded light-skinned blacks and house
servants suspiciously. If covert meetings were disclosed, if obstinate
slaves were punished, derision was aimed at the suspected snitching,
treasonous house slave. Thus was the beginning of a skin-color game
that outlasted slavery.

> Long after slavery ended, a more privileged class of black folks
> who were fairer skinned participated in creating and sustaining
> hierarchical social arrangements where they lorded it over
> their darker counterparts. Since they often lacked concrete
> material privilege, skin color itself became a mark of status.
> — bell hooks

A Time of Unity

After Emancipation, former slaves scrimped, saved, and sacrificed to escape the cruelties of the Deep South and start anew in the North. The fact that they were prohibited from living among whites or patronizing their businesses motivated many to create their own fortunes.

> [After Emancipation] us got together and raised money to buy ground enough for a churchyard and a graveyard for the colored folks. Dat graveyard filled up so fast dat dey had to buy more land several times. Us holped 'em build de fust colored church in Hancock County.
> — Jasper Battle, former slave

In an interview for this book, Steven Pitts, Ph.D., labor policy specialist at the UC Berkeley Center for Labor Research and Education, explained how white society before the 1960s forced blacks into states of unity. "Disunity is part and parcel of the victory over legal segregation which loosened social contraints," Pitts explained. "For instance, there was cohesion in black consumer spending during the era of Jim Crow. What made it so cohesive was the lack of options—we had to 'buy black.'"

Blacks who migrated to Oklahoma exploited new vistas and developed one of the most affluent districts in the country. By 1920, Greenwood Avenue in Tulsa boasted a number of thriving black-owned grocery stores, barbershops, clothing stores, funeral parlors, medical and dental services, and an eclectic mix of professionals. Behind the success of Tulsa's "Black Wall Street"—its bus line, newspapers, theaters, drugstores, hotels, hospital, public library, and more than a dozen churches—was a commitment of professional, blue-collar, and low-income blacks to recycle their wealth.

Tulsa's Black Wall Street was dealt a crushing blow when whites dynamited the district into oblivion during the 1921 Tulsa race riot. The Tulsa incident was not the only example in which whites purposely burned or destroyed black neighborhoods and businesses, stole farmland, or initiated bloody riots when black laborers threatened their livelihoods. Following the riot, city officials passed strict, unaffordable ordinances that forced many black Greenwood residents to relocate. Through violence, intimidation, and race-based legal restrictions, blacks soon came to realize that the safety, stability, and prosperity that usually accompanies innovation, hard work, and determination was, for them, just another dream deferred.

Divided and Conquered

Isolation is a favored weapon of psychological terrorists.
— bell hooks

What's missing from the Black History Month sound bites and inspiring reflections are the stories of division that existed between the groups fighting for social change. Public feuds over class and ideological differences all helped to undermine and cripple many progressive movements. These include the incidents of crabbin' and backstabbin' among the likes of Booker T. Washington and W.E.B. Du Bois, Du Bois and Carter G. Woodson, and Thurgood Marshall and Roy Wilkins's "problem" with Dr. Martin Luther King, Jr.

What could have been a respectful, multifaceted approach to black progress became grounds for exploitation by vengeful government officials, particularly the FBI's J. Edgar Hoover. Aside from "organic and predictable ideological splits among black leaders, Hoover let loose no less than 15,000 agents to disrupt unity efforts between black folk," said Dr. William E. Cross, author of *The Negro to Black Conversion Experience* (1971) and *Shades of Black: Diversity in African-American Identity* (1991), in an interview for this book. "External forces," Cross argues, "spent millions of dollars and devoted untold manpower and resources to keep whatever unity potential blacks had under wraps."

Free at Last

The most powerful social experience for blacks since Reconstruction exploded in the 1960s. The civil rights movement gave hope while it began the upending of the officially racist American social order. It was a moment of unapologetic, authentic ethnicity and self-definition. The Black Power movement represented an effort to reclaim our African history, images, dignity, self-respect, and communities. Yes, sympathetic whites were welcome and active in the cause, but it was unmistakably ours. Blacks were the movement's leaders, its inspiration, and its foot soldiers.

Expanding the teachings of Du Bois, Garvey, Woodson, and other pre–Vietnam War era thinkers, a culturally inspired generation set out to revolutionize the meaning of economic and social cooperation. Representatives of the Black Panther Party and the Nation of Islam, Huey Newton and Malcolm X encouraged blacks to establish their own schools, businesses, and social programs, such as the Panthers' free breakfast program that fed thousands of inner-city children.

While Dr. King and other civil rights leaders peacefully worked to tear down legal barriers and push for integration, other, more militant groups demanded the right to defend themselves as they addressed economic and class issues. Instead of strategizing, playing their diverse strengths, perhaps assuming "good guy/bad guy" roles to share a mutual prize, civil rights and black power movement leaders launched verbal attacks at each other, each jockeying to be the ultimate organization with the ultimate plan for black people. Each organization was so intent on being "the one," they often underestimated the skill of the opposition. The public bickering amounts to slow-pitch softballs lobbed at a grand-slam hitter. With the use of the negative propaganda bat, the seasoned BI team, as usual, won game after game.

Massa's Media

As the feuds festered, the mainstream media sensationalized black divisions, which not only stoked the flames of discontent but solidified popular perceptions that blacks were only capable of disorganized, chaotic, and dangerous leadership.

In September of 1961, more than 30 religious leaders endorsed a letter sent to the Reverend J. H. Jackson, then head of the National Baptist Convention (NBC). The letter beseeched Jackson to retract the public accusations claiming that Dr. King was responsible for the death of one of his supporters.

> Whatever may be our differences within the denomination, this uncalled for and unprovoked attack (credited to you) upon one of the greatest men of our time will only serve the purposes of the segregationist forces in America who are determined to suppress the Negro community all over the nation.

Tensions between King and Jackson had escalated since 1956 when some religious leaders urged King to challenge Jackson for the presidency of the NBC. The men disagreed on civil rights tactics— Jackson advocated redress through the court system in opposition to King's in-your-face method of nonviolent social confrontation.

Pandemonium erupted during the 1961 NBC convention in Kansas City, Missouri, when Jackson and the Reverend Gardner Taylor, whom King supported, both claimed they won the NBC presidency. Among the onstage chaos, one of Jackson's supporters, the Reverend Arthur G. Wright, toppled off the dais, struck his head, and subsequently died from his injuries.

Jackson's allegation that King and his supporter's involvement resulted in "an election campaign so vicious it produced violence" was ripe fruit for the September 10, 1961 *Chicago Tribune* headline: "Calls Dr. King 'Master Mind' of Fatal Riot." The media did an excellent job of portraying not only King, but all black groups at one time or another, as conservative or revolutionary, out-of-touch or philosophically divided, under Communist influence or controlled by militant revolutionaries. As in the days of slavery, the media serves as the propaganda tool to keep blacks wary of potential troublemakers.

A Brief Shining Moment—
Stolen

I remember this one time, there was an internist who happened to be Caucasian. Anyway, he was treating a black patient who needed to see a neurologist. So, the internist referred him to me. The moment this man walked into my office and saw me, he became so angry! Like, "Why did you send me to this black doctor? Is it because I'm black?" He was actually offended that I was black, and assumed that I was subpar because of it. He stormed off in a huff, and only came back because the white internist assured him that I was the best in the field.
— Spencer, neurosurgeon

During the 1967 Southern Christian Leadership Conference convention in Atlanta, Georgia, Dr. Martin Luther King, Jr., sang the praises of a relatively new SCLC initiative destined to create hundreds of jobs, earn the respect of black consumers, and pump millions into urban areas.

Indeed, Operation Breadbasket had such potential. The program, influenced by the "selective buying" campaign of the Reverend Leon Sullivan of Philadelphia, became an economic arm of the SCLC, headed by Jesse Jackson.

Operation Breadbasket's threats of boycotts convinced major Chicago food chains to carry products produced by blacks, such as Joe Louis Milk, Mumbo barbecue sauce, and Diamond Sparkle wax. Under Jackson's leadership the program, within three years, generated more than 3,000 jobs and pumped $22 million into the South Side Chicago area.

The Black Power movement that birthed initiatives like Operation Breadbasket was indeed a brief shining moment. But we mustn't over-romanticize the era. While we experienced its potential, the BI complex campaign worked its voodoo, reminding blacks that the new movement was still an inferior competitor to all its superior brands. At an Operation Breadbasket meeting I attended in the '60s, the

Reverend Willie T. Barrow, later chair of the board emeritus of the Rainbow PUSH Coalition, related that some black folks had remarked that Joe Louis Milk, a black-owned brand, tasted "chalky" compared to white brands, like Dean's and Hawthorne Melody. This taste perception existed, she noted, despite the fact that Joe Louis Milk came from the same processing plant as the other two.

After landmark civil rights laws were passed in the mid-1960s, great sources of potential wealth and stability were discarded when legions of brainwashed blacks abandoned their communities and businesses to chase the "dream" of a newly integrated society. Patronizing and working for popular and prominent white businesses, instead of creating, growing, and supporting their own, became the symbol of progress. Nevertheless, the integration fantasy turned out to be another spiritually uplifting but failed experiment, mostly because we were missing an essential element that makes prosperity possible in the land of opportunity.

The Great Culture Robbery

Why is it that other ethnic groups, some who've suffered atrocities in their native lands, can come to this country, work together in unison, and outperform blacks who've been here for centuries? The answer to that question is also connected to our initial sojourn to America. Had Africans come to this nation voluntarily, with their cultural heritage and languages intact, we could have, like other ethnic groups, adapted those anchors for use in this new land.

Koreans, for example, have transplanted cooperative methods from their native culture to America. The Korean word *kye* refers to an "agreement or bond...a social organization based upon the principle of mutual cooperation and aid with a specific objective. Although there are many different types of *kye,* all collect dues and manage funds." Korean Americans use *kye* as a sort of private banking system within their community. Business owners contribute money to the *kye* to make loans to potential Korean entrepreneurs without application or promissory note.

The Vietnamese use a similar system, called ROCSA (rotating credit and savings association). Vietnamese ROCSA groups utilize the *hui* system—groups meet regularly, with each member bringing a fixed sum of cash to help start or support a Vietnamese business.

Instead of complaining about banks not lending to us, why haven't African Americans been able to create or maintain independent lending systems that sustain community businesses? Perhaps it's because the critical elements of *kye* and *hui* are trust and cultural unity—elements severed from the black experience. All peoples have divisions and internecine battles. However, few other minority groups in America have been conditioned from infancy to view each other through the jaundiced eyes of those who dehumanized them.

The Myth of Individualism

The saddest thing is that in the 35 years of the BE 100 there has not been to date, that I can think of, a significant merger of any kind that brought 2 and 2 together to make 5. I've attempted a couple of them. I've been unsuccessful.
— Bob Johnson, founder and former CEO of BET

Slavery, subjugation, dehumanization, and institutionalized oppression are not the stuff of which strong communal foundations are built. Unlike other ethnic groups, we can only draw on what our American past has taught us.

In the "Buy Now, Pay Later" chapter, we discussed how many blacks define their self-worth through material possessions. The conditioning that feeds that impulse also affects business relationships. Many of us take pride in having our "own thing," doing it our way, no matter how we struggle. It offsets societal forces that remind us of our powerlessness.

The media constantly preaches the sermon of rugged individualism, while whites and other races merge, acquire, form organizations, affiliations, and cabals to control the economic systems that benefit them most.

Fifty years ago, owners of black-owned advertising agencies came together to form an association, like white firms, that would make us stronger and more competitive. Yet even though all of our futures were in peril, we were never able to establish a strong association.

We are challenged to find any major mergers or acquisitions in the black business arena. Oh, there have been successful black companies that have been sold or bought out by white companies. But rarely do you see black businesses, from the corporate to the mom and pop store levels, combine talents and share resources with the intent of dominating an industry or a neighborhood.

When discussing this topic, Derrick Dingle, executive editor of *Black Enterprise* magazine, identified a reason why black entrepreneurs are hesitant to partner or merge: "For the most part, our businesses have been companies where you've had a singular vision. You've had an individual who has done all the spade-work, the hard work, therefore they think, 'Why should I give up a piece of my enterprise after I put in the sweat equity?'"

That model may have worked for us in the past, but the business world is changing. "With our present situation, going into the future, especially in terms of accessing the same size and scale of contracts, out of necessity, we will have to form partnerships," Dingle added. As an example, he mentioned the recent merger between two African American firms, RS Information Systems and 1 Source Consulting Inc. The partnership enabled the two black-owned firms to become a billion-dollar contractor with the federal government.

Getting to that "next level" will be a challenge. While other ethnicities operate on the innate principle of cultural collectivism, we maneuver in the ego-swelling arena of individualism, which is often just a euphemism for isolationism. Because of our disunity, we have disdain for cooperation and coalescence among ourselves. Consequently, we isolate ourselves from the possible benefits of collective development and business sustainability.

Diss-Unity: Connecting the Dots

Contemporary Manifestations	Historical Roots
Crabbin': Complaining about blacks who have moved ahead. And trying to pull them back into the barrel of inferiority. The desire to keep ambitious or visionary blacks in their proper place.	A basic tenet of American chattel slavery was the pitting of blacks against each other. Individuality was discouraged so that racial dominance could be maintained.
Backstabbin': Active jealousy, envy, and hateful behavior toward other blacks. Willingness to sabotage another black person's possible success.	Slavemasters shrewdly "rewarded" blacks for backstabbing, betrayals, and snitching. Blacks' sense of self was perversely enhanced by being a party to this betrayal, because being "closer" to whites made them feel less inferior.
Lack of coalescence: Refusal to unite to create a strong collective. Fear that another black person at your level will threaten your job or upward mobility. Operates independently at a substandard level and never gains traction from collective effort.	Slavemasters aggressively discouraged coalescence among slaves. We were brainwashed to distrust and disrespect other blacks and to diminish black efforts. Since opportunities for blacks in white institutions have always been limited, we viewed another black's success as our personal loss.
Lack of support/mistrust of black goods and services: "The white man's ice is colder." The belief that goods or services created or distributed by blacks are inherently inferior, therefore refusing to support them.	The BI Complex taught that that anything we said, did, or produced was inferior. Throughout history, our mistakes, missteps, and failures have been blown out of proportion, fueling the widespread belief that we are inherently flawed.

Exceptionalism: The "exception to the rule" theory. Feeling special being the only black in all-white circles. Feeling extremely gratified when whites compliment you for being different from other blacks.	When given an opportunity to interact with "superior" people, we felt superior. Modern institutions keep blacks separated by exaggerating and exploiting their differences. We wanted to be the "only one" because it gave us status over the "lowly" rest.

Building a Bridge to Unity

Hundreds of years of schooling in the BI Complex have left us with no affirming, solid cultural ground beneath our feet. We view one another with the same contempt and suspicion with which the majority views us. We laugh at Chris Rock's "blacks versus niggas" routine. It gives those labeled as inferior the luxury to separate themselves from "those people." I suppose there's some benefit to that release but, like everything else, there's a price to pay.

Benefits & Costs of Diss-Unity

Short-term Benefits

1. **Crabbin':** Black folk make me crazy! If I don't complain, I'll explode. It's a great release.

2. **Backstabbin':** Sabotaging another black person makes it possible for me to move ahead. After all, there are only so many opportunities available for black folk. Dog eat dog, right?

3. **Lack of coalescence:** Why bother? Blacks can never do anything right. Why set myself up for obvious failure? It's best to go it alone or team up with white people with the

power, resources, and connections. Besides, if I help elevate another black person, he may become a threat to my upward mobility.

4. **Lack of support/mistrust of black goods and services:** I go out of my way to avoid supporting blacks because they will let me down. Let's be real—whites do everything better. Why give my hard-earned money to a black person when I know the job will not be done correctly?

5. **Exceptionalism:** In a sea of failure, it's quite nice to be considered the exception to the norm. I like having my achievements noticed. When I walk into the boardroom or the social club, I get white folk's instant respect. Obviously I'm "special" or else I wouldn't be there.

Long-term Costs

1. **Crabbin':** Complaining about another black person's achievement is really a self-indictment. The possibility that another black person may move ahead solicits that "if she made it, what's my excuse?" feeling. Crabbing about blacks reinforces negative perceptions and validates the stereotype of our inferior status.

2. **Backstabbin':** Hatred, envy, and sabotage stunt opportunities for other blacks and provide opportunities for other races. Stopping one black person has a domino effect, guaranteeing that others won't benefit from the high-ranking black person's success.

3. **Lack of coalescence:** Disunity makes the collective even more vulnerable. Just as a robust economy is good for the nation, a higher ratio of successful blacks increases opportunities for black communities, schools, and busi-

nesses. Blacks will forever remain on a substandard level if we refuse to coalesce, plan, work together, and share the wealth.

4.   **Lack of support/mistrust of black goods and services:**
     The white man's ice is NOT colder! There are subpar white businesses, services, and products as well as black. Going out of our way not to patronize black businesses helps other races exploit the wealth and resources of black communities, while enriching their families and strengthening their neighborhoods.

5.   **Exceptionalism:** Everyone has the potential to be special. Human beings are not trinkets or display models. Feeling unique in the boardroom or social club is a selfish, counterproductive indulgence. While languishing in your "one and only" status, those around you are doing business and making valuable connections with folks who look and think like them.

Just as there is no "unity meter" to empirically gauge our cohesion, no magic formula exists that will bring us together. Every society and group has its fissures. We have ours. However, it is our duty to ensure that those fissures are not of someone else's making.

Because we have internalized negative propaganda about who we are, we are more likely to treat those who look like us poorly. This is the real source of disunity in the black community.

Diss-Unity Cues

Brotherhood is not for some other hood
We should not be sitting idly by, watching as other groups progress through unity and move up and ahead. We did it before, we can do it again!

The "U" and "I" of unity
I will make it my personal responsibility to be a force for coalescence. A fist is stronger than five open fingers.

Be a yea-sayer
See your glass as half full by learning to value our own abilities and those of other African Americans. We need to envision the unity we seek and be proactively positive. Let's transform our attitude about what is positive.

Don't hate, elevate
Seize the opportunity to encourage the accomplishments of others. As Alex Haley said, "Find the good and praise it."

Collaborative Relationships

It's hard to imagine where I'd be today if not for the National Black McDonald's Operators Association (NBMOA), which is now one of the largest and most influential black business organizations in the nation. In 1968, with race riots blazing across the country after Dr. King's assassination, it dawned on McDonald's Corporation executives that having all white owner/operators and managers at its high-volume restaurants in black neighborhoods might be a dangerous proposition.

Enter Roland Jones, at the time a McDonald's restaurant manager in Washington, D.C. Eager to create black franchises and managers, Jones was promoted to the position of regional consultant in Chicago. In his book, *Standing Up and Standing Out*, Jones writes that he was the first black man to set foot on the McDonald's corporate ladder in Chicago. Jones could have been content in his role as the "only black" on the corporate level at McDonald's. He could have been that richly rewarded, smiling black face in the company who made no waves and opened no doors for other black folk. But that's not the Roland Jones I met in the early 1970s.

Working closely with Herman Petty, who in 1968 became the first black McDonald's owner/operator in Chicago, Jones had officially formed the National Black McDonald's Operators Association (NBMOA). The new organization, originally consisting of five black owners and operators, was dedicated to providing employment for black youth and helping the McDonald's Corporation cultivate partnerships with African American organizations, vendors, and suppliers.

In 1972, Roland arranged for me to make a presentation on behalf of Burrell Advertising, Inc., at what was then NBMOA's 2nd Annual Mid-eastern/Mid-western convention in Chicago. In his book, Roland writes about the event that helped put Burrell Advertising on the map:

> What really got everyone fired up in 1973 was a discussion I led and a presentation by Tom Burrell...Most of the convention attendees knew little about Tom before that meeting, but he was about to change the way black people perceived McDonald's and the way McDonald's marketed itself to the significant portion of its customers who were not white...The collaborative relationship between Tom, NBMOA, and McDonald's proved to be one of the most mutually beneficial that I have ever experienced in business.

The operative words in Roland's statement are *collaborative relationships*. I share this story not to boast about my former clients but to speak of our success and the power of unity. We united in the past and we can do it again—this time we are stronger. We have more information, greater resources, and a firm intention to build a sustainable future.

Don't Hate, Elevate

Today the NBMOA has 33 chapters in 32 states with approximately 375 members. The handful of original members were truly the exception to the rule, because they understood that every link in the chain needed to be reinforced. They set up an organization where

new black owner/operators could learn from their mistakes, marshal resources, and become a strong collective. They committed to a long-term strategy to foster solid partnerships with black businesses that would help stabilize the communities in which they operated.

:::

In my career, I have been blessed to interact with many individuals like Roland and the men and women of the NBMOA. There were others, like former NAACP president Bruce Gordon, who personified the meaning of purposeful unity. Gordon, who sits on several major corporate boards, has never been timid about standing up for black inclusion. It was Gordon, as president of the Retail Markets Division of Verizon, who made it clear that Verizon should do business with minority firms.

We need to let our united good works speak for us. The best revenge for white injustice is black success—products and services that earn a profit. We need collaboration and cooperation inspired by the quiet mantra of "each one, reach and teach one."

With unity, all things are possible. There is no better time than now to heal our divisions, no better time to shift our minds, no better time to pool our resources and talents and soar. Instead of crabbin' and backstabbin,' this generation can be the pioneers who pool their resources and talent. This can be the generation that says, "Enough. The master puppeteer will no longer pull our strings."

Chapter 11

Neo-Coons

Why Is the Joke Always on Us?

Dear Mr. Perry: I appreciate your commitment to giving black folks jobs in front of and behind the camera...but both your shows are marked by old stereotypes of buffoonish, emasculated black men and crass, sassy black women. I'd like to support your work, I really would...but I can't let advertisers and networks think that these stereotypes are acceptable.

— JAMILAH LEMIEUX, SEPTEMBER 11, 2009 NPR

Jamilah Lemieux's open letter to writer/director/producer Tyler Perry received nationwide attention in late 2009 after NPR posted it on its Web site. In the letter, Lemieux thanked Perry for his humor and his "positive messages about self-worth, love, and respect." However, she took issue with the images of black people Perry presents in his TV shows and movies:

> Your most famous character, Madea, is a trash-talking, pistol-waving grandmother played by none other than you. Through her, the country has laughed at one of the most important members of the black community: Mother Dear, the beloved matriarch. I just can't quite get with seeing Mother Dear played by a 6-foot-3 man with prosthetic breasts flopping in the wind. Our mothers and grandmothers deserve much more than that. Heck, our fathers and grandfathers deserve more.

Lemieux acknowledged that Perry had built an "empire on a foundation of love and Christianity." But, she added, his work is mired in "the worst black pathologies and stereotypes." She ended her letter urging Perry to examine his contributions, shift his priorities, and use his talent and Hollywood clout to "revolutionize the world of black film."

Lemieux's open letter is not only relevant to this book; it also reflects another calamity resulting from our unconscious addiction to the BI brand.

First, her missive serves as an example of 21st-century advocacy. Lemieux used the media to call attention to a perceived problem. Her comment, "I can't let advertisers and networks think that these stereotypes are acceptable," gives those who share her concern a viable course of redress. Lastly, she didn't erect barriers with a wholesale trashing of Perry. Instead, Lemieux respectfully encouraged him to be a pioneer in the game instead of just another player. In short, she urged Perry to be his best self.

Still, as much as I support self-responsibility, it's not entirely fair to expect Perry to chart a new course alone. His movies and TV shows would not be so successful if blacks didn't have a raging appetite for messages and images that project us as dysfunctional or incompetent. Nothing that occurred during *Amos 'n' Andy*'s radio and television reign could match the words and actions of black comedies like *Madea* and *The Browns*. Our attraction to self-demeaning images came way before, and goes far beyond, Tyler Perry.

The Nouveau Coon

I don't know how I'ma stop saying "nigger" when it describes some motherfuckers I know so perfectly. Everybody knows that one motherfucker that can only be described as "That nigger there, goddamn, whew!"
— D.L. Hughley

A deep-rooted addiction to the BI brand allows us to laugh at the antics of black entertainers who call us "niggas" and denigrate black men and women in comic routines, songs, and music videos. Woven into the black American experience is a strong thread of avoidance, an aversion to critical thinking, and an abnormal embrace of anything that appeals to our emotions rather than our reasoning. The unspoken trauma of pain and powerlessness has led too many of us to prefer laughter to learning, and pretending over mending. These impulses, mixed with our damaged psyches, have left us ripe for exploitation. If a comedian, actor, or film director strums our emotional chords, we tolerate all sorts of sour notes. In reality, many of these talented, creative, charismatic individuals assume the role of "Neo-Coons"— modern-day jesters and clown princes. They provide superficial, short-term pain relief that impedes permanent healing.

This chapter examines why we choose to laugh instead of think. We will examine comedy and the role of comedians who are responsible for some of the degrading images of black folk that we see across a variety of today's media platforms.

Blacks themselves took over the job of self-ridicule over a century ago. Our goal is to understand fully how this phenomenon came to be. We will also explore the disturbing side of our human need to laugh and how we've come to rely on funny men who too often support the marriage of white superiority and black inferiority.

What's Good for the Group

Since its beginning, the American mass marketing and propaganda system has been the envy of the world. Its unheralded achievement has been creating and sustaining an almost four-century-long campaign that has the American public not only accepting, but also applauding anything that reinforces the original black inferiority brand identity.

For 45 years, I was engaged in the field of systematic persuasion, convincing people through mass communication to buy—buy a product, buy a service, buy an idea. In almost all cases, the means by which people are convinced to buy rarely has anything to do with

reason or logic, and humor is one of the most powerful tools in the arsenal of persuasive communication. It's used to distract, control, and keep people from pondering too long or thinking too critically. For too many of us, our minds are on long-term disability while our emotions are pulling double shifts. Humor has become our way of coping with our sense of degradation. And nothing is off the table—we laugh about slavery, we joke about lynching, and chuckle about police brutality or the shooting of unarmed black men.

Can you visualize any other oppressed group joking about its own oppression? Imagine if Jewish comedians incessantly used the word *kike* or told concentration camp jokes. Why, there would be a crisis alert among Jews. Public and behind-the-scenes pressure would be mobilized immediately to call out the offensive Jewish comedians' material or swiftly end their careers.

Yet with blacks, this type of incendiary material receives cheers and raucous approval. To those in the audience outside the cusp of consciousness, the material is perfectly acceptable. It must be okay to laugh at our woes, they reason, because "Everybody else is laughing."

With "group think," the goal is to make the buyers believe they are not alone. They are part of the popular in-crowd, so it's just fine to laugh at self-deprecating humor. Still, some things that are obviously bad contain a grain of truth that reflects a negative condition. Joking about it makes it less bad…and, unfortunately, more true.

Laughing Too Long and Too Hard

Everything everywhere is comedy material. To watch and view the world via television, newspapers, movies, and music translate our world into funny. There is no subject where funny doesn't exist.
— Katt Williams

Humor and entertainment are proven sedatives. We have been conditioned to disengage from anything resembling critical thinking. In an interview on *The View,* while promoting his film *Madea Goes to*

236

Jail, Tyler Perry told the audience, "We need to laugh." We do. But we've laughed at some things long enough. Consider some of the topics black comedians find "funny":

> *I really want to ask white people, Why don't y'all beat y'all's kids? Beat 'em...whip they motherfuckin' ass. Y'all give y'all kids all kinds of time outs and special places. What the fuck is a special place? To a black child, that's a coma.*
> — Aries Spears

> *I'm from the old school. I'll kick a kid's ass. When a kid get one year's old I believe you have the right to hit 'em in the throat or the stomach. If you grown enough to talk back, you grown enough to get fucked up.*
> — Bernie Mac

During the course of writing this book, I can recall numerous instances of black children shaken to death, beaten, scalded, smothered, and otherwise tortured by adults. Where is the outcry against comedy that celebrates child abuse?

> *Man, it's hard being a athlete. Dammit. You gotta run, jump, block, work out everyday...shit, and that's just dodging child support.*
> — DeRay Davis

> *You know how you know when you lost a fight to your woman? When the cops come to your house and ask you, Do you want to press charges?*
> — Kevin Hart

While black families are mired in layers of dysfunction, we crack jokes about bitchy black women, deadbeat dads, badass kids, and battling black parents.

I bought a gun because "POW POW" sounds a lot better than
"Hey, put that back!"
— Joe Torry

As morgues and prisons fill with black bodies from homicide shootings, we laugh as the jokester riffs about our threatening images, murder, and violence. As the math, reading, and literacy gaps widen between failing black kids and other races, a smorgasbord of jokes celebrates and normalizes underachievement.

I'm a one-year-old bitch, but I know not to take this note home...
this is an ass whoopin' you're pinning on my shirt.
— Mike Epps

Black families suffer disproportionately from diabetes and obesity, yet some black female comedians ridicule so-called "skinny, black bitches." As single-parent homes, divorce, and a host of sexually transmitted diseases ravage black lives, funny folk crack jokes about sexual promiscuity.

I got caught in the bed with my best girlfriend Peaches' [man], and
the bitch gonna get mad at me! Talkin' 'bout, "Sheryl, what you
doin'?" Bitch, I'm trying to help you! The N* said if he don't get
no pussy soon, he gonna leave your ass, and I'm a mother fuckin'
friend to the end, God damn it!
— Sheryl Underwood, *Def Comedy Jam*

My friend caught his wife fucking around. She told this motherfucker
"it just happened." You may just happen to slip and fall. You can
just happen to wear a fucked-up outfit. But you cannot just
happen to get fucked. You can't just walk outside... "I done
slipped in some pussy..."
— Faizon Love, *Def Comedy Jam*

As the economy tanks and the rates of black poverty and unemployment worsen, we laugh at jokes about poverty and irresponsible spending.

[For] black folks, credit means, "Get it." If you got some credit, get
it. I got 11 flat screens in a four-room house.
— Cedric the Entertainer

Millions of blacks will wake up tomorrow to dumbed-way-down syndicated radio. Most will crack up over formulaic sitcoms and reality shows, or laugh until they cry in the comedy clubs and movie theaters when people who share their skin color serve as the butt of derision. The way we act is no accident. I see it as a direct outcome of the branding, brainwashing, and marketing program to keep blacks anesthetized and distracted. Entertainment and humor, in its place, is harmless. However, when interwoven into our everyday interactions and substituted for critical, social dialogue, it becomes self-destructive because it promotes and perpetuates BI.

What we need is more critical and more conscious comedy. We must learn to incorporate critical thinking when dealing with ourselves, our hang-ups and habits, and when dealing with the world we live in. Then we will be better able to laugh through our problems.

Therefore, as much as I admire Lemieux's individual stance, the task is much more daunting. Getting rid of one drug dealer will not eradicate drug addiction. The addict will simply find another source willing to abet an escape from the unfaceable or tolerate the intolerable.

If we are going to address misplaced buffoonery, we must examine the genesis of the Neo-Coon and the trauma that fertilizes his or her prominence in today's society.

Calling Dr. Feel Good

Look, my job is to make motherfuckers laugh, to make them feel
good. Had a bad day? Go to the comedy club. Need to forget all the
shit that's wrong with your sorry-ass life? Come laugh with me.
— Sterling, L.A. comedian

Feeling good is the drug of choice, and for centuries we have turned to black Dr. Feel Goods for our fixes. Many of these practitioners receive free rides on the cultural coattails of a people saddled with an indoctrinated need to paper over their woes. Why do so many of us let our passions govern us so completely and predictably? Why have we set such a low bar of accountability for high-profile buffoonery?

Before exploring those questions, let's further examine what supports Neo-Coonery:

Neo-Coon Dynamics

1. **Laugh leaders:** Public venues, filled with approving audiences, have come to be safe places to tear down and demean black people. We place comedians on pedestals and allow them to express sentiments that would be defined as racist or inappropriate if mouthed by whites. We strike a hands-off bargain with black comedians because we rely on them to express our frustrations about whites and publicly say things about blacks that we quietly endorse.

2. **The joke is on us:** Release of toxic and traumatic emotions through laughter. Comedy provides the safe avenue to strike back at whites and poke fun at blacks, while it also unconsciously reinforces long-held stereotypes about one another.

3. **See no evil:** We are fearful of facing truths about the psychological damage that has resulted from centuries of systemized oppression. We resist questioning authority and of being labeled "stuck in the past." Such anxieties allow us to avoid honest self-examination, which discourages critical thinking. It's simply easier to laugh about what ails us than face and address it.

4. **Assault with a funny weapon:** The need to engage in the kind of self-destructive, self-debasing, and culturally demeaning humor that intensifies the damage done to our psyches and bolsters the myths perpetrated about our inherent inferiority.

Constructing a fertile future from a fractured past is painful, tiresome work. Our craving to feel good *now* trumps our ability to think and prepare for the future. Far too many of us hunger for salty, sugary, greasy, nutritionally deficient brain food pitched as tasty distractions, fantasy thinking that leaves the black mind flabby and malnourished. Unresolved trauma leaves black people today with a tremendous craving to feel better. Like Evilene, the wicked witch in *The Wiz*, we have one overriding wish: "Don't nobody bring me no bad news."

As we laugh and sing about helplessness, mediocrity, and mindlessness, the cycles of dysfunction roll on from one generation to the next. While distracted, the task of reprogramming ourselves to build strong, vibrant psyches with race-based self-esteem goes unattended. If we thoroughly examine the correlation between the Neo-Coon, forced captivity, and institutionalized oppression, we will better understand why we still subconsciously flip on the emotional switch that salves and subdues our painful past and uncomfortable existence.

Our Ignorance, Their Bliss

One of the primary forms of remaining in favor with the slave-master by the slave was to provide entertainment for the master and his household. It is easy to observe that man exults in his superiority over lower animals by teaching them to do tricks and to be entertained by those tricks. Great favors of leniency and special rewards were given to the clowning slave.
— Dr. Na'im Akbar

In spite of what we've absorbed, black America's disproportionate preference for emotion over reason is not inborn. To control slaves and maintain a system of racial superiority, it was imperative to block all pathways to critical analysis. Proponents of the systemized BI branding campaign outlawed education, stifled public dialogue, and employed other psychological restrictions to convince blacks of their own helplessness. Our ignorance was necessary to maintain the slaveholder's security. It was key to the creation of a product that was to be branded and marketed—walking, talking human chattel, without the uniquely human ability to think and reason.

Although slaveowners worked tirelessly to snuff out any semblance of slave thinking, they couldn't control their captives' feelings. Harsh reality could not be changed, but it could be endured with prayer, eased with song, and smothered with laughter. Emotion became the slave's only succor from fear, sorrow, and hopelessness. Slaves found sustenance in the nuggets of amusement and emotional discharge— singing, dancing, laughing, and praying. The "entertainment component of Negro culture," as author Charles Keil coined it, is the "one area in Negro life that was clearly not stripped away or obliterated by slavery..."

In many ways, we were forced to become idiot savants of emotion—we are exceptionally gifted but incredibly disabled. Our overdeveloped ability to express feelings is at the expense of our ability to think and engage critically. Emotional release through music, joking, and religion understandably became a critical part of our survival. Reliance on our emotions helped us survive turbulent times. Such reliance was not, however, supposed to be a permanent substitute for thinking as independent, sentient beings. It was a defense mechanism our ancestors triumphantly used to express their artistry and their staunch commitment to survive.

One of our greatest gifts, our instincts—that gut sense of what was good or bad, safe or dangerous, helpful or harmful—has been systematically anesthetized and blunted.

Originally, we used humor to keep the master from knowing what we were thinking. Today we use humor to avoid thinking altogether. The real question is whether our instinct for survival has been brainwashed away.

Singing Away Da Blues

Slave folkses sung most all the time but we didn' think of what we sang much. We jus' got happy and started singin'. Sometimes we 'ud sing effen we felt sad and lowdown, but soon as we could, we 'ud go off whar we could go to sleep and forgit all 'bout trouble!
— James Bolton, former slave

The seemingly insurmountable reality of slavery produced long-standing coping and communication mechanisms within our psyches. Slaves existed in a perverted realm of "two-ness," wrote W.E.B. Du Bois. The scholar meticulously defined the contradictory state of double consciousness where blacks saw themselves reflected by "a world which yields him no true self-consciousness, but only lets him see himself through the revelation of the other world."

Escape from that other world was virtually impossible. Therefore, slaves learned to cope within it—creating and clinging to any morsel of humanity, dignity, and hope. For many, entertainment became the barricade against painful reality. Music, for instance, was a form of expression slaveowners welcomed and exploited. Singing, dancing slaves complemented the white man's illusion of happy servitude.

Humor also served as one of our only means of redress, relief, and refuge. As Mel Watkins noted in his book, *On the Real Side: A History of African American Comedy from Slavery to Chris Rock*, comedy has always been the quiet equalizer against the notion of inferiority and a means to stave off the brutality of slavery:

> No master could be thoroughly comfortable around a sullen slave and conversely, a master, unless he was utterly humorless could not overwork or brutally treat a jolly fellow, one who could make him laugh.

Strangely, after 144 years of freedom, humor for many African Americans still serves as an outlet for frustration and a means to "get back" at perceived enemies. Author Glenda Carpio, in her book *Laughing Fit to Kill: Black Humor in the Fictions of Slavery*, writes about black comedians who have attempted to flip the script on our tragic

past. *Harvard* magazine cited an example from Carpio's book where she recalled comedian Dave Chappelle's parody of the slave Kunta Kinte from the 1977 miniseries *Roots*:

> [A]s Kunta, he receives interminable lashes for refusing his new, slave name...but just as the lashing begins to become unbearable, Chappelle's Kunta suddenly frees himself from the post to which he is tied, runs to the overseer, and proceeds to beat him. "What did I tell you about getting out of hand!" yells Chappelle, turning his back to reveal the thick padding that protected him from the lashes all along.

Sadly, some comedians have commandeered roles that have nothing to do with comedic relief, at least not for black people. Unbeknownst to them, they have extended a genre crafted long, long ago to keep us psychologically at the back of the bus.

The Founding Coons

In 1896, a man by the name of Ernest Hogan made his fame (and most of his fortune) when he wrote, "All Coons Look Alike to Me."

All coons look alike to me
I've got another beau, you see
And he's just as good to me as you, nig!
Ever tried to be

Think of it as the multi-platinum, Grammy-winning, pop mega hit of its day. Some say it was one of music's first million-sellers. It soon became a standard in every popular band's repertoire. Suddenly Ernest Hogan, who was already a seasoned comedian, singer, and dancer, became a superstar of the new genre called "ragtime."

Coon songs were already proven crowd-pleasers. Hogan just made the most of it. After all, white blackface stars like T.J. "Daddy" Rice (the original Jim Crow) and George Washington Dixon (aka "Zip Coon") weren't simply riding the coon song bandwagon, they were driving it.

Who could blame a talented young Irishman from capitalizing on the craze?

Well, what about a talented young black man?

Hogan's name wasn't even "Hogan," it was Reuben Crowders, and he was as colored as the Sunday funnies.

As catchy as his little ditty was, Crowder/Hogan's dubious distinction was that he not only wrote a hit song, his title became a catch phrase that would hound members of his race (himself included) to this very day. "All Coons Look Alike to Me" gave whites and blacks a handy, all-purpose put-down to whip out for any and all occasions.

Even though it's been written that Hogan regretted his contribution to coonery until the day he died, he also tried to justify it (as his successors do today) by claiming it helped employ many other black composers, singers, and dancers. I tell Crowder/Hogan's long-forgotten tale not because I want to add to his posthumous pain, but because it's relevant to today's comedians and to this discussion.

The Minstrel Show

Although music, merchandise, media, and theatrical and literary efforts reinforced insidious black stereotypes, nothing was as effective and long lasting as the phenomenon of minstrelsy. The humor delivered through this genre served to validate black oppression and inferiority. Whites attending the shows were made to feel superior as they listened and laughed at "nigger dialect" and representations of buffoonish, inept Negroes who loved plantation life.

After the Civil War, many former slaves expressed their newfound independence by taking over the lucrative but demeaning minstrelsy business.

The cooning of African America was just another phase of the massive marketing campaign to reinforce the idea of black inferiority. Not only did it never stop, it morphed into more sophisticated, pervasive, and insidious forms—into what I call "Hogan's (Neo-Coon) Heroes"—blacks who dominate the airwaves, stages, and television screens of our nation in an endless cakewalk through the African American psyche.

245

Why was Hogan so successful? Why, more than 100 years after he died, are today's Hogans still so lavishly rewarded? Hogan's success helps us understand the contemporary marketing that leads us to adore many of today's biggest stars who promote similar demeaning portrayals of black people. It explains why today's comedians can joke about their pimp-like abilities, their sexual prowess, their pitiful "baby's daddy," "crackhead" friends, or "welfare mamas." Hogan's hit demonstrates how adhering to and extending a known brand identity—originally created to justify and market racial slavery—remains a sure path to fame and fortune for many of today's comedic descendants.

What's So Funny, Nigga?

Over the past century, the Coon concept—instead of dying with slavery—has spread like a virus far beyond its blackface minstrel music hall origin. Although many of its most visible promoters today have black bodies as well as faces, they still seem to have the same disregard for themselves as did their painted progenitors.

After clownish TV shows, like *Amos 'n' Andy*, were taken off the air, we continued the tradition of self-deprecation with even more toxic, black-generated comic fodder, as Bill Cosby and Dr. Alvin F. Poussaint observed in their book, *Come on, People: On the Path from Victims to Victors*:

> After Hollywood had put most of the silly or ugly stereotypes behind it, it began resurrecting them. Many black sitcoms in the 1990s reverted to buffoonish stereotypes and black comedians prospered on cable, making liberal use of the N-word. In the world of music videos and their movie spin-offs, the images grew uglier still.

It's clear that humor and comedy served a purpose for the black slave. It was a way to share hard times and hard truths. It sometimes saved them from the lash or from insanity. But was it insanity endured or insanity deferred? What is sane about watching hour after hour of

"Nigga"-laced skits on black stand-up comedy shows? As we laugh along with the jokes, we subliminally notice the underlying notion that "Niggas" aren't equipped to control their lives. An audience of "Niggas" can't possibly walk away determined to challenge the historical woes hidden in the jokes.

Jabari Asim, author of *The N Word: Who Can Say It, Who Shouldn't, and Why,* has little patience with rappers and comedians who insist they have redefined the N-word and taken the negativity out of it. Its contemporary usage, Asim says, is nothing more than a "linguistic extension of white supremacy, differing little from the days of slavery."

Some young entertainers today defend their actions with the claim that we must always "keep it real." I contend that, in our brainwashed state, we have no idea what's "real" or what's simply part of a propaganda campaign designed to make black inferiority a permanent reality.

Driven to Distraction

Ironically, the people who created the conditions that led to African America's insatiable need for diversion are the same people who benefit most from today's mindless amusement.

The disproportion underpinning the emotionally driven entertainment component of African American culture is evident in the fact that in 2003, African Americans watched 23.7 more hours of television per week than the average white viewer, for an average of 76.8 hours per week, according to Initiative Media. It's not just an issue of the amount of TV watched; it is also about the *quality* of what we watch. The five shows ranked highest among black television viewers between August 2008 and October 2009 are:

American Idol (FOX / Wednesday)
House of Payne (syndicated)
Meet the Browns (TBS)
American Idol (FOX / Tuesday)
Dancing with the Stars (ABC)

Those shows, with the inclusion of *CSI: Miami* (CBS) and the rowdy talk show *Maury* (NBC), rounded out the top ten shows in the same time period. In other words, it's a safe bet that black folk are not significantly driving up the viewership over at PBS or C-SPAN.

Of course, today's slick BI campaign comes with a highly polished veneer of glamour, sophistication, sly humor, false fervor, and specious symbolism that conceals blatant psychological fratricide. Yet, with our historical microscope in hand, we clearly see the roots of this campaign.

Neo-Coons: Connecting the Dots

Contemporary Manifestations	Historical Roots
Laugh leaders: Public venues, filled by approving audiences, are safe places to demean black people. Popular black comedians who express sentiments that would otherwise be defined as inappropriate and racist. Black entertainers benefit from our hands-off policy because they express our frustration about whites and endorse our negative feelings about blacks.	The minstrel, or the funny man, was an elevated figure within the black community. He transmuted our pain through the "feel-good" moment, which was our primary medicine then and now.
Laugh factor: Release of toxic and traumatic emotions through laughter. Comedy provides a safe avenue to strike back at whites but also reinforces negative stereotypes of blacks.	Slaves understood that laughter was a protective factor against severe punishment. If we amused the master, we might escape harm. Powerless to hurt whites, we relished the opportunity to participate in hilarious verbal retribution. Comedy provided the opportunity to be clever, creative, and intellectual without deadly repercussions.

See no evil: Fear of facing truths about the psychological damage caused by centuries of oppression. We are reluctant to challenge oppression and discrimination or being labeled "stuck in the past." Such anxieties lead us to avoid honest self-examination, which discourages critical thinking.	Slavery and racial oppression were painful and traumatic. The natural inclination of the human mind is to repress pain, suffering, and trauma. A history of power-lessness has conditioned us to tolerate, and stop questioning that which we feel we cannot control.
Assault with a funny weapon: Self-destructive, self-debasing, and culturally demeaning humor intensifies the damage done to our psyches and bolsters the myths perpetrated about our inherent inferiority.	Brainwashed to hate ourselves, we were taught to admire those who taught us to laugh at our inferiority. They joke about our innate deficiencies, and then we followed suit, ridiculing and demeaning ourselves through humor.

Resolve to Be Better

To this day, I wish I'd never said the word. I felt its lameness. It was misunderstood by people. They didn't get what I was talking about. Neither did I...So I vowed never to say it again.
— Richard Pryor on his decision to stop using the N-word

While discussing resolutions as a guest on the January 12, 2007, *Tavis Smiley* show, Dr. Cornel West encouraged blacks to become "more critically informed" to be able to partake in "something grander than us." West urged that blacks ask themselves what they can do for "God, for justice, for freedom, for equality." There is no question that there is a pressing need for us to do better, to be better. However, what West recommends seems far beyond the reach of a race still laboring under the influence of a trauma that remains untreated because the diagnosis is not yet public.

We think we're joking and laughing at a script of our own design. Instead, we have swallowed a fallacy. The fact is that the script was actually written by those who control the media. They have been clever enough to write it for us, feed it to us, and have us deliver it for them, completely oblivious to the fact that there's nothing bold, new, or authentic about it.

To get to that healthy place of critical reflection and concerted action, we must first untwist the thread of historical brainwashing. This step automatically leads us to reevaluate our addiction to the laughing, singing, and smack-talking Neo-Coon.

The Pros & Cons of Neo-Coons

Short-term Benefits

1. **Laugh leader:** We're lucky to have comedians and entertainers who help us ease our emotional woes. Yes, they can be demeaning and destructive, but it's a small price to pay to avoid confronting our pain.

2. **Laugh factor:** It's best to laugh off the pain. Comedy is our weapon. It allows us to lash out at whites and poke fun at black folk. If anybody gets mad—"Hey, it's just a joke."

3. **See no evil:** No one wants to hear our gripes about racism or oppression. We can cope better if we pretend there has been no psychological damage caused by systemized oppression. Scrutinizing and attacking what's considered funny will only lead to more depression and a greater need for relief.

4. **Assault with a funny weapon:** It feels good to attack black folks with humor. Laughter takes some of the vindictiveness away. Although we share criticisms whites

have about blacks, comedy gives us an out—the fact that we can say "I'm only kidding" separates us from racists who hate black people.

Long-term Costs

1. **Laugh leader:** When comedians define us culturally as spokespersons, we risk endorsing any demeaning act. Dependence makes us vulnerable to emotional manipulation. Reliance on outside forces, as funny as they may be, is part of the BI campaign designed to blunt critical thinking.

2. **Laugh factor:** Comedy is not a weapon, it's a temporary fix. Laughing at the pain only prolongs the pain. Lashing out at whites and making fun of blacks is no joke. In communal settings, it only validates the status quo. The suppression of anger and frustration prevents us from moving toward self-love and empowered action.

3. **See no evil:** Ignoring systemized oppression or pretending it doesn't exist won't change reality or bring peace of mind. Questioning authority is an adult's prerogative and part of critical thinking. To be labeled as "stuck in the past" devalues our history. No other culture is encouraged to forget its history.

4. **Assault with a funny weapon:** The need to validate criticisms whites have about blacks, even through humor, is a reflection of inferiority brainwashing. To say "I'm only kidding" doesn't separate anyone from the racist; it validates racist perceptions. Complicit laughter not only condones the stereotype, it adds an element of truth to negatives designed to demean, belittle, and oppress black people.

Destroying Our Inner Coon

According to the news media, comedian Dave Chappelle had clearly lost his mind when he walked away from *Chappelle's Show* and his reported $50 million contract. As a guest on the *Oprah Winfrey Show* in 2006, Chappelle attempted to set the record straight. He left the show, Chappelle said, because he grew tired of playing "socially irresponsible" roles: "I felt like some kind of prostitute or something."

Chappelle seems to have recognized the fine line between Neo-Coonery and dignity, and took steps to break the psychological cycle. It takes guts to recognize symptoms of deep-rooted ailments, especially when it means sacrificing a life of emotional and financial reward. Chappelle's act of defiance underscores this chapter's mission. We have identified the age-old game of manipulated inferiority, the genesis of our entertainment addiction, and the quick fix provided by the unwitting Neo-Coon. Now is the time to defeat the forces that promote our communal affliction.

This is not a call to rebuke entertainers. I'm calling for a psychological revolution—and the destruction of our inner Neo-Coons—a planned reprogramming process designed to reshape our receptors to block BI conditioning no matter how funny the joke may seem. This process comes complete with positive propaganda tools.

"No Neo-Coon" Positive Propaganda Cues

Stand-up against put-downs
When a joke reinforces negative attitudes and behaviors, it is harmful. When you realize that the joke is harmful, speak up or tune it out.

Stop yuk-in' and jivin'
For those people who have the stage, don't fan the flames of BI propaganda.

Don't laugh to keep from thinking
Don't use laughter to avoid dealing with the important racial issues.

Laugh at your own risk
Some jokes actually do hurt and reinforce existing internalized feelings of black inferiority.

Once we shift our loyalty and place comedy and entertainment in their proper perspective, we no longer follow the lead of misguided celebrities. Disturbing messages may not seem so funny once they are strained through newly implanted critical-thinking filters.

The Last Word

The media is powerful. Those in the business of making people laugh are also powerful. We have an abundance of creative, hard working, charismatic black personalities. I'm confident they can produce material that makes people laugh without being destructive or chipping away at our self-esteem.

With her 2009 HBO comedy special, *I'ma Be Me*, Wanda Sykes presented about 90 minutes of observational humor on politics, anti-gay legislation, personal relationships, getting older, and erectile dysfunction ads without a hint of BI Complex–inspired self-degradation.

We must also challenge black Hollywood to step outside the parameters that keep us see-sawing between buffoonery and pathology. Black comedians can rise to the challenge and it's our job as the audience to recognize and reward those who do the right thing, and hold accountable those who don't. For those who tell the joke, and for those who listen, the litmus test should be:

Does this move us forward?
Does it move us backward?
Does it keep us in the same place and in the same brainwashed state?

Given the severity of our situation, it is vital that we work to have more in the "move us forward" category. I'm asking all African Americans who've been blessed with the combination of luck, talent, and tenacity that put them in positions of influence to really think about what we've discussed here and their parts in perpetuating the idea of inferiority, and to change.

As our griots have said, *Once you know better, you have to do better.*

Chapter 12

Yes, We Must!

Healing from the Inside Out

The final chapter of Brainwashed *cannot—
must not—be a conclusion.*

— DEBORAH COWELL, 40, WRITER

Dear Mr. Burrell,

*I am both honored and humbled to have had the opportunity
to be an early reviewer of* Brainwashed: Challenging the Myth
of Black Inferiority. *The most important thing about this book
is its use of history as evidence. There has been a brainwashing
campaign of epic proportions going on for the longest time and
the proof is absolutely everywhere. You don't even have to go as far
back as Thomas Jefferson. J. Edgar Hoover went on record making
it clear that the objective of the United States government was to
stop the rise of a black messiah at all costs. Hence COINTELPRO.
This is not conspiracy theory. This is fact. History is the proof.*

*While digesting this book, I had the opportunity to be in close
proximity and had intense discussions with a few 20-somethings.
The experience has been eye-opening. I am about to turn 40 and
a couple of these 20-somethings have noted that I am either the*

same age as, or, a year younger than their mothers. This does more than give me pause. It saddens me. It scares me. Everyone needs to have a clear idea of what exactly is at stake. What I know is that there is another generation of kids who are on the brink of being lost.

There is a book called The Black Woman: An Anthology *by Toni Cade Bambara and Eleanor W. Traylor, that targeted young folks who had come of age during the Black Power movement. The book, in a very specific way, was the call to action of its time. One call urged black folk to prepare for the revolution by "breeding an army," or so the discourse went.*

Fast forward and we get a clear picture of what someone else planned for our "army." Colored contact lenses, new and improved hair relaxers, crack cocaine, poverty, teen pregnancy, AIDS, imprisonment, death, and more dysfunction and disunity than ever. Thank God we had hip-hop, until the record moguls realized that money could be made through the perpetration of violence and defamation of women. Thank God for "spoken word," until television folks got hold of it and turned it into an exaggerated curse fest. Thank God, we have black authors and black books until publishers discovered there was a greater black market for street lit than Danticat, Morrison, or Mosley.

Thank God for the Internet. We have yet to see what the "until" will be. Because the brainwashing campaign has been so deeply pervasive and so insidious, that generation is cross cultural—it's not "just us," it's all of us. Put madness in music, set it to a wonderful beat and white folks play it in their headphones, too. Put crazy images of black folks on television and in movies and white folks lap it up, too. Incessantly repeat that blacks are inferior and that, too, becomes a universal reality.

Brainwashed *is more than a discussion about "what happened to us," it is a call to action—not a call to arms, but a call to action. And the time is now.*

The letter from writer Deborah Cowell arrived as I was tweaking the final chapter of this book. Parts of her letter have been included in this chapter because her insights, passions, and concerns speak to the mission I've attempted to put forth here. She notes the "almost there" potential of the Black Power movement and how it, too, was flipped on us and used to further our mental demise. She voices concern that a golden opportunity to use new media and fresh, unbridled talent will once again become part of the BI Complex arsenal.

As an example Cowell cited the newly released film, *Precious*, based on the 1996 novel *Push* by the poet Sapphire, directed by Lee Daniels and executive produced by Tyler Perry and Oprah Winfrey. The movie tells the story of an obese and horribly abused black teenage girl in Harlem. Precious's fantasies of being a celebrity, a BET dancer, and a model with a light-skinned boyfriend speak to the state of black confusion we have explored so far. Director Daniels received a standing ovation at the Cannes Film Festival and the Grand Jury prize at the Sundance Film Festival in 2009.

In her letter, Cowell also expressed concern about the praise heaped on those involved with the film:

> *The reality of black life ... right? When I heard the film garnered a fifteen-minute standing ovation at the film festival, I was horrified. To have not one, but a few conversations with folks who said it was an important, must-see movie, became more than I can stand. I can't help but wonder—did* Finding Forrester *get the same response?*

In his Variety review, John Anderson described *Precious* as "an urban nightmare with a surfeit of soul," like "a diamond—clear, bright, but oh so hard." Clay Cane, writing for BET.com predicted the film will "go down as one of the great films in American cinema." In contrast, the urban web site MediaTakeOut.com, criticized the film's "blatant colorism in casting," noting that the "good characters" were either white or biracial, while all "the evil characters" were played by "dark skinned Black actors." Armond White, in a scathing *New York Press* review, described the movie as a "Klansman's fantasy" that allows whites to enjoy a "sense of superiority—and relief":

"Not since The Birth of a Nation has a mainstream movie demeaned the idea of black American life as much as Precious. Full of brazenly racist clichés (Precious steals and eats an entire bucket of fried chicken), it is a sociological horror show. Offering racist hysteria masquerading as social sensitivity, it's been acclaimed on the international festival circuit that usually disdains movies about black Americans as somehow inartistic and unworthy."

The varying reviews, no doubt, reflect the diverse and complex reactions of black audiences. We are not monolithic people. Some of us were insulted by the exaggeration of black pathologies and color coded casting, while others lauded the quality of the acting and bold attempt to bring subjects like incest and sexual and physical abuse among blacks into the public arena.

Debates will continue about Winfrey's and Perry's involvement with the film but our concerns must go far beyond the offerings of any single individuals. Will this powerful film of unspeakable trauma and redemption serve to increase perceptions of our compassion and strengths or simply reinforce the stigma of our community's pathology in the wider world? Damaging content can indeed come in beautiful packages. We must always be ready to ask ourselves the hard questions. No matter which side of the fence you land on, a film like Precious provides an unprecedented teachable moment and a reminder that none of us can afford to abandon our critical thinking capacities.

It also speaks to the power of propaganda. The film was a "must see" mostly because the media noticed it was connected with powerful black names in Hollywood and it exposed and propagated exaggerated but palatable black pathologies.

In real life, Gabourey Sidibe, the star of the film, defies the stereotypical role of downtrodden, abused and hopeless Precious. At the time of filming, Sidibe, a psychology major, attended City College in New York. We will have truly "arrived" when the black powers-that-be realize the value of promoting the potential of black women like Sidibe instead of the over-hyped pathologies of Precious.

Because We Are
All *Precious*

How will we use what we've learned here to enact changes in our lives, relationships, and communities? What can we do as individuals to combat something so sophisticated and so entrenched in our society? What will it take to gather diverse forces who will rise above historic divisions, combine their talents, and launch a collective, cohesive anti-brainwashing media campaign?

Of all the disciplines and forces there are for major change, none is more powerful (for good or evil) than propaganda: the strategic planning and placement of words and images. The right words, in the right place, at the right time, have exponential value. Jefferson's five words, "all men are created equal" survived all his attempts to rescind them through contradictory deeds and writings. Indeed, a picture can be worth infinitely *more* than a thousand words. Linking the right pictures and words at the right time has a potent ability to persuade, influence behaviors, and engender the courage to change the world.

These closing pages will outline a multi-tiered, action-oriented strategy designed to finally terminate the four-century-old BI campaign. But, without concrete buy-in and radical action from Hollywood to the hood, all we've done is recycle the black identity problem. That's not enough. My goal is to join with like-minded others to plan and implement the most aggressive marketing campaign that we've ever engaged in. I'm not asking you to put foot to pavement, but I am asking you to put your mind where our future can be. In other words, this is not just a book, it's a mission—one that no single individual can accomplish alone.

As Cowell said, *"the final chapter of Brainwashed cannot—must not be a conclusion!"* It won't be. Consider these final pages a rallying cry to the young and not-so-young; a communal call to cease seeing ourselves as victims, to roll up our sleeves, utilize our talents, honor our ancestors, and finally, *finally* regain control of our lives, our destinies, and our minds.

Question, Analyze, Unplug, Reprogram

Up to now, this book has been about the myth of our inferiority and how, why, and by whom it was sold to blacks and America at-large—in short, how we became brainwashed.

I've shared what I've learned as a black man who made his living studying black people and understanding the power of propaganda. Unlike even the best-funded, most massive advertising campaigns, the BI crusade used every institution of American society, including media, education, law, religion, and science to seed and promote its propaganda. The major difference between the past and now is that the campaign is more sophisticated, insidious, and persuasive than ever. Most critically, its major perpetrators are blacks, not whites.

In *Africans at the Crossroads: Notes for a World African Revolution,* historian John Henrik Clarke examined the propaganda that was central to the European domination of the planet in the 15th and 16th centuries. "The greatest achievement was the conquest of the minds of most of the people of the world," Clarke surmised. Clarke didn't need any media literacy training when he called for a plan to counteract white corporate media's brainwashing campaign. He instinctively suggested we adhere to a powerful four-step mandate: "Question, Analyze, Rethink, and Unplug." Clarke's advice serves as my springboard. But, considering the urgency of our mission and the advances in media technology, I add an addendum: "Question, Analyze, Unplug, and Reprogram."

If you've come this far, you've been prepped for the next phase of our journey. The dots have been connected. We've examined the historical roots and modern manifestations of words and images that perpetuate black inferiority. We have answered and analyzed the tough questions—why we can't build strong families; why we still promote black sexual stereotypes; why "black" and "beauty" are still contradictions; why we kill one another at astronomical rates; and how denial, risky behavior, and poor eating habits are sending so many of us to early graves. We now know why we can't stop shopping; why we instinctively expect so little from each other and our children; why we so easily give up our power; why we can't work together; and we understand the painful and shameful motivators that beg for humorous distraction.

The end of each chapter was constructed to further the four-step process. We've examined the costs and benefits of each negative manifestation. Awareness is the first step. We must make sure our receivers are powered up to detect and dissect the avalanche of daily media messages. The simplest means to accomplish this task is to ask three basic questions:

"Does it hurt black self-esteem?"
"Does it help black self-esteem?"
"Does it have no effect on black self-esteem?"

Positive propaganda cues were provided at the end of each chapter to help prepare our minds to rethink, challenge, and unplug from the onslaught of negative stimuli. With these cues, we are better equipped.

10 ANTIDOTES TO END MENTAL SLAVERY TODAY

1.   Recognize and acknowledge that you have been brainwashed.

2.   Use your mind and think for yourself. Don't go along with the brainwashing program.

3.   Stop looking to other races to do for you. Do for self.

4.   Demand accountability from our leaders, be they preachers, teachers, politicians, or entertainers.

5.   Don't settle for seconds. Be a first-class citizen, consumer, parent, etc.

6. Ask, "What's so funny?" Before you laugh at any friend's or professional comedian's jokes, ask yourself if the laugh's really on you...and other black folks.

7. When you hear lyrics or see videos that denigrate or demean through misogyny or the glorification of violence ask, "Why am I participating in this?" "Why am I sitting still for this?"

8. Demand a return on your investment. Support individuals and organizations dedicated to solving, not just treating, the race problem.

9. Be outraged at white-on-black injustice but be even more outraged at black-on-black injustice.

10. Understand that you are the center of your own control. You don't need permission. You are a self-appointed leader.

We have questioned, analyzed, and begun the unplugging process. It is time to reprogram.

The greatest social movements in history began with a change of consciousness. And make no mistake about it, propaganda, still is the most effective tool in creating new consciousness. Thanks to positive propaganda, smoking cigarettes is no longer hip; it's now widely considered disgusting and deadly. "Saving our planet" is no longer a cause just for tree huggers and environmentalists. Almost everyone now knows we can't keep trashing our world.

This is why, after nearly four centuries, I'm calling for a new campaign that markets multi-dimensional, fully developed, non-destructive visions and images of ourselves. I'm calling for a movement created by African Americans specifically for African Americans but curative for all infected by the BI brand. This is the beginning of a campaign to change black minds.

The Campaign to Change Black Minds

There is another election coming up in 2012. Twenty-somethings will be five years older. The images on television and in movies will matter much less than the information distributed on the web. You cannot just say to a generation of kids, "This is what's wrong. Fix it. Good night."
—Deborah Cowell, 40, writer

Our immediate challenge is evident in Cowell's observation. No matter how tech-savvy, energetic, talented, or creative they may be, we cannot expect the next generation to just "fix it." Nor can we afford to disregard or dismiss the experience, tenacity, or the wealth and wisdom of the 30-, 40-, 70- or 80-somethings. Our grassroots marketing campaign must be engineered in a way that allows everyone with the will to play respected and valuable roles.

I've discussed the damaging effects of sex- and violence-laden hip-hop lyrics and videos, but along with that criticism comes an acknowledgment of tremendous accomplishment. Say what you will about the music but it cannot be disputed that young black people created a multibillion-dollar industry that's just as significant as jazz, rock 'n' roll, or rhythm & blues. More importantly, they started this exciting new genre in backyards, on the corners, in the subways, on the beach, and in the clubs without anyone's permission.

I didn't wait for permission to start my own advertising and marketing firm. I just did it. Historic social movements weren't permitted; they were demanded. Throughout this book, we have talked about ways to foster self-motivated change agents who operate without the permission of teachers, ministers, or members of the old guard of the civil rights era. There's something necessary about that youthful spirit of creativity and independence pulsating through the hip-hop community. It must be harnessed and used for our new media campaign.

The Internet provides a level, global playing field. With the Internet and a unified mission, our churches, black organizations, neighborhood centers, and individual homes become bases of strategic reform and replenishment. With an organized effort, anyone and everyone with ideas, talent, and courage can be empowered without anybody's permission.

Here we must be careful to avoid the "diss-unity" trap. Valuing new energy doesn't mean we discard those who have fought and are still fighting the hard fight mentoring, educating, and nurturing black kids, and who are actively engaged in other efforts to change negative conditions.

Great social movements require a great change in consciousness. By fate, profession, or life experience, I am unabashedly race-conscious. Therefore, I'm calling for a new generation of race-consciousness—but in a new way. Disengaging ourselves from the word "inferiority" and replacing it with its opposite, "black superiority," will be just as damaging, just as illusory, and just as counterproductive for us as it has been for whites. Our mission is more complex than a label. We tried "Black Power" and "black is beautiful." We've been emancipated, liberated, and integrated; now we supposedly live in a post-racial society. Those labels gave some of us hope and helped us feel momentarily better. None, however, have been strong enough to truly convince us that we are as beautiful, as resourceful, and as equal as whites.

New race consciousness moves us beyond labeling. It introduces a new game board. It's no longer about changing white folks' minds—it's about changing our collective mindset. It's about people dedicated to destroying the myth of black inferiority with a powerful new media campaign.

New race consciousness creates the opportunity for brilliant, creative minds to collaborate. It challenges the Jeremiah Wrights to jam with the Jay-Zs; the Angela Davises to hook up with the Alicia Keyses; the Andrew Youngs to team up with the Akons; the Iyanla Vanzants to strategize with the Van Joneses; and the Wests (Cornel and Kanye) to harmonize together.

If we have reached consensus that brainwashing is real and it must end NOW, age or stature won't trump energy and commitment, and no one will be expected to "fix it" alone.

The Resolution Will Not Be Televised

Thankfully, the brainwashing campaign got an egregious derailment. The level of brilliance attached to the Obama candidacy will be studied for centuries to come. The revolution was not televised. It happened over the Internet. Honestly, I believe that what we did on November 4, 2008 helped save the nation. Now we need to do the same thing with technology to help save ourselves.
—Deborah Cowell, 40, writer

We have an opportunity here like no other—to put into practice what we have learned through our collective effort to help get the right candidate elected to the most powerful position in the world. Age, race, social or economic stature, gender—none of those things mattered. Obama and a group of creative, limitless thinkers used modern technology to trounce ancient prejudices, age-old stereotypes, and ingrained fears. The words "Yes we can!" linked with the right images nudged a divided nation into changing the course of history.

In 2007, I created the Resolution Project with a goal of sparking intra-racial dialogue and sharing ideas about ways we can challenge and change how we perceive ourselves. This book is the Resolution Project's first tangible product. Our task is to use propaganda to eradicate negative images and replace them with a bombardment of positive words and images.

Branding got us into this mess. Branding can get us out. Only this time we're branding ourselves. I've worked with a creative team to come up with one prototypical advertising campaign that will attack some of the issues we've addressed in this book. For our purposes here, we'll call it the "New Black Brains" or "*New B*'s" campaign. The theme is meant to provide a hip, attractive, fashionable symbol for our desired actions. Part of the problem with what has been said or written (even in this book) about our issues is that, out of necessity, the conversations veer toward the creation, development, or consequence of the problem. There's been a lot of time spent telling us what's "wrong with us."

The *New B's* Campaign is designed to not only show us what's right, but make it hot, sexy, hip—all the things almost any person wants to be. Like historic efforts to change the black image—Du Bois's Talented Tenth, the Harlem Renaissance's "New Negro"—our campaign proposes drastic social change but will use the power of propaganda and media to attract and evangelize. Unlike others, our campaign is not exclusive to those with certain degrees or of celebrated status. All that's needed to join the *New B's* is a new way of thinking and acting.

The *New B's* is only meant to serve as a catalyst to stimulate thought and more dialogue. It is offered here as an example of how powerful, positive ad campaigns can work. In the end, we may develop something different but just as effective. With that said, let us examine positive propaganda as a means to replace the myth of our inferiority with the reality of our greatness.

Create & Promote the *New B* Image

Launch an online campaign backed by posters, slogans, lyrics, and images that promote the *New B* image. This campaign even allows us to set up a boogeyman—people who act as though they have "Old Black Brains." *New B's* aren't violent, demeaning, or destructive. They are depicted in loving relationships with their spouses and children. They are actively involved in their communities and engaged in efforts to promote better health and safe, economically thriving, self-sustaining communities. Appealing *New B* images, songs, and catchphrases should be incorporated in daily life.

Develop the Black Bill of Responsibilities

Instead of only talking about our rights, we should produce and circulate a *New B* "Bill of Rights and Responsibilities" card and poster to remind us of our rights. We have the right to be healthy, happy, and fully engaged citizens without living under the shadow of racial inferiority. We have the right to create images and communities of our own design. This professionally designed, laminated card will serve as a visual reminder that we are part of a larger collective, fully engaged in an ongoing campaign to reclaim our minds.

Create a Sovereign State (of Mind) Campaign

Part of our problem in America is that we have never been independent citizens of our own sovereign state. We have been associated with slavery, segregation, and integration. Whatever relationship we had to any other nation was severed centuries ago. To succeed together, we must see ourselves as a distinct and powerful culture, instead of a temporary, inferior subculture that depends on white America for sustenance. The "Sovereign State of Mind" campaign reinforces our uniqueness, our proud past and our right to develop an independent system that addresses our distinct needs and desires.

Create and/or Support Locus of Control Centers

We can no longer allow schools and educators, influenced by the BI Complex, to underestimate the power and potential of black communities and black children. We must support schools that teach kids to effect change in their communities. This part of the *New B* campaign supports and celebrates schools that do it right and offer after-school or in-home curricula and activities for students not exposed to this valuable information.

Create a Black Truth Squad

Establish an African American Anti-Defamation League Cultural Commission, or "Black Truth Squad" organization. Like the Jewish Anti-Defamation League, the role of this online organization is to combat all forms of negative, stereotypical imagery through social network sharing, publicity, boycotts, and other legal actions. The "Truth Squad" will promote positive aspects of African American culture and try to contain and eliminate negative, demeaning holdovers from slavery and segregation. Unlike the JADL, however, the AADLCC will initially go after black folk. This campaign isn't geared to change white folks' minds. Its mission is to create a new black mindset.

Develop and Introduce the 'For Example' Award
This is not an award for perfect people. If so, it would never be given. The For Example Award will be presented to everyday people who have contributed positive value to African Americans in particular and the human race in general. Since all of us are capable of doing both good and bad, the For Example Award will be given to those individuals who have done—and are doing—the most good.

Introduce the *New B* Wonder Awards Ceremony
This annual awards gala (named after Stevie Wonder) honors entertainers who exhibit the highest level of positive artistry without resorting to exploitative, negative, or denigrating tactics.

Create the Neo-Coon Award
Like the Mr. Blackwell "Worst Dressed Award," this annual virtual award goes to the institution or persons that has done the most to reshackle our minds.

Establish the Black Brains Think Tank
This virtual, online university is the place where scholars, professionals, and the black public at large can study, share ideas, and develop new ways of creating a new black American culture. It would also be charged with developing a "Resolution Plan."

Sponsor the Black Future Contest
We know our past. Now it's time to invite young minds to create our future. The "Black Future Contest" provides a cash award or scholarship to young contestants who come up with scenarios for African American future achievement and advancement. This *New B* contest should be sponsored by blacks and incorporated in the nations' schools. If that's a challenge, we incorporate through our network of churches, organizations, and the Internet.

Create a Great Black Images (or Missing Images) Hall of Fame, Traveling Exhibit and/or Web Site

The most beautiful, positive, and life-affirming photographs, art, books, poetry, films, music, etc. and the people who created them (or who exemplify these traits) will be displayed along with the most positive aspects of black culture and achievement. Many of the artifacts (like the photos of middle-class, healthy black families in the late 1890s through the early '60s) that were hidden from the public would get their first wide public exposure. The "Great Black Images" *New B*'s exhibit will be another tool to stimulate dialogue and inspire independent action and collective change.

Other *New B* Concepts and Possibilities May Include:

State of Black Leadership Annual Report Card

This evaluation addresses all aspects of African American leadership in all industries and fields, and gives honest, bottom-up assessments of the effectiveness of each individual or group.

Organize the Creation of *New B*'s MySpace, Facebook, Twitter, and Other Social Networking Sites

These sites will be launched for the *New B*'s "Change your mind. Change your environment. Change your friends" continuous dialogue campaign.

Establish Annual Regional and National *New B* Conferences Held at African American-Owned Venues

Of course, propaganda, no matter how powerful, can't work by itself. To be successful, we need your input, feedback, and active involvement in the New B's Campaign as we focus on four specific goals:

Mastering Media literacy
Challenging and eliminating negative propaganda
Creating and disseminating positive propaganda
Mainstreaming our new messages to the world

Technology has changed the way we communicate. Social networking Web sites have become much more than a means to find new mates and long-lost high school buddies. Facebook, Twitter, MySpace, and LinkedIn represent virtual communities of millions with shared interests. Corporations and organizations have discovered that generating conversations and discussions on these sites creates brand awareness and drives traffic to their own online sites.

With technology, we have the opportunity to institute a new communication model, elevate cultural dialogue and reward positive thinking. Consider Jamilah Lemieux's open letter to Tyler Perry. After posting it on her blog, NPR republished the letter on its Web site. Lemieux expanded the dialogue and received international attention simply because she had the temerity to speak up.

Likewise, with new media technology and awareness, we can analyze, respond, create news and reward contributors. We can dissect the tentacles and alliances of negative propaganda disguised as entertainment. New B's can commit to daily online conversations detailing how they recognized and overcame various aspects of the black inferiority conditioning. Groups can regulate media assignments, monitoring and flagging the positive or negative contributions of morning talk radio shows, children's programs, or new movies and television shows.

Most importantly, we can have fun. Imagine reaching young kids before the brainwashing is too deeply embedded. As our efforts to create sophisticated positive propaganda becomes newsworthy, we can call on enlightened popular artists to support the effort. Imagine a 15-minute positive propaganda YouTube spot featuring the likes of Jay-Z, Nas, Mary J., Tina Turner, or Aretha Franklin. With a sophisticated social network of hundreds of thousands, we have the power to create new success stories and launch our own "New B" careers in music and the arts.

I envision a coast-to-coast community of committed individuals harnessing the Internet to unleash unprecedented "no-victims-allowed" dialogue. The Resolution Project will serve as a hub, a gathering place for networking, strategizing, and transforming reality through innovative marketing and advertising campaigns dedicated to ending the BI Complex because we will dare to hold ourselves and the world to a new standard. The Resolution Project Virtual Channel will encourage people to utilize new media as both consumers and producers.

The Resolution Project didn't require anyone's permission. The seeds have been planted. Now it's up to each of us to do the work required to create a fruitful yield.

Yes, We Must!

The election of Barack Obama, the novelty of "the first black president," has worn off. Already, BI-influenced whites (and blacks) are actively trying to undermine the magic of that historic moment.

Deborah Cowell, hopefully one of our newest Resolution Project recruits, strikes the appropriate tone of urgency. Obama gave us hope, but hope pitted against a seasoned, masterfully trained brainwashing champion has been KO'd in the past.

We need more than hope, more than symbolism.

President Obama, as gifted an orator as he is, didn't win the election on oratory skills alone. With new-age technology, word-of-mouth activity, with young volunteers energized by the testimonials of entertainers and street beats from geniuses like Will-i-am, Obama's "truth" touched souls ranging from 90-year-old grandmothers to 18-year-old first-time voters.

Make no mistake about it, the most powerful weapon in the brainwash arsenal is media—everything, audio or visual, via television, radio, film, music videos, billboard, print, the Internet, or cell phones—that influence our minds. It is an arsenal now at our disposal.

The anti-BI campaign is not an attack on white people—they, too, are BI victims. This is not an attempt to ostracize or replace traditional black institutions or individuals. On the contrary, our success ultimately is everybody's success. This is a call to coalesce, unify, improve, and end a detrimental campaign that has gone unrecognized and unaddressed for too long. This is a declaration: "We are watching. We're no longer helpless. We plan to defend ourselves through the power of our untapped genius and the best communication mediums available!"

I believe that once we change the image of ourselves, we will change the image of humanity, and subsequently deflate a debilitating power structure. We will blaze a new path of unlimited possibilities for future generations free of the BI influence. There is no better time, no better opportunity, than now.

"We may not have all the power we want, but we have all the power we need!"

Acknowledgments

Birthing *Brainwashed* was not an easy task, and I am deeply grateful to all who helped to bring it to life.

I would first like to thank my wife, Madeleine, whom amazing fortune brought into my life. She has been constantly by my side on this journey, as major contributor, loving guardrail, and guiding light.

Publisher Tavis Smiley for recognizing my passion.

SmileyBooks president and my editor Cheryl Woodruff, whose extraordinary commitment and wise counsel kept me going (and growing) throughout this journey. Having been warmed by her fire, and inspired by her tenacious dedication to professional excellence, I am forever in her debt.

Undaunted by adversity, laser-focused, and committed to the end, my newfound blood brother Sylvester Brown, Jr. showed me how to spin straw into gold. I look forward to watching him spread his creative wings and soaring for many years to come.

Without the day-to-day organizational, technical, research, and creative skills of the incomparable Willow Wells, this book would not have been done as well, nor finished as soon.

Special thanks to the indefatigable SmileyBooks team, especially John McWilliams, Rose Jefferson-Frazier, Carl Arnold, and Hay House's Amy Gingery for their exceptional efforts.

Thanks to the multi-talented Lowell Thompson, who, among his many contributions, created the visual concept for the Timeline; and Angela Dodson for her early technical guidance and moral support.

Boundless gratitude to Juan Roberts of Creative Lunacy for creating our arresting cover, and to graphic designer Terry Barnes and photo researcher Diane Allford-Trotman for their heroic and outstanding contributions to the *Brainwashed* Timeline.

Applause to my comrade-in-arms, Deborah Cowell, for her inspiring contribution to "Yes, We Must."

Pat Ward, a trusted and constant provider of calming, user-friendly wisdom, kept us centered and on track through it all.

For helping to make the difficult eminently doable, I extend my sincere thanks to Sarah Burroughs, Ronnie Reese, Atsede Elegba, Joyce McGriff, Leonce Gaiter, Diane Weathers, asha bendele, Nick Chiles, Todd Burroughs, Esther Franklin, Johnathon Briggs, Susie Ward, Tegan and Adam Moore, Lisa Riley, Mike Smith, Nancy Davis, Cheeraz Gormon, Sergio Mims, Bob Sayles, Barbara Allen, Morris "Butch" Stewart, Janice Kelly, Leslie Cole, Jun Mhoon, Anita Burson, Fay Ferguson, George Curry, Fern Gillespie, and Herb Boyd.

Special thanks to dearest friends and uplifters Ed and Carolyn Lewis; Susan L. Taylor, for always encouraging my forward movement; David Bloom, Donna Pierce, Bill Sharp, Frantz and McGhee Osse, Denise Bradley, and Steve Durchslag. Thanks for words of wisdom from Na'im Akbar, Randall Robinson, Joy DeGruy, Boyd James, Derrick and Janet Bell, Anderson Thompson, Carl Bell, Adelaide Sanford, and Natasha Tarpley.

I proudly and gratefully stand between the strength and the promise of my mother, Evelyn Burrell; my daughters Bonita and Alexandra; and my son, Jason. I strive to make them as proud of me as I am of them.

And finally, my heart goes out to all the ancestors who withstood so much, sacrificed so much, and made so much possible. This book is just the beginning in my pledge to make your sacrifice redemptive through conscious and committed resolution.

Endnotes

Chapter 1: The Scorch at the Bottom of the Melting Pot
1. W. E. B. Du Bois, *W. E. B. Du Bois: A Reader*, edited by David Levering Lewis (Holt Paperbacks, February 15, 1995)
2. Norman Coombs, *The Immigrant Heritage of America* (Twayne Press, 1972).

Chapter 2: Relationship Wrecks
1. Dr. King citation from "Black Families: Surviving Slavery," TIME.com, Nov. 22, 1976, http://www.time.com/time/magazine/article/0,9171,914677,00.html
2. Obama's Father's Day Remarks, Transcript, New York Times, June 15, 2008
3. "Papa Was a Rollin' Stone" by The Temptations, released 1972, Hitsville U.S.A.
4. Margaret Mead, "The Negro Family: The Case for National Action," The Moynihan Report (1965), Office of Policy Planning and Research, United States Department of Labor, March 1965, http://www.blackpast.org/?q=primary/moynihan-report-1965
5. Brenda L. Richardson and Dr. Brenda Wade, *What Mama Couldn't Tell Us About Love* (Harper Paperbacks, July 3, 2000)
6. "My Man," recorded by Billie Holiday (Brunswick 1937 and Decca Records 1948)
7. E. Franklin Frazier, *Negro Family in the United States* (revised paperback, University of Notre Dame Press, January 2001)
8. Kevin Powell, *Open Letters to America: Essays by Kevin Powell* (Soft Skull Press, October 20, 2009)
9. Dr. Arlett Malvo, "Black Females Raising Black Males," July, 7, 2008, http://www.myfoxwfld.com/myvoicedc/2008/07/18/tv-one-series-black-men-revealed-back-with-a-hot-season/
10. Orlando Patterson, *Rituals of Blood: The Consequences of Slavery In Two American Centuries* (Basic Civitas Books, December 9, 1999)
11. Institute on Domestic Violence in the African American Community (IDVAAC), University of Minnesota, http://www.dvinstitute.org/media/publications/FactSheet.IDVAAC_AAPCFV-Community%20Insights.pdf
12. Black & Married With Kids.com, http://blackandmarriedwithkids.com/

Chapter 3: Studs and Sluts
1. Thomas Jefferson, *Notes on the State of Virginia, 1743–1826*, Electronic Text Center, University of Virginia Library, http://etext.virginia.edu/toc/modeng/public/JefVirg.html

2. "LeBron James Criticized for Vogue Cover: ESPN columnist sees racist undertones in photograph with supermodel." EURWEB.com, March 26, 2008, http://www.eurweb.com/story/eur42039.cfm

3. "Race and the ape image," opinion by Phillip Atiba Goff and Jennifer L. Eberhardt, *Los Angeles Times*, February 28, 2009, http://www.latimes.com/news/opinion/commentary/la-oe-goff28-2009feb28,0,1418895.story

4. A. Elaine Brown Crawford, *Hope in the Holler: A Womanist Theology* (Louisville: Westminster John Knox Press, 2002)

5. Jabari Asim, *The N Word: Who Can Say It, Who Shouldn't, and Why* (Houghton Mifflin Harcourt, March 26, 2007). Asim cites White's *An Account of the Regular Gradation in Man, and in Different Animals and Vegetables; and from the Former to the Latter* (1799)

6. Deborah Gray White, *Ar'n't I a Woman?: Female Slaves in the Plantation South* (W.W. Norton & Co., revised edition, February 17, 1999)

7. "Trina," http://www.wikimusicguide.com/Trina

8. "Nelly in Hot Water over Video," MTV Networks European, Jan. 10, 2001, http://www.mtv.tv/article/10800_Nelly_in_hot_water_over_video.htm

9. "The Attitudes and Behavior of Young Black Americans," University of Chicago
Center for the Study of Race, Politics, and Culture, http://www-news.uchicago.edu/releases/07/pdf/070201.cohen-byp.pdf

10. Earni Young, "Urban lit goes legit: authors headline new ventures to bring street cred into the world of corporate publishing," *Black Issues Book Review*, Sept–Oct 2006, http://findarticles.com/p/articles/mi_m0HST/is_5_8/ai_n27026371/

11. George M. Fredrickson, *The Black Image in the White Mind: The Debate on Afro-American Character and Destiny, 1817–1914*, (Wesleyan, March 15, 1987)

12. Donald Bogle, *Toms, Coons, Mulattoes, Mammies, & Bucks: An Interpretive History of Blacks in American Films*, (New York: Continuum, 1994)

13. April Silver, "Beneath Low: BET, Lil Wayne Set the Stage for Child Pornography," Clutch Magazine Online, July 2, 2009, http://clutchmagonline.com/newsgossipinfo/beneath-low-bet-lil-wayne-set-the-stage-for-child-pornography/#1

14. Michel Marriott,"Black Erotica Challenges Black Tradition," New York Times, Sunday, June 1, 1997, http://www.nytimes.com/1997/06/01/style/black-erotica-challenges-black-tradition.html?pagewanted=all

15. "Will Smith on Playing Muhammad Ali: The Fight of Will Smith's Life," ABC News.com, Dec. 3, 2001, http://abcnews.go.com/Primetime/Story?id=132161&page=2)

Chapter 4: Uglified

1. bell hooks, *Sisters of the Yam: Black Women and Self-Recovery* (South End Press, July 1, 1999)

2. Hazel Trice Edney, "New 'doll test' produces ugly results," FinalCall.com, Sep 14, 2006, http://www.finalcall.com/artman/publish/National_News_2/

New_doll_test_produces_ugly_results_2919.shtml

3. Burrell interview with author and journalist asha bandele

4. A'lelia Bundles, *On Her Own Ground: The Life and Times of Madam C.J. Walker* (Scribner January 2, 2002)

5. Alex Haley, The Autobiography of Malcolm X: As Told to Alex Haley (Ballantine Books, October 12, 1987)

6. Kimberly Davis, "Why more blacks are choosing plastic surgery," *Ebony*, August, 2004, http://findarticles.com/p/articles/mi_m1077/is_10_59/ai_n6119096/?tag=content;col1

7. "Glamour Editor To Lady Lawyers: Being Black Is Kinda A Corporate 'Don't,'" jezebel.com: http://jezebel.com/289268/glamour-editor-to-lady-lawyers-being-black-is-kinda-a-corporate-dont

8. "Hairy Advice, Glamour Stirs Another Racial Debate" by Monica Harris, blackcollegeview.com, Sept. 09, 2000, http://media.www.blackcollegeview.com/media/storage/paper928/news/2007/09/09/News/Hairy.Advice-2945315.shtml7

9. "Mamas Wear Your Hair Natural," by K. Danielle Edwards, BlackCommentator.com
(http://www.blackcommentator.com/274/274_ftf_mammas_wear_hair_natural.html)

10. *Oprah Winfrey Show*, Sept. 30, 2009, YouTube clip: http://www.youtube.com/watch?v=mQINvD2O6b0)

11. Laquita Thomas-Banks, "The Power of the Fro" clutchmagonline, Monday Jul 13, 2009, http://clutchmagonline.com/beauty/the-power-of-the-fro/#2

Chapter 5: Homey-cide

1. "Justice for the Jena Six—Take Action Now," naacp.org, http://www.naacp.org/youth/college/jena6/

2. "Morehouse student convicted of murder," Associated Press, published in the *Athens Banner-Herald*, 8/28/2009, http://chat.athensnewspapers.com/stories/082909/new_487253058.shtml

3. Fox Butterfield, *All God's Children* (Harper Perennial November 1, 1996)

4. Eugene D. Genovese, *Roll Jordon Roll: The World That the Slaves Made* (Vintage; 1st edition January 12, 1976)

5. Ralph Ellison, *Invisible Man* (Vintage, April 23, 1989)

6. Benjamin Mays, *Born to Rebel: An Autobiography* (University of Georgia Press, April 14, 2003)

7. Shaun L. Gabbidon and Helen T. Greene, *Race, Crime, and Justice: A Reader* (Routledge, 2005)

8. Gordon Berry, "Media Effects on African Americans," Encyclopedia of Children, Adolescents and the Media, 2007

9. The Sentencing Project: Research and Advocacy for Reform, http://www.sentencingproject.org/template/page.cfm?id=122

10. "Jim Webb's courage v. the 'pragmatism' excuse for politicians," Salon.com, March 28, 2009,http://www.salon.com/opinion/greenwald/2009/03/28/webb/index.html

11. "Criminalization of Black Children," Marian Wright Edelman, Blackstarnews, Nov. 23, 2007, http://www.blackstarnews.com/?c=135&a=3934

12. Carlos Sadovi, Kayce Ataiyero, and Sbr Angela Rozas, "Teens: 'No more funerals' Chicago students join public officials' call for solutions to ongoing teen killings," April 2, 2008, Chicagotribune.com,http://archives.chicagotribune.com/2008/apr/02/news/chi-chicago-school-protest_02apr02

Chapter 6: Slow Suicide

1. More African-Americans Die from Causes that Can Be Prevented or Treated, News Medical.Net, April 23, 2009, http://www.news-medical.net/news/2009/04/23/48783.aspx

2. Centers for Disease Control and Prevention (CDC), "Health of Black or African American Population," http://www.cdc.gov/nchs/fastats/black_health.htm

3. Janice Billingsley, "Randy Jackson Takes Aim at Diabetes," HealthDay Reporter, *HealthDay News*, October 4, 2007

4. Jawanza Kunjufu, *Satan! I'm Taking Back My Health*, (African American Images, June 2000)

5. Terrie Williams, *Black Pain: It Just Looks Like We're Not Hurting*, (Scribner, Jan. 6, 2009)

6. *When in Doubt, Add Bacon and Cheese: How the Food Industry Hijacked Our Brains and Made Us Fat*, Amy Goodman interview with Dr. David Kessler and Arun Gupta, *Democracy Now!*, August 10, 2009

7. Susan C. Duerksen, Amy Mikail, Laura Tom, Annie Patton, Janina Lopez, Xavier Amador, Reynaldo Vargas, Maria Victorio, Brenda Kustin, and Georgia Robins Sadler, Health disparities and advertising content of women's magazines: a cross-sectional study, http://www.biomedcentral.com/content/pdf/1471-2458-5-85.pdf

8. "Root of the Problem," The Center for Minority Health (CMH), May 14, 2009, http://www.cmh.pitt.edu/news_051409.asp

9. Income, Poverty and Health Insurance Coverage in the United States: 2008, U.S. Census Bureau, http://www.census.gov/Press-Release/www/releases/archives/income_wealth/014227.html

10. "The Cost of Cancer," blackenterprise.com, Sept. 2008, http://www.blackenterprise.com/lifestyle/health-wellness/2008/09/19/the-costs-of-cancer

11. TaRessa Stovall, "Racism Contributes to Health Disparities and Early Death, Research Says," The Defenders OnLine, http://www.thedefendersonline.com/2009/07/07/racism-contributes-to-health-disparities-and-early-death-research-says/)

12. Harriet A. Washington, *Medical Apartheid: The Dark History of Medical Experimentation on Black Americans from Colonial Times to the Present* (Doubleday, January 9, 2007)

Chapter 7: Buy Now, Pay Later

1. Dave Feschuk, "NBA players' financial security no slam dunk," January 31, 2008, The Star.Com, *Toronto Star*, http://www.thestar.com/article/299119

2 "African Americans and Latinos: The Future Middle Class," June 7, 2005, Demos.org, http://archive.demos.org/pubs/costly_credit_300.pdf

3. Johnnie L. Roberts, "The King's Ransom," Jun 26, 2009, *Newsweek* Web Exclusive, http://www.newsweek.com/id/204011 and "Michael Jackson, Style Icon," *Women's Wear Daily* Reports, June 25, 2009 http://www.theinsider.com/news/2307503_Women_s_Wear_Daily_Reports_Michael_Jackson_Style_Icon

4. Alexis Stodghill, "The Real Houswives of Atlanta Really Are Broke," BlackVoices.com, Aug 7, 2009,
http://www.bvonmoney.com/2009/08/07/real-houswives-of-atlanta-broke/

5. Barbara Ehrenreich and Dedrick Muhammad, "The Economic Fallout Has Decimated the Black Middle Class," Barbaraehrenreich.com, August 10, 2009, http://www.alternet.org/story/141825/

6. Jason Szep, "Blacks suffer most in U.S. foreclosure surge," March 20, 2007, Reuters, http://www.reuters.com/article/domesticNews/idUSN1931892620070320

7. Javier Silva and Rebecca Epstein, "Costly Credit: African Americans and Latinos in Debt," News America Media, May 11, 2005, http://archive.demos.org/pubs/costly_credit_300.pdf

8. "Payday Lending 'Debt Trap' Siphons $3.4 Billion from Borrowers," http://www.responsiblelending.org/media-center/press-releases/archives/payday-lending-debt-trap-siphons-3-4-billion-from-borrowers.html

9. Jake Lewis, "Renting to Owe: Rent-to-Own Companies Prey on Low-Income Consumers," October 1, 2001, Multinational Monitor, http://www.allbusiness.com/human-resources/employee-development/828365-1.html

10. "Marketing Luxury Brands Q&A," July 2, 2009, Branding Strategy, The Branding blog, http://www.brandingstrategyinsider.com/2009/07/marketing-luxury-brands-qa.html

11. "Hip-Hop Culture Drives Brand Name Shopping in Suburbia, says New Report" May 23, 2008, Report Buyer, http://www.reportbuyer.com/go/PKF00113

12. Terry Mattingly, Gail Lowe interviewed in "Sunday hats and links to the past," June 20, 1998, Scripps Howard News Service

13. Jean Ann Fox, Director of Consumer Protection Federation, Hearing on Foreclosure, Predatory Lending and Payday Lending in America's Cities, March 21, 2007,
http://www.consumerfed.org/pdfs/PDL_Kucinich_Hearing_Testimony032107.pdf

14. Lorenzo Richardson, Sharing the wealth—investment clubs, *Black Enterprise*, June, 2001, / http://findarticles.com/p/articles/mi_m1365/is_11_31/ai_75090990/

15. "Beyonce's 'Frugal' Spending," February 21, 2009, Female First.com, http://www.femalefirst.co.uk/entertainment/Beyonce+Knowles-63852.html

16. Jeffrey A. Trachtenberg, "Magic Johnson on Succeeding in Business and Finding Balance," Nov. 24, 2008, WSJ.com, http://online.wsj.com/article/SB122754159250353209.html

Chapter 8: D's Will Do

1. Angela P. Dodson, "Community Colleges May Be Best Hope to Close Achievement Gap," June 1, 2007, DIVERSE http://216.97.229.165/diverse/business/web/site3/article/7397/1.php

2. Nanette Asimov, O'Connell, "Summit called to address racial disparities in academic performance," *San Francisco* Chronicle (SFGate), November 12, 2007, http://www.sfgate.com/cgi-bin/article.cgi?file=/c/a/2007/11/12/MNH8T5LTC.DTL

3. Bruce Fuller quoted in "The 'Achievement Gap' Gets Wider, Despite Changes," Larry Abramson, Nov. 15, 2006, NPR.org, http://www.npr.org/templates/story/story.php?storyId=6493050

4. "Harlem Children's Zone Breaks Poverty Pattern," July 28, 2009, NPR: Talk of the Nation, http://www.npr.org/templates/transcript/transcript.php?storyId=111193340

5. *"Mike Tomlin: A man of his words,"* by Chuck Finder, July 22, 2007, Pittsburgh Post-Gazette, http://www.post-gazette.com/pg/07203/803522-66.stm

6. Douglass, Frederick, *Narrative of the Life of Frederick Douglass, an American Slave* (1845), Barnes & Noble Books "Classics" August 1, 2005

7. Williams, Heather Andrea, *Self-Taught: African American Education in Slavery and Freedom* (UNC Press, 2005) Interview, http://www.uncpress.unc.edu/browse/page/144

8. "Lincoln's Fourth Debate with Douglas at Charleston (1858), Learner.org. http://www.learner.org/workshops/primarysources/emancipation/docs/fourthdebate.html

9. "Slavery a Positive Good," John C. Calhoun (February 6, 1837) Teaching American History.org, http://teachingamericanhistory.org/library/index.asp?document=71

10. Carter G. Woodson, *The Mis-Education of The Negro* (Africa World Press, 1990)

11. Proposal for Free Standing Africana Studies Major Program at Ramapo College of New Jersey 2007, http://192.107.108.17/libfiles/fa/Arch_Announce/Ramapo%20Africana%20Studies%20Proposal%20for%20Major%202007-2008.doc.

12. Dr. Terrence Roberts, "Little Rock Nine" interview with Tavis Smiley September 12, 2007, PBS.org, http://www.pbs.org/kcet/tavissmiley/special/littlerock.html

13. Barbara A. Sizemore, *Walking in Circles: The Black Struggle for School Reform* (Third World Press, 2008)

14. Julian Weissglass, "Racism and the Achievement Gap," August 8, 2001, EdWeek.org, http://www.edweek.org/login.html?source=http://www.edweek.org/ew/articles/2001/08/08/43weissglass.h20.html&destination=http://www.edweek.org/ew/articles/2001/08/08/43weissglass.h20.html&levelId=2100

15. Temple Hemphill, "For poet and publisher Haki Madhubuti, success has been hard-earned," September 01, 2007 Echo Online edition; and "Ed Gordon talks with writer and publisher Haki Madhubuti about new autobiography, *Yellow Black: The First Twenty-One Years of a Poet's Life,"*

November 2, 2005, NPR.org, http://www.npr.org/templates/story/story.php?storyId=4986191

16. Dr. Williams and University of Michigan research cited in "How Do Educators' Cultural Belief Systems Affect Underserved Students' Pursuit of Postsecondary Education?" Pathways to College Network, 2003, http://www.pathwaystocollege.net/pdf/EducatorsCulturalBeliefs.pdf

17. Stacy A. Teicher, "Audrey Bullard and J.S. Chick elementary: An African-centered success story," June 8, 2006, *The Christian Science Monitor*, http://www.csmonitor.com/2006/0608/p14s01-legn.html#

Chapter 9: Bred to Be Led

1. Juanita Bynum (video) at the Full Gospel Baptist Conference in Atlanta, GA 2007, http://www.higherpraisetube.com/video/7167/Juanita-Bynum-ministering-at-Atlanta-conference

2. Christine E. Smith, Reginald Hopkins, "Mitigating the impact of stereotypes on academic performance: the effects of cultural identity and attributions for success among African American college students" *Western Journal of Black Studies*, Spring 2004, http://findarticles.com/p/articles/mi_go2877/is_1_28/ai_n29149891/

3. Tom Krattenmaker, "Why Christians should seek MLK's dream," January 21, 2008, *USA Today*, http://blogs.usatoday.com/oped/2008/01/why-christians.html

4. WPA Slave Narratives: William Moore, http://memory.loc.gov/ammem/snhtml/snvoices07.html

5. John Hope Franklin, "Propaganda as History," in *Race and History: Selected essays 1938–1988* (Louisiana State University Press, 1989)

6. William Banks, *Black Intellectuals: Race and Responsibility in American Life* (W. W. Norton & Company, 1996), http://www.washingtonpost.com/wp-srv/style/longterm/books/chap1/blackintellectuals.htm

7. Bruce Lambert, "Warmoth T. Gibbs, Educator Who Backed Civil Rights Protests," obituary, New York Times, April 22, 1993

8. Maura Sheehy, "Salvage Mission for the Inner City," March 8, 1993, *Christian Science Monitor*, http://www.csmonitor.com/1993/0308/08151.html

9. "Slavery in the United States," Encarta/MSN, http://encarta.msn.com/text_761580652__1/Slavery_in_the_United_States.html

Chapter 10: Diss-Unity

1. "Andrew Young Says Obama Lacks Experience to Be President," Dec. 10, 2007, FOX News, http://www.foxnews.com/printer_friendly_story/0,3566,316366,00.html

2. Katharine Q. Seely, "BET Founder Slams Obama in South Carolina, January 13, 2008, New York Times http://thecaucus.blogs.nytimes.com/2008/01/13/bet-chief-raps-obama-in-sc/

3. Chris Rock: "Niggas vs. Black People" from the 1997 album *Roll with the New* and the 1996 HBO special *Bring the Pain*

4. Na'Im Akbar, *Chains and Images of Psychological Slavery* (New Mind Productions, January, 1984)

5. Charles Joyner, *Down by the Riverside: A South Carolina Slave Community* (University of Illinois Press January, 1986, pg. 68)

6. Thomas Jefferson Foundation; Monticello, http://classroom.monticello.org/teachers/resources/profile/261/Plantation-Economy/

7. William E. Wiethoff, *Crafting the Overseer's Image* (University of South Carolina Press, December 30, 2006)

8. William Wells Brown, *Clotel, or the President's Daughter*, (Penguin Books, 2004, edited with an introduction and notes by M. Guilia Fabi/ pgs.5-6)

9. Gregory A. Freeman, *Lay This Body Down: The 1921 Murder of Eleven Plantation Slaves* (Chicago Review Press, Inc., Sept. 1999)

10. hooks, bell, *Rock my soul: Black people and self-esteem* (Atria, December 24, 2002)

11. Trina Jones, "Shades of Brown: The Law of Skin Color," http://www.law.duke.edu/shell/cite.pl?49+Duke+L.+J.+1487#H2N1

12. "Rare Bias Case Involves Dark Skin Color of African American Employee," EEOC press release, August 7, 2003, http://www.eeoc.gov/press/8-07-03.html

13. Jasper Battle, former slave, *Slave Narratives: A Folk History of the United States from Interviews with Former Slaves, Georgia Narratives, Part 1*, by Works Projects Administration

14. NBC letter to Rev. Joe H. Jackson, Research & Education Institute, http://mlk-kpp01.stanford.edu/index.php/encyclopedia/encyclopedia/enc_jackson_joseph_harrison_19001990/

15. Korean Family Customs: Cooperative Organizations, Asianinfo.org, http://www.asianinfo.org/asianinfo/korea/family_customs.htm

16. "Microfinance in Vietnam," http://www.scribd.com/doc/4304801/Microfinance-in-Vietnam; and "Micro Finance in Vietnam: Three Case Studies" Ruth Putzeys, Hanoi, May 2002, http://www2.btcctb.org/vietnam/docs/microfinance.pdf

17. Roland Jones, *Standing up and Standing Out* (World Solutions, Inc., Sept. 2006)

Chapter 11: Neo-Coons

1. "An Open Letter To Tyler Perry" by Jamilah Lemieux, September 11, 2009, NPR.org., http://www.npr.org/templates/story/story.php?storyId=112760404

2. Charles Keil, Urban Blues (Phoenix Books, 1966, re-issue University Of Chicago Press, 1992)

3. Mel Watkins, *On the Real Side: A History of African American Comedy from Slavery to Chris Rock*, (Lawrence Hill Books, May 1, 1999)

4. Glenda Carpio, *Laughing Fit to Kill: Black Humor in the Fictions of Slavery* (Oxford University Press, USA; illustrated edition, July 1, 2008); and "Subverting Stereotypes: Laughing at Slavery," by Craig Lambert, *Harvard Magazine*, March–April 2009, http://harvardmagazine.com/2009/03/laughing-slavery

5. Bill Cosby and Alvin F. Poussaint, *Come on, People! On the Path from Victims to Victors* (Thomas Nelson, 2007, Hardcover)

6. *"The N-word: Sordid past, confusing present,"* interview with author Jabari Asim, *St. Louis Post-Dispatch*, April 29, 2007

7. Neilsen National Television Index, Oct. 08–Aug.09

8. Derrick Z. Jackson, "The N-word and Richard Pryor," December 15, 2005, *New York Times*, http://www.nytimes.com/2005/12/15/opinion/15iht-edjackson.html

9. Interview with Dr. Cornel West, Tavis Smiley show, January 12, 2007, http://www.pbs.org/kcet/tavissmiley/archive/200701/20070112_west.html

10. Interview with Dave Chappelle, February 2006, *Oprah Winfrey Show*, http://www.oprah.com/tows/pastshows/200602/tows_past_20060203.jhtml

notes

notes

notes

notes

notes

notes

notes